For *Direct from Death Row, the Scottsboro Boys*:

"A work of searing truth and staggering theatricality, this Midwest premiere of Mark Stein's important, ingeniously conceived play—with a wonderfully warped use of traditional songs, plus original music and lyrics by Harley White Jr.—is a magnificent achievement."
—HEDY WEISS, *Chicago Sun-Times*

For *American Panic: A History of Who Scares Us and Why*:

"An informative tour through some of the country's most notable spasms of fear."
—*Wall Street Journal*

For *Housesitter*:

"Pound for pound there are more laughs to be had from [*Housesitter*] than one might expect . . . mainly due to Mark Stein's nicely turned screenplay which is skillfully delivered by Steve Martin and Goldie Hawn."
—*Cinephilia*

"*Housesitter* wins the cigar as the decade's most imaginative screwball comedy."
—*USA Today*

THE PRESIDENTIAL FRINGE

★ ★ ★ ★ ★ ★ ★ ★ ★ ★ ★ ★ ★ ★ ★ ★

★ ★ ★ MARK STEIN ★ ★ ★

THE PRESIDENTIAL

FRINGE

★ ★ ★ ★ ★ ★ ★ ★ ★ ★ ★ ★ ★ ★ ★ ★

QUESTING *and* JESTING *for the* OVAL OFFICE

★ ★ ★ ★ ★ ★ ★ ★ ★ ★ ★ ★ ★ ★

Potomac Books

AN IMPRINT OF THE UNIVERSITY OF NEBRASKA PRESS

All rights reserved. Potomac Books is an imprint of the
University of Nebraska Press.
Manufactured in the United States of America.

Library of Congress Cataloging-in-Publication Data
Names: Stein, Mark, 1951– author.
Title: The presidential fringe: questing and jesting for the Oval Office /
Mark Stein.
Description: [Lincoln, Nebraska]: Potomac Books, an imprint of the
University of Nebraska Press, [2020] | Includes bibliographical
references and index.
Identifiers: LCCN 2018003952
ISBN 9781640120327 (cloth: alk. paper)
ISBN 9781640121232 (epub)
ISBN 9781640121249 (mobi)
ISBN 9781640121256 (pdf)
Subjects: LCSH: Presidential candidates—United States—Biography. |
Presidents—United States—Election—History. | United States—Politics
and government.
Classification: LCC E176 .S835 2020 | DDC 324.973 324.973—dc23
LC record available at https://lccn.loc.gov/2018003952

Set in Minion Pro by Laura Ebbeka.
Designed by Roger B.

CONTENTS

Part 4. Clowns and Quixotes Stampede
the Internet and Cable TV

ILLUSTRATIONS

ACKNOWLEDGMENTS

First and foremost (and yet again) I want to thank Arlene Balkansky at the Library of Congress Serial and Government Publications Division for assistance with newspaper and magazine articles and with providing guidance through the maze of extraordinary materials in the various divisions of the Library of Congress, as well as guidance through life's maze for forty-plus years of marriage.

I also want to thank her colleagues, Eric Frazier from the Rare Book and Special Collections Division of the Library of Congress and, at the Federal Election Commission, Christian Hilland. Little-known fact: federal employees such as these are part of a workforce that, given its enormity, is efficient and helpful far more often than not—indeed far more often than other huge organizations—and far too often unjustly maligned.

For similarly valuable assistance at other libraries, I am grateful to Jennifer Bibb from the Special Collections Division of the University of North Florida; Joanne Bloom, photographic resources librarian at Harvard University Fine Arts Library; and American University's Bender Library for extending borrowing privileges to me.

As in the past, my agent, Alec Shane, provided insights and posed questions that were of immeasurable value in my finding the common denominator that linked the variety of fringe candidates included in this book. Similarly I am once again grateful to my editor at the University of Nebraska Press/Potomac Books, Tom Swanson, for spotting, amid the upheaval of the 2016 election, the value of exploring fringe candidates. My thanks as well to the entire team at University of Nebraska Press, with whom it has once again been a pleasure to work, with a particular shout-out to Mark Heineke for his input and special appreciation to copyeditor Judith Hoover for catching countless missteps without stepping on tone.

My thanks also to those whose comments, suggestions, questions, or answers to questions greatly aided me: Pat Behling, Bari Biern, Elizabeth Copeland, Daniel L. Goldberg, Bastian Hermisson, Bryan McGovern, Eric Meyers, and (alphabetically last but far from least) Harry Stein.

THE PRESIDENTIAL FRINGE

★ ★ ★ ★ ★ ★ ★ ★ ★ ★ ★ ★ ★ ★ ★ ★

Before We Begin—Political Tickets, Please

IN 1848 JOHN DONKEY, A CARTOON CHARACTER (UNRELATED to the donkey that later represented the Democratic Party), announced his candidacy for the presidency.[1] That same year a delegate to the Whig Convention proposed Gen. Zachary Taylor's horse, Old Whitey, for vice president—though the delegates ultimately opted, for better or for worse, to nominate Millard Fillmore as Taylor's running mate. That gag is also as old as those gag candidates. A news item from the time commenting on the convention's choice of Fillmore as Taylor's running mate told readers that the Whigs "have placed on the ticket with him, instead of a horse, a most consummate ass."[2]

The supporters of the fictional John Donkey for president and of Zachary Taylor's horse for vice president were, in fact, serious in their ridiculousness. If nothing else (though there was something else), they saw the circus that elections were becoming a few decades after the nation's birth. These fringe candidates who "campaigned" as clowns sought to call the nation's attention to this unfunny danger by taking the stage with the political equivalent of a big red nose. The more that mainstream candidates behaved as political equivalents of P. T. Barnum, the patriarch of American hucksters, the more clown candidates honked their noses.

In the years that followed John Donkey, fringe candidates used slogans appropriate to the age in which they lived, such as the arguably age-inappropriate "Lick Bush," "Live Forever," "We Want Our Money Back," and "Just a common, ordinary, simple savior of America's destiny." Similarly such candidates represented a variety of political parties—often self-created—including the Universal Flying Saucer Party, the Theocratic Party, the Surprise Party, or the Rent Is Too Damn High Party. As some of these slogans suggest, not all fringe candidates were running for laughs.

While some fringe candidate were famous, such as Mark Twain, Will Rogers, Gracie Allen, and Stephen Colbert, most were not—and a few were virtually anonymous, such as presidential contenders Naked Cowboy and Inmate No. 11593-051. But before dismissing as lunatics the likes of Naked Cowboy and Inmate No. 11593-051, or other pseudonymous candidates for the Oval Office such as Vermin Supreme or Deez Nuts, keep in mind another quixotic character—in fact the granddaddy of quixotic characters—Don Quixote himself. He too was considered a lunatic. And maybe he was. But in that difficult distinction resided a quest to bring justice to the world that has remained significant since that gallant knight errant absurdly embarked on his "impossible dream" in 1605.

In the case of fringe candidates, not all the dreams at which they tilted in battle have been impossible. In the 1872 election, for example, Victoria Woodhull's presidential campaign elicited laughs because she was a woman. Not so the later presidential quests of Shirley Chisholm, Jill Stein, or Hillary Clinton. In addition to exerting an influence on political substance, fringe candidates have also impacted political style. Guess which presidential candidate said, "Everything's going to be beautiful. Everything is so tough in this country. We're going to make it so easy—to get health care, so easy to get jobs. It's so simple! . . . The answers are all so simple and they're right in front of us." Congratulations if you said Donald Trump, for the closest-to-correct answer. Trump amazed Americans, supporters and opponents, by his ability to sense not just discontents but also yearnings that were largely overlooked by the other presidential aspirants in 2016. The quote, however, was a statement made in 1992 by fringe candidate for president Joan Jett Blakk. She was (and as of this writing still is) the professional persona of Terence Smith.[3] Who, by the way, is African American. And who, as we shall see, was attuned to—and used performances and a good deal of humor to convey—the feelings of a multitude of groups that felt left out.

Before embarking it's fair to ask: What constitutes a "fringe" candidate? It is not only that they ran under banners other than those of the major political parties but also that, whether or not they sought laughs, their candidacies were received by the general public with laughs. Few people today remember Verne L. Reynolds, who ran for president in 1928 as the nominee of the Socialist Labor Party (not to be confused with that era's Socialist Party), and few people voted for him. But even fewer ridiculed him or his party's rejection not only of Wall Street but also of the Soviet Union. Hence, though he was a peripheral candidate, in terms of this book's use of the term, he would be a "third party" candidate, not a "fringe" candidate. While this distinction separates "fringe" candidates from "third party" candidates, it remains subjective, as will be seen in several of the candidates included in this book.

Which, in turn, raises a final question: Who's in and who's not in this book? There have been countless fringe candidates in this nation—and not just recently. In 1872, for example, there were at least five fringe candidates for president in addition to the nonfringe nominees of the (are you ready?) Democratic Party, Republican Party, Liberal Republican Party, Liberal Republican/Democratic Party, and Southern Democratic Party.[4] Jumping to the 2012 campaign, the Federal Election Commission recorded 439 candidates for president. In 2016 that number grew to 1,853.[5]

Included in this book are those fringe candidates who received widespread attention—but not simply for that reason. To the extent that a fringe candidate receives attention—even in the form of ridicule—it is because his or her candidacy resonates with something in the nation's political landscape. By virtue of being on the fringe, the candidacy *amplifies* that aspect which is otherwise less, if at all, detected.

The greater that amplification, the greater the ability of fringe candidates to plant seeds in voters' views. Over time a number of those seeds sprouted in the attitudes of mainstream candidates, subsequently spreading into realms that expanded opportunities for those lesser heard Americans, including those who'd been lesser heard presidential candidates—eventually blooming in the Oval Office.

PART 1

Fringe Candidates in the Eighteenth
to Early Twentieth Centuries

The First Fringe Candidates

"Scattered" and "Other"

WHEN ANDREW JACKSON RAN AGAINST JOHN QUINCY Adams in 1828, 4,568 of the 1,148,018 votes were cast for, in the language of that era's news reports, "Scattering."[1] No record remains of who composed that category, but an absence of information can in itself be information. One reason for the absence of information about fringe candidates is that voting in the early years of the United States was conducted very differently than today; back then there was no equivalent of a Federal Election Commission. Nor, in the earliest years of the republic, did states have procedures for office seekers getting their names on the ballot. In many jurisdictions eligible voters (also very differently from today) simply gathered at an appointed time and place and voted by voice or holding up a hand. It is very likely that when, for example, John Adams ran against Thomas Jefferson in 1796, local election officials simply ignored any isolated voices calling out for Yankee Doodle or the town drunk. American democracy soon took a step forward by providing greater privacy. In an increasing number of jurisdictions in the early nineteenth century, voters came to the polls with the names of their chosen candidates already written down on their personal ballots, which they placed in a box. A remnant of this system remains in today's prepared ballots via the write-in option, as does the news media's reporting of isolated votes under a category such as "Other" or some equivalent to "Scattering."

One can well imagine, however, that with the birth of the United States, some number of quirky candidates availed themselves of this new democracy. But in fact they precede the creation of the United States. Just as democracy was evolving in monarchical England, so too its embryo existed in colonial America. While

England's monarchs appointed and empowered colonial governors, colonists elected representatives to legislatures that exercised limited home rule. And among those seeking to be elected there already were, evidently, fringe candidates. How else to explain the first stage comedy to be written by an American, *The Candidates*, by Robert Munford?

Munford wrote the play in or around 1770, when what would become the American Revolution was starting to bubble up in that year's Boston Massacre and in violence erupting in New York between British soldiers and the Sons of Liberty. Writing in the stylized traditions of Restoration Comedy, Munford named the mainstream candidates Mr. Wou'dbe and Mr. Worthy. The fringe candidates seeking office—unsuccessfully but, if you're into his kind of writing, hilariously—were Sir John Toddy, a drunk; Mr. Strutabout, an egomaniac; and Mr. Smallhopes, a single-issue candidate whose issue was horsemanship.

Although these characters were fictional, Munford did not create them out of thin air. Indeed he was sufficiently concerned that the actual likes of such candidates might take action against him that he put an eighteenth-century version of today's disclaimer—*Any resemblance to actual persons, living or dead, is purely coincidental*—in the play's prologue. Which, in his words, was this:

> While some may make malicious explanations,
> And know them all still living in the nation . . .
> I boldly answer, how could he mean you,
> Who, when he wrote, about you nothing knew?

As it turned out, Munford need not have worried. Being the first American known to have written a comedy did not mean his writing was good. Assessed as, at best, an amateur effort with amusing moments, *The Candidates* was never produced.[2]

John Donkey

America's First Cartoon Candidate

ON APRIL 22, 1848, JOHN DONKEY, AT THE URGING OF
many and against his will (or so he claimed), declared his candidacy for president of the United States. Mr. Donkey's name was
initially mentioned (or, one might argue, self-mentioned) as a
candidate months earlier, when it was speculated in the pages of
a national magazine called *The John-Donkey*, an American periodical that sought to replicate England's widely admired satiric
magazine, *Punch*. According to *The John-Donkey*, "The free and
independent citizens of Ann Arbor, Michigan . . . have unanimously
nominated our venerable and beloved patron, the great and good
JOHN DONKEY, for the Vice Presidency." Not the presidency. But
being, by design, a political ass, he responded only to the part he
wanted to answer when he replied, "If I am elected President . . ."[1]
And soon after, he was off and running.

"Off and running" resonates with the significance of the fact
that John Donkey ran for president in 1848. After the Revolution
the United States was a new nation and, more important, a new
democracy—indeed the first of its kind since the Roman Republic
and Ancient Greece. Consequently the oratory of politicians seeking the presidency was now also being newly developed. Clearly,
however, by 1848 Americans had begun to recognize patterns in
such political rhetoric, as for example: "The various and conflicting
reports which my friends have at various times, constantly against
my will, caused to be circulated in regard to my intentions with
respect [to] the approaching canvass in relation to the next presidency, appear to me to furnish a proper occasion for a full, free,
frank, and explicit exposition of my feelings, sensations, emotions,
desires, hopes, wishes, views and expectations on that subject."

John Donkey? Daniel Webster? Or Stephen A. Douglas?

Whichever one you answered answers the question, since one could correctly say oratorical hot air now wafted over the political landscape. And in so saying one would have used an idiom, "hot air," which the *Oxford English Dictionary* identifies as a term originating in the United States in the mid-nineteenth century.

The quote, for the record, was from John Donkey.[2]

He may have been a joke candidate, but it was no joke that John Donkey's candidacy resonated with and amplified realizations and attitudes easily overlooked in this era of American history.

Not all of John Donkey's presidential campaign was aimed at ridiculing politicians. Nor was his humor entirely benign. In replying to his "supporters" in Ann Arbor—whose unanimous vote, according to *The John-Donkey*, was reported in "the *B'hoy's Eagle*"—the reluctant candidate stated, "In regard to the . . . great questions of national interest, I have never had time to form an opinion, being for the most part engaged in chasing up the cockneys with blood-hounds and the dunces of my own country." Back in the day, "b'hoy" was a derogatory term for an Irish male, though it came to be embraced by a variety of urban toughs. His mention of the "cockneys" he'd been engaged in chasing was a similarly derogatory reference to lower-class British immigrants. Ann Arbor, Michigan, arising at the time as a regional railway hub, was home to a great many immigrants, particularly among the Irish fleeing starvation resulting from that nation's potato famine in the 1840s. Not true, however, was the occurrence of any such convention in Ann Arbor, nor the existence of a newspaper called the *B'hoy's Eagle*. Both creations, with their whacks at the Irish, were just for laughs.

Laughter, however, is serious business. And good for business—a fact borne out by the number of newspapers that sought to boost readership by reprinting John Donkey's declaration of his candidacy.[3] Other newspapers capitalized on his candidacy with their own tongue-in-cheek articles and editorials. "Must be [that] John Donkey . . . has seen our advertisement for a candidate to be run on the Federal Republican Democratic Whig Taylor ticket," boasted a column in Missouri's *Democratic Banner*.[4] The "Federal Republican Democratic Whig Party" was this article's satiric amalgam of that era's political parties, through which the paper poked fun at Whig nominee Zachary Taylor's avowal not to hew to any party line. A number of the nation's more staid newspapers glommed on by reporting his candidacy poker-faced, as in the June 1, 1848, *Indiana State Sentinel*:

PRESIDENTIAL CANDIDATES

The Democrats having made their nominations, the candidates in the field may be summed up as follows: *Whigs*—Daniel Webster, Henry Clay, John McLean, General Scott, Tom Corwin. *Abolition*— John P. Hale, Wm. Lloyd Garrison, and Abby Kelly. *Independent Whigs*—General Taylor, John Donkey, James Gordon Bennett, Joseph Lawson.

John Donkey did not, of course, simply spring from a pot of ink. He was the creation of his magazine's editors, George G. Foster and Thomas Dunn English. They were as oddball a publishing partnership as John Donkey was a candidate. English commenced his career as a physician, trained at the University of Pennsylvania. But his father did not view medicine as a worthy occupation and urged his son to learn carpentry. He did, but while doing so he also studied law on the side, and not long after was admitted to the Pennsylvania bar. All these endeavors were sidelined, however, during an illness in which, to keep occupied, he took up writing, penning a play that was produced by one of that era's preeminent actor-managers, Junius Booth (whose son John would grow up to become the nation's preeminent assassin). Despite *The John-Donkey*'s mockery of politicians, English later ran successfully for the New Jersey legislature and afterward was elected to Congress. Throughout he continued to write plays, poetry, nonfiction, and literary criticism—including criticism of Edgar Allen Poe that led to their having a lengthy literary snowball fight and one fist fight, which, alas, predated iPhone videos. Poe claimed to have given the cocreator of John Donkey "a flogging which he will remember to the day of his death," which English not only didn't remember but denied.[5]

English's coeditor, Foster, was described in his *New York Times* obituary as a "remarkable example of a brilliant talent unguided by moral purpose or a decent regard for the conventions and proprieties of civilized society." And to think that's putting it respectfully. Like English, he too was a playwright and author of nonfiction, but with some differences. Foster's nonfiction explored the underbelly of urban life in ways (also in the words of his obituary) "to exclude them from the hands of [fastidious] readers." His work in the theater differed as well from that of English in Foster's additionally having been an actor, musician, and forger of a wealthy actor-manager's signature—for which he spent a year in the clink.[6]

In the 1848 election Zachary Taylor received upward of 47 percent of the 2,876,818 votes, edging out his two major competitors, Democrat Lewis Cass and former president Martin Van Buren, who ran as a candidate for the antislavery Free Soil Party. As for John Donkey, it is not known how many of that year's 121 write-in votes he received. But 121 votes, taken together, represented just over 0 percent of the voters—a fact that is significant when, in later elections, a far larger percentage of Americans voted for particular fringe candidates.

Joseph Smith

Cult Candidate?

JOSEPH SMITH WAS NO JOHN DONKEY. HE WAS THE FOUNDER and leader of the Church of Jesus Christ of Latter-day Saints, more commonly known as the Mormons. Nevertheless when he ran for president in 1844, he contributed to John Donkey's 1848 campaign, which satirically amplified the nation's discontent with political b.s.

In announcing his candidacy Smith declared, "I would not have suffered my name to have been used by my friends on anywise as President of the United States, or candidate for that office   but for the general good of mankind."[1] Compare that statement to the b.s. (or d.s.?) in John Donkey's declaration, "With a strong disinclination to the use of my name in connection with that office (which my past life has so strikingly illustrated) . . . my friends, seeing the direction in which my inclinations pointed, have represented to me . . . that I was the only hope of the country."[2]

At the time Smith ran for president, the Mormons were widely viewed as a cult. Today the leadership of this far more widely respected religion is centered in Salt Lake City, Utah, the place to which Mormons fled to escape mob violence in Nauvoo, Illinois, a town founded in 1839 by Joseph Smith, whom Mormons view as one of God's prophets. Many Americans, however, viewed that view of Smith as laughable. The *Baton Rouge Gazette*, for example, quipped in regard to the two leading presidential contenders in the 1844 election, "[Henry] Clay and [Martin] Van Buren may now hide their diminished heads, for a prophet is now come up for judgement before the people."[3] But Smith was not running as a prophet. Indeed had there been bumper stickers back then, his could have read, "Pick Your Own Prophet—Smith for President," since he was campaigning for religious freedom.

Whether or not he was truly a prophet, Smith was truly intelligent—profoundly so. In the run-up to the 1844 election, he spotted an opportunity for a campaign that could begin on the edge of the stage but had the possibility of moving to the spotlight. Henry Clay faced little opposition in the Whig Party, but among the Democrats, President John Tyler faced reelection challenges from former president Martin Van Buren, Secretary of War Lewis Cass, Senator John C. Calhoun of South Carolina, and Senator James Buchanan of Pennsylvania. An impressive array. Unable to agree, the Democrats opted instead for a peripheral member of their party, a former congressman who went on to serve one term as governor of Tennessee before losing reelection, James K. Polk. The idea was that he'd never get elected, so the major players could take another shot four years later. And if by some fluke he did win, Polk had to promise not to run again. Which he did—win, and not run again.

During this scrum among Democrats as they headed (and elbowed and kneed) their way toward their nominating convention, Smith perceived, as few others did—including those who nominated Polk—the degree to which the presidency could be up for grabs. In January of that year he shared this perception with his inner circle and sought their view on throwing his hat in the ring. He made clear to them what the task ahead would entail if they approved and joined this effort to turn a fringe candidacy into one by a genuinely contending third party: "If you attempt to accomplish this, you must send every man in the city who is able to speak in public through the land to electioneer and . . . have General Conferences all over the nation, and I will attend as many as convenient. Tell the people we have had Whig and Democratic Presidents long enough; we want a President of the United States. If I ever get into the presidential chair, I will protect [all] the people in their rights and liberties."[4] The members of his inner circle agreed to give it a go.

At the outset the press reflected the nation's widespread derision of Mormons. "On mature deliberation," one newspaper wisecracked by its winking reference to maturity, "the Mormons do not intend to cast their votes either for Van Buren or Clay, but for

General Joe Smith."[5] One of the few newspapers to devote more than a smirk in reporting the announcement of his candidacy was the *Washington (DC) Globe*, though its coverage began by condescendingly stating, "We have cast our eye hastily over General Smith's (Mormon Joe) 'Views of the Powers and Policy of the Government of the United States.'"[6] In addition to religious freedom, Smith's platform addressed all the major issues of the day. In response to his proposals the editorialist clowned around, using derision to hide the fact that he actually agreed with Smith. For example, Smith stated his views on the hot-button topic of monetary policy in regard to a national bank, the equivalent of which would become the Federal Reserve. Sarcastically calling him the "great financier," the author wrote, "We think Joe's plan has decided advantages over those of Messrs. Clay and Webster." Quite a compliment, even as that newspaper, or any other, would never have referred to Messrs. Clay or Webster as Hank or Dan. Smith also supported the annexation of Texas and the nation's expansion to the Pacific coast, but added the stipulation "when we have the red man's consent."[7] And he stepped up to the plate on slavery, calling for its abolition but compensating slave owners to minimize their economic loss. This last plank the *Globe* opted not to mention. Being published in a city where slavery was allowed, its editors may have feared the issue too hot handle. Even the article's conclusion, which expressed admiration for Smith, snidely italicized a word to hide (perhaps even from themselves) how seriously it meant: "We will do *General* Smith the justice to state that we think . . . his views more honest and his scheme more feasible than those of the hypocrites and quacks who, supported by a great party, have fleeced the country."

Which brings us to why the repeated bestowal of this highest military rank on Smith ranked as ridicule. Anti-Mormon sentiments, marked by violence, commenced prior to their settlement at Nauvoo, a wilderness to which they had fled to escape mob violence at their original settlement in Missouri. With that state's governor turning a deaf ear to their pleas for the militia to intercede, the Mormons formed a military-style defense unit under Smith's leadership. Hence the use of "General."

Ultimately those opposing the Mormons forced them to flee for their lives. In Illinois, however, events unfolded much as they had in Missouri. Once the Mormons again began to prosper, rumors and accusations spread regarding theft, murder, and, new to the list, polygamy. Still debated is the degree to which there was justification for the accusations and counteraccusations. But no matter what the degree of fact, it is a fact that there were fears. Three days before Smith and his inner circle decided to put him forth as a candidate, the *New York Herald* told readers, "The Mormons are indeed making progress in every point of view. . . . Money is increasing amongst them—increasing industry—population rapidly increasing. They have already, we believe, a military force of nearly two thousand strong, armed and equipped."[8] Amid such fears the snickers at Smith's bid for the White House served to avoid the serious questions his campaign raised.

As he had in Missouri, Smith appealed to the governor for protection. And as in Missouri, Illinois's governor sat on his hands. Though morally wrong, politically it made reprehensible sense. "The Mormons are numerous enough in the State of Illinois to control the character of its vote," the *New York Herald* article noted. "If they control the vote of that state, they will succeed in great measure in controlling the vote of the whole western country." The article then stated more presciently than it realized, "It therefore will be seen that this insignificant body of men may, in the event of the next Presidency, control the destinies of all the candidates."

Which may be exactly what Smith sought to do by throwing his hat in the ring. Though he never said so in the diary he assiduously kept, he may have run for president to work his way into the spotlight with the major candidates and, empowered by the growing number of Mormons, force one or both of those candidates to guarantee military protection. Or, by using that platform to appeal to the nation at large, he may have perceived a possibility of securing a plurality of the votes and himself become the next president.

While Smith's candidacy resulted from his efforts to protect the Mormons in Illinois, it also added fuel to the fire of those opposed to their presence. One newspaper reported during the time of his campaign, "They [people in Illinois] talk openly of the extermination of the Mormons as the only means of securing their own safety."[9] As incidents of violence began to flare, with both sides blaming the other, the nation increasingly paid attention to events in Nauvoo and to the Smith presidential campaign. "When it is considered that four years since this place [Nauvoo] was a desert . . . numbering twenty souls in all," the *New York Tribune* observed, "and that now the population undoubtedly exceeds fifteen thousand . . . surely it will strike the mind of the most ordinary observer that these people, whatever else may be thought of them, cannot . . . [be] deemed beneath notice."[10] The article then went on to say, "You have seen it announced that Joseph Smith is a candidate for the Presidency of the United States. Many think this is a hoax—not so with Joe and the Mormons." Smith's campaign, it reported, was dispatching organizers to every state, not only soliciting votes but also seeking delegates for a national convention to take place in Baltimore, where both the Whig and Democratic conventions were slated to take place later that year. By choosing that city as well, Smith was now clearly seeking to address the nation from center stage.

Which, in Illinois, added to the panic of those opposed to Mormons. On June 27 the *Cleveland Herald* wrote, "We fear ere this that blood has been shed in the city of the Prophet. . . . The 19th had been set by the exasperated enemies of the Mormons to rendezvous preparatory to the opening the campaign."[11] The campaign to which the article referred was not Smith's presidential campaign but rather a euphemism for massacre. Smith knew from the outset that *his* campaign could increase the risk of mob violence and up the odds that the death threats to which he'd become accustomed might be enacted. Back when he first spoke about running for president he'd confided, "If I lose my life in a good cause, I am willing to be sacrificed on the altar of virtue, righteousness, and truth in maintaining the laws and Constitution of the United States."[12] Prophetically, on the very day the *Cleveland Herald* feared blood had been shed, Smith was shot and killed by a mob.

In the years to come, numerous fringe candidates for president would run on campaigns entirely based on the foundations of a particular religion. The next candidate to be discussed, Leonard "Live Forever" Jones, was such a candidate, one whose path crossed that of the Mormons. But while Smith was the founder of a particular religion, the fact that he campaigned on a foundation of religious freedom reveals the extent to which religious tolerance was limited in the United States at that time.

But it also reveals more. The Mormons were derided out of fear of their potential political power. Likewise in this nation's past, Catholics and Jews faced derision arising from similar fears. Currently Muslims are derided by many Americans as a result of such fear. The fringe candidacy of Smith not only amplified an un-American discord in the American Way, as it were; it also enables us to hear that discord continuing to resonate today.

Leonard "Live Forever" Jones

High Moral Party

FRINGE CANDIDATES IN THE 1848 PRESIDENTIAL ELECTION
were not confined to horses and asses. Also running that year—
and in every subsequent presidential election up through 1868–
was Leonard Jones.[1] More commonly known as Live Forever Jones,
this perennial candidate from the self-created High Moral Party
based his campaign on a single pledge: Through faith and adherence to a completely moral life, you can live forever.

While Americans were, and remain, reluctant to laugh at others' religious beliefs (though not so reluctant to castigate certain
religions), many responded to Live Forever Jones with the age-
old technique to avoid laughing at a person by humoring him or
her. "Sometimes a band of music would undertake to play him
down," one reporter wrote regarding Jones's campaign speeches,
going on to add, "He always waited and had his say to the rollick-
ing, shouting crowd that was ever ready to applaud and extol him."[2]
Suppressed laughs can also be detected from an incident in 1833,
when Jones sought federal funds to create an "endless life" settlement. That session of the U.S. Senate's transcript noted that the
debate, if one could call it that, "was couched in respectful language."[3] Respectful, but the request was rejected.

To some extent it is difficult to assess Live Forever Jones. On the
one hand, reporters could not resist remarks such as "Live Forever
Jones favored our citizens with one of his characteristic speeches.
He is still a candidate for the presidency."[4] On the other hand, in
this article as in others, none of the content of his speeches was
included. Back to the first hand, the press *did* mention that the
exclusion of his remarks in news reports greatly irritated him.[5] In
addition no writings by Jones were ever published, though there's

reason to believe he did write. In 1852 Congressman Edson Olds told of an instance (possibly apocryphal) in which Jones asked an acquaintance for his opinion of an essay he'd written. After reading it, this person said he was unable to grasp the point, to which Jones is said to have replied, "That's just what I want; for when I make a point, they are always sure to get me on that point."[6] Maybe it happened, maybe not, but neither the essay nor any other writing by Jones has survived. Most of what we know of him comes from reminiscences published, ironically, at the time of his death. Not all the details fit together neatly, however. Some said "his information was limited and gained only from his long and varied life rather than from study," while others remembered him as a former attorney and as "having been a constant reader."[7]

This much is known: Live Forever Jones amused a considerable number of Americans but amassed only a few followers and, there is reason to believe, no votes. Not even his own if, as one obituary reported, "he always went to the polls on Election Day, and the judges would receive his ballot and pretend to deposit it."[8] The generally agreed upon assessment was that Jones was nutty but not nuts. "The physicians assert that he was not insane," one newspaper reported, "and incline to the belief that his mind was in a state of 'quasi deformity.'"[9]

Whether or not his mind was deformed, Jones was not alone in his era for espousing nontraditional spiritual views. During his lifetime the newly formed Mormon Church was attracting many thousands of adherents to the prophecy of its founder (and one-time presidential candidate) Joseph Smith that Christ would return to the world's New Jerusalem: the United States. Thousands also flocked to the Shaker movement as word spread that one of its leaders, Ann Lee (known as Mother Ann), was herself the Second Coming of Christ. On the pessimistic side, thousands were drawn to the preaching of William Miller, who predicted that God would end the world in 1843. When God didn't, Miller rechecked his math and declared 1844 to be the end of days. Wrong again, as it turned out. Amid all of which emerged Leonard "Live Forever" Jones.

What was it in the social landscape of that era that produced this bumper crop of apocalyptic and messianic views? And how did a guy who claimed we can live forever fit into that?

Leonard Jones was not the first person (nor the last) to espouse the possibility that human beings could live forever.[10] Likewise, messianic and apocalyptic fervors were not new to the world, either, but dated back to the earliest recorded times in multiple cultures. Worth noting in regard to Jones's era is that the advent of Christ occurred at a time when the Jews, under the domination of the Roman Empire, so feared the extinction of their culture many placed their faith entirely in God's sending a savior. While many believed (and, of course, still do) Jesus to be the Messiah, other Jews at the time believed the messiah was Simon Bar Kochba, the leader of a failed Judean revolt. In the United States, when the Lakota feared in the late nineteenth century that their culture and nationhood faced extinction, many joined in the Ghost Dance movement, which sought to summon a messiah who would reunite them with their ancestors while covering the Earth with new soil that would both replenish the wildlife and bury the white people.[11]

Seeking to understand the new religious sects emerging in the first half of the nineteenth century, scholars have posited a variety of views, all of which are based on existential fears at that time similar to those felt by Jews during the Roman Empire and the Lakota in the run-up to the 1890 massacre at Wounded Knee. These scholars have identified social impacts resulting from geographic change as Americans trekked into new regions and the nation's rapidly increasing industrialization caused great economic changes, while others have examined discontent with established churches having failed to bring about the promise of a New Jerusalem in the United States.[12] Yet another element was demographic change, as immigration to the United States in these years went from flowing to flooding. Many of these new arrivals were Irish Catholics, seeking opportunities created by industrialization. Under the headline "Popery in the United States," one newspaper told readers in 1843, "This degrading superstition [Catholicism], which the good and wise Lafayette predicted many years ago would eventually become the dangerous enemy to the liberties of this Republic, is increasing among us with great rapidity." While there is dispute as to whether or not Lafayette, himself a Catholic, ever made such a statement, it is indisputable that the statement was first cited, factually or not, during Jones's era to buttress fears that Catholic immigrants threatened the foundations of the United States.[13]

Industrialization and the social shifts it spawned were not, of course, limited to the United States. By the same token, neither were the era's apocalyptic fears. The British writer Mary Shelley, most remembered as the author of *Frankenstein*, published *The Last Man* in 1826, the first literary work in which the end of the world is based more on human choices than biblical prophecy. On these shores Edgar Allen Poe wrote an end-of-the-world story, "The Conversation of Eiros and Charmion," in 1839.

Fears of doom were endemic. Among those affected was the young Leonard Jones, as he migrated from Virginia, where he was raised in a Methodist family, to Kentucky and soon joined a community of Shakers. During this time, by some accounts, Jones practiced law and, by all accounts, engaged in land speculation— and (by one account) land swindles. He soon grew disenchanted with the Shakers for reasons that, all accounts agree, had more to do with a failed love affair than a failure of faith. After leaving the Shakers he was briefly attracted to the Mormons but lost interest when unable to speak in tongues.[14] He next became entranced with a man remembered only by his last name, McDaniel, who preached the "live forever" doctrine that Jones embraced the rest of his life. They formed a team in the early 1830s and soon after made their attempt to create a "live forever" colony. It lasted only briefly, however, losing whatever followers it had when McDaniel upped and died.[15]

Jones, however, did not lose his belief that, through strictly moral behavior, one can elude death, nor did he lose his sense of humor that enabled him to tickle so many Americans through his repeated political campaigns. When asked about his reaction to McDaniel's death, he was remembered as saying that his faith remained, but, he added, "I was very much embarrassed to preach his funeral."[16]

Still, the most essential question remains: What led Jones to run for president? Might it have been, at some subconscious level, a desire to live forever either physically or, if that didn't pan out, historically? Either way, immortality was clearly the driving passion in his life. And therein is one of the key insights provided by his presidential candidacy since, in this respect, *he did not differ from mainstream presidential candidates.* Abraham Lincoln, for example, confided in despair to a friend when he was a young man "that he had done nothing to make any human remember that he had lived, and that to connect his name with . . . something that would redound . . . was what he desired to live for."[17]

Most significant, however, is what the candidacy of Live Forever Jones brings into focus regarding the political shape of the nation at that time. Just as Joseph Smith preached a particularly American theology by virtue of believing this land to be the latter-day Zion to which Christ would return, so too Jones, despite so many in his day believing the end of the world was near, preached an optimism that grew from that same political soil of "American exceptionalism."

Few Americans, however, shared his larger-than-life view. Or cared. When Jones died during his 1868 quest for the presidency, none were at his funeral other than the sextons who prepared his grave.[18]

George Francis Train

"Spread-Eagleism"

FOR THOSE OPEN TO THE POSSIBILITY OF REINCARNATION, the life of George Francis Train, who ran for president in 1872, may persuade you. As the self-proclaimed candidate on behalf of what he termed "Spread-Eagleism," Train bears an uncanny resemblance to Donald Trump. Resemblance, however, does not mean identical. Along with some differences in character, the most significant difference between them is that one was a fringe candidate and the other was elected. Therein lies the importance of Train as a fringe candidate amplifier of views that, at the time, were in the equivalent of a larval state beneath the nation's political landscape.

Let's begin with the case for reincarnation. "The Philadelphia Record calls George Francis Train 'a political clown,'" a Louisiana newspaper told readers in January 1872. "Clown Runs for Prez" headlined the front page of the *New York Daily News* on June 17, 2015, accompanied by an image of Trump as a clown—one of several front-page images in that newspaper of Trump as a clown.[1] Of Train another newspaper quipped, "The all absorbing theme of [his] discourse was George Francis Train." Even the sedate *New York Times* described a campaign speech he gave in that city by saying, "George Francis Train . . . strutted and fretted his little hour on the stage. . . . His various observations appeared to be that all the world was sunk . . . and only one man could save it, and he was GEORGE FRANCIS TRAIN." Eerily similar to Trump's declaring at the 2016 Republican Convention, "I alone can fix it."[2]

Also much like Trump, Train was a highly successful businessman who amassed great wealth that spanned the globe. Where Trump rose through the ranks of his father's real estate business,

Train rose through the ranks of his uncle's overseas shipping company. Both envisioned far greater possibilities for their respective companies. Train, at the age of twenty, foresaw that his uncle's company would have to use packet ships twice the size of those then in existence in order to acquire a competitive edge—advice that the company followed, to its enormous profit.[3]

Or so he claimed. He also claimed that, to better enable impoverished Irishmen to emigrate and become longshoremen for the company, he "invented the prepaid passenger certificate and also the small one-pound, English money, bill of exchange."[4] Which must have been news to the Bank of England, being under the impression it had begun issuing £1 notes in 1797.

"In Train's life . . . it was never quite clear where real life experience left off and legend began; the exaggeration was quickly accepted as fact," the historian Dennis B. Downey wrote in a biographical sketch of Train. As to how widely the public accepted Train's claims, Downey aptly described the arc of Train's reputation when he went on to say he "was variously hailed as a financial wizard, astute political philosopher, defender of womanhood, an oddball bent on self-aggrandizement, and a declared lunatic."[5]

Even discounting for exaggeration and, possibly, mental illness, Train clearly possessed considerable business acumen. In 1850 his uncle entrusted him to oversee the company's operations in the bustling British port of Liverpool and, in 1853, dispatched him to Australia to extend the company's routes to ports in the South Pacific. When a group of Americans there held a Fourth of July banquet, Train took the opportunity to deliver an oration, the entire text of which appeared on the front page of his hometown newspaper, the *Boston Post*. What the article did not report was that the Australian correspondent for the *Post* was none other than George Francis Train.[6]

When speaking of his time in Australia, Train frequently mentioned his overseeing the construction of a six-story warehouse for his company that, in point of fact, was two and a half stories—much as Trump Tower in New York was billed by its namesake as having sixty-eight stories, ten of which are also fiction.[7] Not surprisingly with such accomplishments, Train went on to become the president of Australia's Chamber of Commerce and, amid political turmoil taking place in the gold mine region of Ballarat, the leaders of what has come to be known as the Eureka Rebellion offered him the nation's presidency—although newspapers from the time, later historians, and the Australian Chamber of Commerce have never mentioned either achievement.[8]

Returning to the United States in 1856, Train wrote the first of what would eventually be fourteen books during his seventy-four-year life, detailing his experiences and political views. Here he compares unfavorably with Trump, who published *twenty-five* such books by age seventy. Also at this time Train saw that big money could be made in, well, trains. With new railroads branching out in the United States, he put his entrepreneurial skills to work and secured financing to build a railroad in Ohio that joined several existing lines to create a new entity called the Great Western Railroad. He then envisioned a fortune to be made by introducing street railways into England to replace horse-drawn omnibuses. As in America, some resisted this innovation due to dangers it created; also in England Train faced additional resistance due to support he had expressed for independence movements in Ireland and Australia. Nevertheless he persisted and, ultimately, succeeded.

With the United States on the brink of civil war, Train spotted a new opportunity: politics. In 1859 he published *Spread-Eagleism*, a term from that era that referred to pride in the nation's uniqueness, today termed "American exceptionalism." Train, however, employed the phrase to convey a somewhat different perspective. His book's introduction commenced with a recitation of the favorable reviews he got in England for his first book, *Young America Abroad*. He then complained about the negative reviews he received in the American press for his next book, *Young America in Wall Street*.

From that springboard he dove into the book's topic. "Spread-Eagleism is an Institution," he wrote. "Young America is the vanguard of change—the coming age. . . . He despises Humbug—Exaggeration [?!?]—Hypocrisy."[9] From which he turned to the essence of his political viewpoint:

The fact is, if a man don't have a good opinion of himself, who will care for him? I know of no one better pleased with number one than I. . . . This is my theory: As there are so many young men in the world who don't like to go over and around it; who don't like to know the languages, make books, and be in the newspapers, I say, as there are so many of these modest, unassuming men, who are not ambitious, I maintain there is no harm to mankind, no moral wrong committed, in having one superlative exception.[10]

If his readers wondered who that superlative exception might be, the chapters that followed eliminated any doubt. Chapter 1 was titled "Review of Young America from 'Illustrated London News,' Nov. 20, 1958." Chapter 2: "Sketch of the Author from 'New York Herald,' 1856." All the subsequent chapters were speeches Train had delivered, with two exceptions, one being his correspondence with British officials, the other a chapter titled "Opinions of the British Press." Spread-Eagleism, in this context, might best be defined as Spread-Trainism.

In fairness Train did not always speak in platitudes or in praise of himself. In *Young America in Wall Street*, for example, he offered his strategy in that 1857 book for avoiding secession by the slaveholding states: "Since my remembrance, this country has been agitated by legislating for the 'blacks.' The whites have been neglected. . . . Now, while I have the best possible feelings toward the 'blacks,' I have also the highest respect for the whites. . . . In times such as these, the futile discussion of the slave question had better be thrown under the table, not to be taken up again till Congress has legislated on some of the practical questions of the day. The whites demand a hearing."[11] For working-class whites, the leading issues at the time were the need for laws or labor agreements limiting the workday to eight hours and the right to form unions with the right to strike, all of which Train consistently supported.

Not surprisingly Train's view on slavery was well received in the South. "It develops a very substantial truth," a Baton Rouge newspaper told readers in a front-page article on *Young America in Wall Street* that reprinted his plan to avert national catastrophe.[12]

Perhaps because the book received so many negative reviews

in the North, Train did not reiterate this plan in *Spread-Eagleism*. Indeed this first foray of his into the whitewater of politics capsized at an 1862 Republican state convention in Massachusetts. While all in attendance were supportive of President Lincoln, the convention's leadership sought to avoid differences among Republicans regarding abolition, which Lincoln had recently announced in his soon-to-take-effect Emancipation Proclamation. Train, who opposed abolition, sought to reply to a speech by Senator Charles Sumner that contained remarks Train believed were directed at him. But the convention's leaders forbade Train to speak and quickly adjourned. Train took the stage anyway, at which point the party bosses called the cops, and in the ensuing uproar Train was arrested. Needless to say, his struggle at the convention was heartily applauded in the South. "The Conflict Commenced in Boston—George Francis Train Mobbed by Sumner's Supporters—No Free Speech" headlined the report that appeared in the *Richmond Dispatch*. Among those opposed to Train, however, a term began to surface that would plague him the rest of his life: "Train is acknowledged to be a lunatic," the *New York Times* declared.[13]

Train retreated for a time to his original turf, entrepreneurship. In 1863 he organized the Union Pacific Railroad. Or said he did. In everyone else's reality he was only a minority investor.[14] Having accomplished that Herculean task, he contributed his unbounded energy to several movements by underdogs (though never underdogs of African lineage). From 1867 to 1870 he was often on the podium for woman suffrage, accompanying Susan B. Anthony and Elizabeth Cady Stanton on speaking tours across the nation.

Traveling to Ireland in 1868, Train lent his support to those seeking independence from England. So influential had he become that some twenty thousand residents of Cork escorted him through the streets to prevent his arrest. Or, once again, so he said. Neither historians nor Irish newspapers ever mentioned the event; its brief mention several years later in the American press bore no attribution, raising suspicion that the source was George Francis Train.[15] "If Train had anywhere near 20,000 following him in Cork, I have no doubt it would have been printed somewhere," states Bryan

McGovern, a leading scholar on the Fenian Rebellion, adding, "I have never come across the story. Compare that to the 30,000 who showed up in Dublin for the Fenian-sponsored funeral of the little-known Terence MacManus in the early 1860s. That was covered in numerous papers on both sides of the Atlantic."[16]

Later that (election) year Train returned to the United States to take another shot at political office. This time he tried his luck running for a New York congressional seat as an independent against that city's well-entrenched Tammany machine. He received 1 percent of the vote, the overwhelming majority going to incumbent John Morrissey, the Tammany candidate, a bare-knuckle boxer turned casino owner.[17]

Undeterred Train continued his quest. Scoping out a new railroad project in California, he spoke on behalf of Chinese immigrants, who faced massive and frequently violent opposition. In San Francisco—ground zero for Chinese arrivals—Train declared he "found the Chinese to be more advanced in civilization than the English." He went on to relate, "I saw in Batavia [a Dutch colonial city, present-day Jakarta, Indonesia] one hundred thousand Chinese. The Chinese were gathered in a square with military cannon all around them, with the pretense of making a treaty with them, and the Dutch officers left them, on the pretense of going for a paper to complete the treaty when the military were ordered to fire upon them, which they did until not one of them was left alive."[18]

In this instance there was indeed a massacre of the Chinese in Batavia, though it differed in several details, one being that *it occurred in 1740*. No evidence exists of the atrocity Train described. Indeed he himself makes no reference to any such shocking event in any of his subsequent books.

In 1870 Train turned up in France during the revolutionary upheaval that resulted in the Paris Commune, offering his expertise to those then called "communards." Amid the violence and turmoil he came to be regarded by the revolutionaries as the ruler of France. No doubt refutation no longer need be said. What was significant, however, is that Americans were now doubting Train's claims. "Mr. Train's description of the manner in which he became ruler of France was original in the extreme," a Memphis newspaper told readers, despite Train's popularity in the South for having opposed abolition.[19]

Significant in the opposite direction of growing awareness of Train's lies was his apparently remaining so *unaware* of himself. One realm in which this was particularly vivid was his racism—though such oblivion was not uncommon in his day (or the present day). In addition to the racism inherent in his plan to avoid a civil war, Train was not averse to the occasional racist joke in his speeches, yet perplexed when African Americans did not hop aboard his presidential bandwagon. To a very sparse turnout at a campaign speech he gave for African Americans, Train declared, "I have ever been your friend. What is the reason that so few of you are present here tonight?" When someone called out, "Because you called us 'cocoanuts' in the newspapers," Train acknowledged the statement appeared but claimed it was "a lie invented by . . . the sensational press"—in modern parlance, fake news.[20]

The African American vote was the least of Train's problems in his 1872 bid for the presidency. By then his time had passed. For some years public consensus had been building along the lines of that expressed in a Cleveland newspaper: "Train belongs to a large and growing class of individuals who believe that they are born with a mission from heaven to administer the affairs of their native country."[21] Echoing this view not long after, a newspaper in Olympia, Washington, told readers, "Train is quite as much mistaken about himself as are his other admirers. . . . He is, after all, no imposter but simply a talking fool who honestly believes himself a great man."[22] In the same vein the press could not resist tidbits of ridicule along these lines: "Skilled navigators have been sent out to bring Cape Horn to the coming [centennial] Jubilee, and George Francis Train has been engaged to blow it."[23] Most damaging, however, was a one-sentence item that surfaced nationwide at the outset of 1872: "An uncle of George Francis Train has made an oath that Francis is a lunatic, and has asked to be appointed over him."[24]

Train, ever thin-skinned to criticism, declared war on the press. Appearing days later in newspapers nationwide was a similarly brief item: "George Francis Train is about to sue all the newspapers that have published him as being crazy. Damage, $50,000 each." To which the press added a closing zinger: "We want no other proof of his lunacy."[25]

To be sure, Train did still have admirers. "George Francis Train has been in the city three or four days and has had an ovation such as no other man ever had here," a Memphis newspaper reported in April 1871, going on to declare, "The ideas propagated by the Northern press that he is crazy is [*sic*] utterly dissipated. . . . He is a miracle of thought, action, and elocution. . . . Train is a great genius."[26] Yet it was on the *same page* of that newspaper that the article appeared describing his explanation of being ruler of France as "original in the extreme." What is most notable in this regard is that this newspaper *recognized but discounted* Train's flights of fancy. Similarly a Nashville newspaper wrote of his upcoming visit to that city, "It is anticipated that there will be a great rush for places to hear the most eccentric genius, the sanest lunatic in the world."[27]

But how many of those who attended his campaign speeches were supporters and how many came for the spectacle? One attendee told a reporter, "He struts like a game cock; he talks like an egotist. He is the best 'trained' buffoon in the world. . . . The same amount of vanity has, perhaps, never been vouchsafed to any other mortal. But George is a success—a triumphant success. . . . We defy the world to beat him."[28]

Similar appeal would later vault Trump to victory over opposition from nearly all political insiders, even in his Republican Party. But in 1872 the outcome was different. Reports on the nationwide vote commingled whatever votes Train received with those of other incidental candidates under the category "Other," which contained a total of 10,473 votes, representing 0.2 percent of the total.[29] How much of that percentage may have gone to Train can be estimated by a sample of the county-by-county votes locally reported in the Train-friendly state of Tennessee. Zero.[30]

But don't let the vote count fool you. Train exited the presidential spotlight in a nationally observed blaze of glory. One week after the election he offered to post bail for a competing fringe candidate in that 1872 election, Victoria Woodhull. Among those opposed to the candidacy of Woodhull was the powerful leader of the New York Society for the Suppression of Vice, Anthony Comstock. It was he who effected Woodhull's arrest for publishing obscene material when the newspaper she and her sister published ran an exposé of an adulterous affair between a prominent minister and a woman from New York City's upper crust. Though Woodhull opted to remain in jail, Train continued to voice his support in the pages of *Train Ligue*, a newspaper he published at the time. For which Comstock had him thrown in the clink as well.[31]

What followed was a tangle of court proceedings as to the obscenity charge and, before that could proceed, to determine the sanity of George Francis Train. While jailed in New York's notorious Tombs, Train went full loco. He declared himself the jail's "dictator" and warned that within sixty days the Tombs would be pulled down "and the streets would run with blood."[32] But where one physician testified that "Mr. Train was laboring under the insane delusion of personal greatness," the prison doctor believed "Mr. Train to be a man of strong powers of mind and highly cultivated, but a strong inclination to get up sensations, and would do almost anything to create them."[33]

Clearly these two opposing views resonate with later debates over aspects of Trump's character. Those seeking decisive insight from Train's case, however, will be disappointed. Train was judged to be sane and, consequently, fit to stand trial on the obscenity charge. At that trial, however, he was shocked when his attorney opted to plead him not guilty by reason of insanity, and, despite vocal objection from Train, the judge directed the jury to return that verdict.[34]

Through the lens of George Francis Train we can see in the political landscape of the time why he drew such large crowds during his presidential campaign while nevertheless remaining a fringe candidate. Though the last act of the Civil War, Reconstruction, would not officially end until 1877, a number of the federal controls imposed on the South after the war had been lifted by 1872. Thirteen formerly disenfranchised Confederate generals, for example, were now members of Congress and, under the administration of

President Ulysses S. Grant, the use of the military to protect African Americans from violence abated.[35] "The present campaign . . . is essentially of but an ordinary degree of importance," the *North American Review* declared in 1872. "Something has been gained by the great elemental epoch from which we are just emerging. . . . All that seems to be wanted is the quiet continuance of the present opportunities and dominant influences, in order that the great settlement may complete itself."[36]

Whereas in 2016 social rifts were widening, quite the opposite was occurring in 1872. And while everyone loves a sensational show, Americans across the political spectrum in 1872 were not looking for a president to create sensation.

In the years that followed, Train attempted several swan songs. In 1877 he drew some three hundred people to a lecture he titled "The Foreshadowing of Great of Events." The foreshadowing, as the *New York Times* reported, turned out to be the "wonders he had accomplished." Still the *Times* had to admit, "All these great achievements he related to the great amusement of his audience."[37] Ten years later Train again ascended the stage, this time speaking out on behalf of seven leftists sentenced to death in a dubious trial in which they were charged with complicity in a Chicago bombing known as the Haymarket Affair. The quality of mercy being strained by puns, the *New York Times* headlined its report "Train on the Platform."[38]

For the remainder of his days Train continued as he had all his adult life, vastly exaggerating his achievements and, despite his career as a wealthy capitalist, voicing support for the downtrodden— though still blind to the struggles of African Americans. In 1894 he was arrested after speaking out in support of Coxey's Army, a nationwide march of the unemployed seeking to converge on Washington DC, their right to assemble being precluded by federal troops.[39] The year before, Train told a *New York Times* reporter that he'd been importuned to save the World's Columbian Exposition in Chicago from financial collapse. "They have put about $25,000,000 into it," he told the reporter. "They cannot get it back except by the use of psychic force. If this force were properly used it would bring millions of people to Chicago."[40]

Wacky, yes. Wacko? You decide. But keep one other thing in mind. When Train went to Chicago in 1887 to speak out on behalf of the Haymarket defendants, he was seen handing out candy and apples to a crowd of impoverished children.[41] He told the *New York Times* of his being asked to use his psychic force to save the World's Columbian Exposition when the reporter came upon him skipping rope with a group of girls in a New York City park. Clearly the comparison of Train and Trump has limits.

Victoria Woodhull

First Woman to Run for President

BECAUSE SHE WAS FEMALE, PRESIDENTIAL CANDIDATE
Victoria Woodhull could not vote for herself in the 1872 election. Needless to say, by throwing a woman's hat in that ring, she invited considerable ridicule. The *Memphis Appeal*, for example, wrote of "one of the most remarkable compounds of shrewdness and sublime folly, of . . . nonsense, of impudence," then sprang their punch line: "We do not refer to Mrs. Victoria Woodhull." Rather the paper was referring to George Francis Train, knowing readers would assume they meant Woodhull. After that era's preeminent African American leader, Frederick Douglass, turned down the offer of being Victoria Woodhull's running mate, a Portland, Oregon, newspaper quipped, "We suggest that she substitute in Mr. Douglass' stead the name of Little Bear, Spotted Tail, George Francis Train, or some other noble savage."[1]

The fact that many viewed Woodhull and Train as comparably nutty serves in its own right to sharpen the focus on the shape the nation was in at that time. Through the lens of Woodhull's campaign, however, that focus become even more acute since, unlike Train's fringe candidacy, Woodhull's campaign resided on the cusp of fringe and third party insofar as it was, on the one hand, ridiculed by a great many Americans while, on the other hand, given serious attention by a great many other Americans, even if not given their votes.

Let's begin with the ridicule—quips that back then were, for many, real knee-slappers. Here's an item from the *New Orleans Republican*, published shortly after Woodhull declared her intention to run: "'What is the difference between you and me?' asked

Victoria Woodhull of Judge Bingham in Washington the other day. 'I cannot conceive, madam,' responded the gallant opponent of woman suffrage."[2]

Not hilarious now but, c'mon, still kind of cute. Others were less so. As for instance from the *Idaho World*: "Victoria Woodhull wants to know 'why women of sound mind cannot vote.' That is precisely the class of women that has not asked for the privilege of voting."[3]

Apparently, however, many of that class did, which led jokesters to mock them. The resident wag at the *New Orleans Republican* wrote, "The English journals are amazed at the nomination of Victoria C. Woodhull for the Presidency, regarding it as a serious matter." As Election Day approached, even the humor fell away as one newspaper declared, "Imagine Victoria Woodhull elected to the Presidency of the United States! True, it requires a very great exercise of various qualities of the mind to imagine a thing so absurd and ridiculous."[4]

Even in those ostensibly more moral times, there were remarks that were the era's equivalent of what was termed in the 2016 election "grabbing her pussy." For example, one Oregon newspaper reported, "The editor of the Owyhee, Idaho, *Avalanche* favors Victoria Woodhull for President, and hoists her petticoat to the masthead of his paper."[5]

Similarly crude but alluding to an additional issue that hampered Woodhull's campaign was a Kentucky newspaper's misogynistic metaphor: "Victoria Woodhull and Tennie Clafin [her business partner and sister] are going to give a series of oratorical *can-cans* in Europe."[6] The can-can is a hem-lifting dance associated at the time with licentious performers in Paris. The "oratorical can-cans" to which the statement referred were lectures by Woodhull advocating that century's Free Love movement.

In addition many newspapers used epithets to ridicule Woodhull. Most frequently employed were phrases along the lines of "a petticoat president."[7] More explicit were those aimed at her views on marriage, such as "the Free Love Queen."[8] In fairness to the news media, it should be said they attacked her in the same way they attacked male candidates with whom they disagreed. Which is to say, often taking remarks out of context and imputing views to the candidate which that person did not advocate.

Here too let's begin with the quips. "A trotting mare has been named after Victoria Woodhull. She is also very fast."[9] And: "The irrepressible Mrs. Victoria Woodhull . . . says that both the great political parties are positively without issue. Notwithstanding she has two or three husbands, and we don't know how many affinities, so far as we are aware she is in the same condition."[10]

As far as they were aware was, in fact, not very far, since virtually all of the details of Woodhull's marital history had been previously reported nationwide.[11] In point of fact Victoria Woodhull had *one* husband. Admittedly, though not unusually, he was her second husband. She divorced her first husband, whom her parents had forced her to marry at the age of fourteen. He turned out to be an alcoholic who buttressed his drunkenness with opium and further destabilized their marriage by, shall we say, buttressing other women. His sole means of support was Woodhull and her sister, when they formed an investment company through which they became the first women to acquire a seat on the New York Stock Exchange. In exchange for which her now ex-husband came to live with her and her second husband in order to take care of the son from that first marriage, who was severely disabled. So much for the issue of having no issue. Woodhull also, as was easily known, had a daughter by her first husband. Also previously and widely reported in the press, Woodhull and her husband eventually evicted her rarely sober ex-husband.[12] Awareness, however, made little difference. One of the news articles conveying the bulk of these details was the one previously mentioned bearing the headline "The Free Love Queen."

Likewise there was absence of awareness in news accounts of her "wholly lascivious lecture." Despite its being delivered before a standing-room-only audience at New York's Steinway Hall in November 1871, "wholly lascivious" was the entirety of the details provided in newspapers such as Ohio's *Painesville Journal*.[13] For which, in fairness, it apologized when explaining why it had not provided the facts: "An apology would the rather have been in place had we given an elaborate account of the voluptuousness of her sentiments and the audacious sophistry by which she endeavored to support it." That must have been one spicy speech—hot enough for the newspaper to set fire to the First Amendment when it added, "Lectures such as these should be suppressed."

The *Painesville Journal* was not alone. "These ideas are as indecent and shocking as any that could have been promulgated in the corrupt ages of Caligula and Louis XV," another newspaper reported. "Woman's 'Rights'—Free Love and Prostitution Claimed as Rights of the Sex—Very Plain Talk from Mrs. Woodhull" headlined yet another.[14]

This is too good to miss. Let's listen in to the spiciest moments from her talk, parts of which did appear in some newspapers and all of which soon appeared in published form: "Over the sexual relations, marriages have endeavored to preserve sway and hold the people in subjection to what has been considered a standard of moral purity. Whether this has been successful or not may be determined from the fact that there are *scores of thousands* of women who are denominated prostitutes, and who are supported by *hundreds of thousands* of *men* who should, for like reasons, also be denominated prostitutes."[15] Even proponents of marriage could not deny what she said, though they could suppress it.

But Woodhull was just warming up. "People may be married by law and all love be lacking," she went on to say. "Law cannot change what nature has determined. . . . Law cannot compel two to love." Which may sound like orgies over order—and the press was as quick then as now to run with such hot headlines—but Woodhull *was not advocating the abolition of marriage.* "Marriage laws that would be consistent with the theory of individual rights would be such as would regulate these relations, such as regulate all other associations of people," she declared—apparently pornographically, in the view of numerous (male) editors. "They should only be obliged to file marriage articles, containing whatever provisions may be agreed upon as to their personal rights, rights of property, of children, or whatever else they may deem proper for them to agree upon." The role of government in marriage would be the same, in this view, as in the enforcement of any other contract. And since contracts may be binding "for an hour, a day, a week, a year, a decade or a life," Woodhull argued, "why should the social relations of the sexes be made subject to a different theory?"[16]

But there is another inconvenient fact, one Woodhull had to confront or suppress. The desire for the committed affection of another person is different from the desire for the commitment of a kitchen remodeler. Which, to her credit, Woodhull recognized and did not seek to evade.

> How can a third class of cases be justified in which but one of the parties desire the separation, while the other clings to the unity? . . . Can any real good or happiness possibly result from an enforced contrivance of marriage upon the part of one party thereto? . . . Now let me ask, would it not rather be the Christian way, in such cases, to say to the disaffected party: "Since you no longer love me, go your way and be happy, and make those to whom you go happy also?"[17]

In terms of pornography, I've read better. In terms of marriage, Woodhull raised issues that, to this day, profoundly challenge the status quo. Many sought to dodge that challenge by accusing her of being, in the words of one newspaper, "a domestic monstrosity . . . rotten, festering, polluted, and abominable."[18] Of the many similar news reports, she said, "The press have stigmatized me . . . [and] the doctrine of Free Love, upon which they have placed their stamp of moral deformity. . . . This conclusion is no more legitimate and reasonable one than that which should call the Golden Rule a general license to all sorts of debauch."[19]

Personally I would not want to debate this woman. But those who did so by ridiculing her presidential bid on the basis of her views on marriage not only overlooked her actual views on the subject but also overlooked the fact that *she was not running on a Free Love platform*. Her platform was equal rights. And, by the way, not just equal rights for women, as can be gleaned from the headline "'Victoria' on the Stump—She Says Christ Was a Communist."[20]

Not all of those who ridiculed Woodhull's candidacy did so on the basis of her sex or her marital views. Some did so on the basis of her spiritual views. When the *Chicago Tribune* headlined a report on Woodhull "The Queen of Quacks" and the *Charleston Daily News* ran a piece on her previously excerpted speech headed "Demosthenes at Steinway Hall," they were alluding to the fact that Woodhull was an adherent to Spiritualism, the belief in communication with those whose earthly life had ended. As such, Woodhull believed herself to be periodically in contact with Demosthenes, a statesman in the days of Ancient Greece.[21]

"Demosthenes assures her that she will be the next President of the United States," Washington DC's *Evening Star* told readers. "Demosthenes declares it to be the correct thing for the American Victoria to live with two husbands."[22] Yeah, except, not.

"Religious freedom does, in a measure, exist in this country, but not yet perfectly," Woodhull replied to such slurs on her beliefs. "That is to say, a person is not entirely independent of public opinion regarding matters of conscience." As significant is *when* she said this: in her so-called Free Love speech at Steinway Hall.[23] Indeed that speech is a fitting monument to her candidacy in that it was *not*, despite news reports, promoting sexual promiscuity and was *not* only about Free Love, and the news coverage of the speech did *not* include her views on religious freedom, women's rights, and the distribution of wealth. At the risk of a bad pun, Woodhull's quest for the presidency brings into focus the variety of ways in which women were tied up in *nots*.

On the other hand, here's a fun fact: the principal opponent to President Grant's reelection that year was Horace Greeley, the founder and editor of the highly regarded *New York Tribune*. Greeley is most remembered today for popularizing the phrase *Go west, young man*, and least remembered (since the press kept it under wraps despite Greeley's never trying to hide it) for being entranced with Spiritualism.[24]

Here's a less fun fact: Woodhull was not running for president on behalf of Spiritualists. And while her platform did primarily advocate women's rights, she was not running with the endorsement of the National Woman Suffrage Association, from which she and her supporters had broken away to conduct their own convention in 1872. As for the National Woman Suffrage Association, it was established in opposition to the American Woman Suffrage Association.

This organizational splintering among woman suffrage advocates reflected the shape the nation was in at that time. The mainstream candidates for president in that year's election included not only Grant (Republican Party) and Greeley (Liberal Republican/Democratic Party splinter) but also Benjamin Gratz Brown (Liberal Republican/Democratic Party splinter), Thomas A. Hendricks (Democratic Party splinter), Charles J. Jenkins (Democratic Party splinter), David Davis (Liberal Republican Party), Charles O'Conor (Bourbon Democratic Party), and James Black (Prohibition Party).

The shattering of political parties in the aftershocks of the Civil War reveals why 1872 was the year the first woman ran for president. Reporting on Woodhull and her supporters breaking away from the National Woman Suffrage Association at its 1872 convention, Portland, Oregon's *New Northwest* explained:

> That this Presidential Campaign brings the nation to one of those crises . . . of general political disintegration, when many new combinations will be formed and several candidates run for the Pres idency, they [the National Woman Suffrage Association] thought it a good time for further agitation, to share in some direct way in the general excitement and party re-organization . . . and demand recognition of each. . . . Mrs. Woodhull's plan, however, differed widely from this, and her action defeated the whole purpose of the combination. She proposed . . . a new Constitution, a new party, a new platform . . . all to be crowned with herself for President.[25]

In this regard Woodhull's candidacy reveals a fact from the past (and present) often overlooked: *not all feminists are alike*. It was also in this regard that Woodhull's candidacy veered into the realm of fringe.

Viewed by many Americans as a fringe candidate, Woodhull's campaign crashed in a way that it may have avoided had public opinion been tipped more toward perceiving her as a legitimate candidate. Three days before the election she and her sister were arrested and jailed, charged with sending obscene material through the U.S. Post Office. The pornography, as it turned out, was an exposé of an adulterous affair between a highly respected minister, Henry Ward Beecher, and the wife of Theodore Tilton, an upper-crust New York poet and journalist. Beecher was prominent for having been a leading abolitionist as well as the brother of Harriet Beecher Stowe, author of *Uncle Tom's Cabin*. Thus *Woodhull & Clafin's Weekly* revealed that a supposedly highly righteous man was a marital hypocrite.

The timing of the arrest was not calculated by opponents of her campaign; rather Woodhull timed the exposé to provide a last-minute burst to her campaign. Previously she had declared, "The whole social state is honeycombed with social irregularities and outrages. . . . Everybody knows that everybody else knows it, and yet everybody pretends to conceal the fact that everybody knows it. Hypocrisy is settling like a mildew on every individual character."[26] Virtually verifying this accusation, no newspaper or public figure responded; they pretended not to hear it. Woodhull then forced them to hear by outing one of the nation's preeminent religious leaders and offering him as Exhibit A in her claim of marital hypocrisy. Unable to ignore such evidence, the nation's public figures were forced either to acknowledge that her attack on marriage had an element of truth or declare her attack so salacious as to be legally obscene.

We can see which they chose. What they did not count on, however, was that the arrest and pretrial confinement of Woodhull and her sister in the dank Ludlow Street Jail turned out to be hot stuff for selling newspapers—so much so that the authorities ended up dropping the charges.[27]

As for the election, what few votes Woodhull may have received have been lost in the category of "Other."

After the dust settled, Woodhull resettled, moving to England, divorcing her second husband and marrying a third, this one a wealthy British banker. Over the ensuing years she and her daughter published the *Humanitarian Magazine*, and with money no longer an object, Woodhull became a benefactor of Sulgrave Manor, the home of George Washington's ancestors. As women began to acquire rights, Woodhull spoke out in favor of sex education, in opposition to abortion, and in favor of eugenics. She was not, in other words, in agreement with most modern-day feminists regarding abortion or with virtually all Americans, post–Nazi Germany, regarding eugenics.

In 1892 Woodhull returned to the United States to a take another shot at that year's presidential election. Her announcement was greeted by so many quips they were combined into a nationwide news article featuring the top nine, followed soon after by the top ten of a new slew.[28] Recognizing reality, Woodhull ended her quest, resumed her activities in England, and passed away in 1927 at the age of eighty-eight.

James B. Walker

From Mainstream to Fringe—Anti-Masonic Party

JAMES B. WALKER RAN FOR PRESIDENT IN 1876 AS THE nominee of the National Christian Association. Or the American Party. Its members never quite settled on an official name. While their platform contained a number of planks, their primary issue was the enactment of laws to prohibit the Freemasons, an organization they viewed as a threat to democracy. Yes, the guy down the street who parades in a sequined fez to raise funds for charitable causes. Back in the day, they were feared by multitudes of Americans on account of their secret rituals and oaths.

But that was back in the days before Walker's day, which is what makes his fringe candidacy significant. It reveals how views that were once mainstream can later be fringe. Through Walker's campaign we can bring into focus not only what changed but, more important, *why.*

Who, for starters, was James B. Walker? Perhaps the best answer appeared that election year in the *Cincinnati Star*: "James B. Walker, of Illinois, and Donald Kirkpatrick, of New York, are the candidates of the National Christian Association—anti–secret society— for President and Vice President. . . . Now who are these Walker and Kirkpatrick, please?"[1] Evidently not famous is who they were. And in that respect Walker differed significantly from the candidate nominated by his party in the previous presidential election, the well-known politician and diplomat, Charles Francis Adams, son of John Quincy Adams, who in turn was the son of this nation's second president, John Adams. Despite the pedigree he brought to his anti–secret society candidacy, Charles Francis Adams received less than 1 percent of the vote—way less. We know, for example, how many votes he received in Indiana (one); the numbers from the other states got mixed in the bin of "Other."[2] Similarly we know that, four years later, Walker garnered seventy-two votes in Michigan—not bad compared to Adams in Indiana, though still roughly .02 percent of that state's total 317,528 votes.[3] Compare these numbers to the first anti-Masonic presidential nominee, Attorney General William Wirt, who received nearly 8 percent of the vote nationwide. He, however, ran four decades earlier, in the 1832 presidential election.

Part of the difference between Wirt's small but noteworthy number of votes and the negligible showing by Adams and Walker in the 1870s can be attributed to a headline-grabbing mystery in that earlier era. In 1828 William Morgan, a former member of a Masonic lodge in Rochester, New York, was denied membership in the Batavia, New York, lodge when he relocated there. In retaliation Morgan threatened to publish a book revealing the secret rituals and oaths of the Freemasons. Before doing so, however, he was abducted and never seen again, making national headlines. A second round of headlines kept the nation's attention when a decomposed body washed up on the New York shore of Lake Ontario. Still, all those headlines were mere kindling to the political wildfire that ensued. As one New York newspaper reported, "The antimasonic feeling seems spreading . . . nor is this excitement confined to our state." The article went on to explain the suspicion echoing through much of the country that Freemasons secretly swore an oath of mutual favoritism and protection. "When, in addition to the boldness and atrocity of the crime," it declared, "the mystery in which its perpetrators as well as its details are involved, and the absolute nullity of the law in its efforts to seek out and punish the guilty parties are considered, it can scarcely be wondered at that the populace should be almost fanatical and phrenzied [*sic*] upon such a subject."[4]

This fear took the form of a political party called the Anti-Masonic Party. A measure of its significance can be seen in the fact that its first presidential nominating convention, in 1831, dominated nearly an entire page of coverage in newspapers in the nation's capital, where politics were most closely followed, but also in newspapers in major urban centers, such as the *New York Spectator*, and in rural regions, such as Pennsylvania's *Gettysburg Star*.[5]

By the next presidential election, however, Morgan's disappearance was old news; other issues had elbowed their way to the forefront, and the best the Anti-Masonic Party could do in 1836 was seek influence by endorsing the nominee from the well-established Whig Party, William Henry Harrison. After that the Anti-Masonic Party was kaput.

Fast-forward to five years after the Civil War. "Some very curious proceedings have been lately had in this city by an organization which styles itself the National Christian Anti-Secret Society Convention," the *Cincinnati Enquirer* told readers in 1870, dismissing their effort with this characterization: "Those who are in this crusade hope to revive the old anti-Masonic feeling . . . [from] a third of a century ago."[6] It was these proceedings that set in motion the nomination of Charles Francis Adams as their presidential candidate in the next election.

"Crazy Candidates" headlined an 1872 article in Indiana's *Fort Wayne Daily Sentinel*. It took potshots at what it considered that year's looniest contenders for the White House, its shortlist consisting of George Francis Train, "a man named James Black" (considered wacky for campaigning to prohibit alcohol), Victoria Woodhull, and Charles Francis Adams.[7]

Expressing the prevailing view of Freemasons, the *Chicago Tribune* declared in an article reprinted nationwide:

> We have no more sympathy with Masonry than the Anti-Secret Society has; but if a man wants to put on a white apron and other silly toggery, march around with a square and compass behind a brass band . . . let him do it and have as many secrets as he pleases to keep from his wife. Ten to one where he has one secret she will have a dozen. Silly as Masons may be, the height of silliness is reached by these Anti-Secret Society individuals who . . . go into spasms every time they see a square and a compass.[8]

As the 1876 election approached, and despite the fact that the Adams candidacy had flopped, the not-very-merry band of anti-

Masons played on, now receiving even more guffaws. "The members of these secret societies have no objections to these mild lunatics enjoying themselves in their own way," an Illinois newspaper declared, "especially as their fulminations can hurt no one. This is a free country."[9]

Understandably Adams was not up for more mockery by running again as the standard-bearer of a party that was little more than a political punching bag. The best they could come up with was James B. Walker, a minister from Wheaton, Illinois, who had recently retired.[10] While his name appeared on the ballot nationwide, there is no evidence Walker ever left home to rouse voters—possibly because of his age (seventy-one), possibly because as the campaign season was just getting started, his wife passed away. As a politician Walker was indeed a fringe candidate; as a person he was a locally respected elderly man who had lived a productive and upright life.

Why, then, was a political party that once was mainstream now on the fringe? Indeed why—given that the original party collapsed—did it even reappear? And why did it reappear when it did?

Both the original Anti-Masonic Party in 1828–38 and the second, never precisely named party in 1870–76 appeared during periods when there was heightened concern as to whether the American experiment in democracy would work. In both eras social uncertainties resulted from a relatively sudden change in commerce that, in turn, led to major shifts in population and demographics. The completion of the Erie Canal in 1825 turned the Great Lakes into highways of commerce from the hinterland to the sea via this new waterway through western New York (where, by the way, William Morgan disappeared). As many Americans relocated and immigrants arrived to avail themselves of the economic opportunities created by the canal, old social bonds withered and organizations such as the Freemasons provided opportunities for new bonds to be formed.[11]

In addition, during this earlier era the torch of leadership was being passed from the founders of the United States to the next generation. From, for example, John Adams to John Quincy Adams.

From highly cultured patricians such as Thomas Jefferson to men of more common stock such as Andrew Jackson. Raising a very real concern: Would they—would we—be up to the task? Would we be able to follow in the footsteps of the nation's revered founders? Might our democracy be done in by members of societies whose secret oaths will undermine the integrity of those who govern— judges, jurors, legislators, governors, possibly even presidents?

Similarly, following the Civil War one could well wonder whether the nation's democracy could work. Clearly it had failed in regard to slavery; only violence and destruction were able to put an end to that question. And it was certainly fair to wonder if that use of brute force damaged, if not destroyed, our democracy itself.

Similarly as well, soon after the Civil War the transcontinental railroad was completed—the spine from which sprang multiple new rail lines. As with the Erie Canal, these railways were followed by shifts in population and demographics. Once again organizations such as the Freemasons enjoyed an increase in popularity, followed once again by an increase in those concerned about it and other secret societies. For it was also in this era of major social and economic change that other fraternal organizations were springing up to provide a sense of community amid rapid change, such as—among the less generous—the Ku Klux Klan.[12]

Similarly as well, then, there was again reason to ask if we would be up to the task of following in the footsteps of the nation's founders. With this in mind, it is not surprising that the first choice for president of those who feared secret societies this second time around was the son of a president who was the son of a president. And whose *second* choice was a man who had lived his life ethically and honestly, in no small part because he had never ventured into politics nor sought fame.

Why, then, didn't America care this second time around? For reasons which, through another fringe candidate, we've already seen. While these social and economic shifts were akin to those that spawned the first anti-Masonic movement, there was now a new issue that was far more dominant: *healing the wounds of the Civil War*. Worth repeating from the discussion of George Francis Train (from the same election whose list of "Crazy Candidates" included Charles Francis Adams) is the statement previously cited from that year's *North American Review*: "All that seems to be wanted is the quiet continuance of the present opportunities and dominant influences, in order that the great settlement may complete itself."[13]

Through the candidacy of James B. Walker we are able to see more clearly just how accurately that 1872 insight from the *North American Review* captured its era and today serves to illuminate why Walker's presidential campaign and that of Adams in the previous election were on the fringe.

Mark Twain

First Celebrity Candidate

"I HAVE PRETTY MUCH MADE UP MY MIND TO RUN FOR President," Mark Twain wrote in an 1879 article that was syndicated in newspapers nationwide.[1] A satiric piece by the nation's preeminent humorist, it constituted the entirety of his "contemplated" presidential bid. In contrast to the reaction that followed the similarly satiric candidacy of John Donkey in 1848, neither the press nor politicians responded to Twain's comic bid for the White House with comments or jokes of their own—raising the question *Why?* Other aspects, too, of Twain's brief feint at becoming a candidate raise questions that yield insights.

Significant in its own right, Twain's "candidacy" broke new ground that cleared the way for humorists such as Will Rogers in 1928 and comedians ranging from Gracie Allen in 1940, Pat Paulsen in 1968, Stephen Colbert in 2008, and others taking their acts to the presidential stage. Just as we'll see how each of these comic candidates provides separate insights into the shape of the nation in those eras, Twain provides us with a window through which we are able to detect subtleties in the political landscape in his day.

Given the rise in recent times of negative ads attacking rival candidates, many may be surprised to know such attacks were the target of Twain's 1879 satire. "What the country wants is a candidate who cannot be injured by investigation of his past history, so that enemies of the party will be unable to rake up anything against him that nobody ever heard of before," he wrote in his syndicated newspaper article. Twain then announced, "I am going to own up in advance . . . and if any Congressional committee is disposed to prowl around my biography in hope of discovering any dark and deadly deed that I have secreted, let it prowl."

And own up he did, as only Twain, one of nineteenth-century America's masters of fiction, could. Among the skeletons in his closet to which he "confessed" were these:

> I ran away at the battle of Gettysburg. . . . I was scared. I wanted my country saved, but I preferred to have somebody else save it. . . .
>
> My financial views . . . do not insist upon the special supremacy of rag money or hard money. The great fundamental principle of my life is to take any kind I can get. . . .
>
> I also admit that I am not a friend of the poor man. I regard the poor man, in his present condition, as so much wasted raw material. . . . My campaign will be: "Desiccate the poor workingman; stuff him into sausages."

Running away from battle at Gettysburg? What made Twain think that would get a laugh, particularly back then, from either Northerners or Southerners? Therein, however, is a key that explains the political mud being slung at the time (and, as told by David Mark in *Going Dirty*, all the way back to nastiness and "alternative facts" being hurled by the Founding Fathers).

In the presidential campaign that preceded Twain's piece, the Republicans' nominee, former Ohio governor Rutherford B. Hayes, squared off against the Democrats' candidate, former New York governor Samuel J. Tilden. Among the accusations leveled against Tilden was that he avoided service in the Civil War other than lip service.[2] Also satirized in Twain's essay were accusations that Tilden's fundamental financial view was to take any kind of money he could get. He was accused of tax evasion and a variety of fraudulent financial transactions, along with perjury during investigations into those accusations.[3]

Nor was Hayes exempt in that 1876 contest. He too was accused of shameful behavior during the Civil War—in his case, holding money for safekeeping on behalf of a soldier under his command, then keeping the money after the soldier died in battle and subsequently lying about it.[4] Hayes too was accused of graft, in his case accepting congressional back pay to which he was not entitled.[5] And while not accused of planning to turn workingmen into sausages, Hayes was accused of planning to deprive them of enough money for bread in order to benefit their wealthy (usually Republican) factory owners.[6]

In short, the jokes were keyed to current events. Still, Twain's brief foray into the upcoming presidential contest provides further insight by virtue of being so brief. Twain could have taken the political bull by the horns and run with it, especially as he was immensely successful on stage in what would later be called stand-up comedy. Why didn't he? Since we cannot climb inside Twain's mind, we can only speculate, then see if those speculations add further dimensions to the issues he skewered.

Had Twain turned his newspaper piece into material he could take on tour, what had been a laugh would have become a satiric campaign. Similarly, had politicians or the press reacted with comments or jokes of their own, they too would have turned comedy into crusade. But the issue of political mud-slinging was not likely to get a lot of traction or laughs during the upcoming 1880 campaign since the 1876 election had ended up hurling more than mud—democracy itself got hurled. Tilden won more than 50 percent of the votes and a plurality of the votes in the Electoral College. After a series of backroom deals, however, Hayes emerged as the winner. Thus negative campaigning was not at the top of America's agenda in the upcoming contest between the highly respected and incorruptible general, Winfield Scott Hancock (named after but not related to the previously eminent general) and a former general turned semi-corruptible congressman from Ohio named James Garfield.[7]

Moreover even a comic campaign against negative campaigning ran the risk of losing laughs to the extent that accusations such as those in the previous election turned out to be true. In the case of the winner, Hayes had in fact played fast and loose with one thousand dollars entrusted to him by a soldier named Nelson J. LeRoy. And as president, Hayes indeed turned out to be no friend to the workingman, dispatching the U.S. Army to suppress a nationwide railroad strike that ensued after repeated reductions in wages.

That Hayes oversaw policies that benefited wealthy Americans provides what may be the primary reason Twain refrained from taking this material to the stage. He was among those wealthy

Americans. While *Tom Sawyer* and *Huckleberry Finn* made Twain and his hometown of Hannibal, Missouri, famous, he now lived in a grand home in tony Hartford, Connecticut. Moreover *he himself had campaigned for Hayes.*[8]

Twain may also have wondered how many laughs he could get from his predominantly well-to-do audiences, for whom things were going so swimmingly but so clearly at the expense of others. The signature "achievement" of the Hayes administration was ending Reconstruction by removing the troops that had remained in the South to enforce compliance with federal laws. Not only was the military subsequently used to battle striking workers; its departure from the South enabled the denial of rights and often deadly persecution of African Americans.

Maybe best to get the laugh and leave it at that.

Whether or not that thought was in Twain's mind, the fact that he did not take his mock campaign essay and turn it into an act amplifies for us today the complexities the nation faced at that time.

Twenty years later Twain made another gag about seeking the presidency. Returning from a world tour of five years, he arrived less than a month before the 1900 presidential election—a rematch between Republican William McKinley, the incumbent president, and the Democrats' charismatic orator, former Nebraska congressman William Jennings Bryan. Asked upon his arrival which candidate he supported, Twain replied that he was undecided and also uncertain if he was still a registered voter. "If I find that I cannot vote," he then quipped, "I shall run for President. A patriotic American must do something around election time."[9]

That was all there was to that. A quip unattached to any issue. Twain, in fact, made a point of detaching it from the issues of the day, preceding his candidacy gag by telling the reporters gathered at the pier, "Don't ask political questions, for all I know about them is from English papers."[10] Times had changed, and Twain knew better than to set foot on what, after his long absence, was an uncertain stage.

While Twain had been abroad, President McKinley and his new running mate in 1900, Theodore Roosevelt, had recently led the charge into the Spanish-American War. Even if the charges were fictitious, the United States wrested from Spain its possession of Cuba, Puerto Rico, the Philippines, and Guam. To keep or not to keep was the question of the day. In addition McKinley signed into law the annexation of Hawaii, whose queen had been overthrown in a revolution for "democracy," spearheaded by Americans backed by the presence of the U.S. Marines. Many Americans strongly opposed the nation becoming kin with Europe's far-flung empires. Others, McKinley and Roosevelt included, viewed such expansion as necessary for security in a transforming world.

Twain knew of this shifting shape in American views, and he experienced it within himself, telling reporters, "I think that I am an anti-imperialist. I was not, though, until some time ago, for when I first heard of the acquisition of the present Pacific possessions I thought it was a good thing for a country like America to release those people from a bondage of suffering and oppression that had lasted 200 years."[11]

Traveling around the world for the past five years, however, Twain had seen lands under foreign rule, including Ceylon (present-day Sri Lanka), India, South Africa, and Tasmania (now part of Australia). Revealed by the tentativeness in this second candidacy gag is Twain's awareness that imperialism may not be a laughing matter. Indeed this brief feint at candidacy revealed how the United States had changed in relation to the world but also how the world had changed Mark Twain.

George Edwin Taylor

First African American Candidate

IN 1904 GEORGE EDWIN TAYLOR, A FARMER AND FORMER
newspaper editor from rural Iowa, ran for president of the United
States. In 2011 the historian Bruce L. Mouser published a biography, *George Edwin Taylor: His Historic Run for the White House*.
The reason this all but forgotten candidate from America's political periphery was worthy of a biography is that he was the first
African American to run for the presidency.

By contrast, Mark Twain's run for the presidency is only briefly
noted in his biographies, when noted at all—and appropriately so,
as Twain was just making a joke. Taylor was serious. As to their
racial difference, Taylor's candidacy reveals that it actually occludes
more insightful distinctions that reveal the shape of racial views
back then being far less simple than many today may assume. Twain
identified with the interests of wealthy Americans, most of whom
voted Republican, but so too did most African Americans, continuing to hew to the party of Lincoln. Taylor likewise identified
with fellow African Americans, but he also saw common cause
with farmers and industrial workers, most of whom were Democrats and many of whom were racist. Nevertheless Taylor aligned
with and was active in the Democratic Party.

Until his presidential bid.

Following the official end of Reconstruction in 1877, the powers-
that-were in the South before the Civil War became the powers-
that-be via their formerly dominant Democratic Party. But they
now had to deal with the enactment in 1868 of the Fourteenth
Amendment, which granted citizenship to former slaves. To combat this amendment when rebuilding their party's platform, they
included trap doors to impede African Americans from voting.

Among the ways they devised, and that were subsequently enacted by their state legislatures, were poll taxes and literacy tests—deemed legal since, ostensibly, they applied to everyone. At the national level the Republicans did nothing to intervene on behalf of African Americans being deprived of their rights. By the 1904 presidential election enough African Americans despaired of making inroads in the Republican Party that they convened in St. Louis to form the National Liberty Party for the purpose of nominating their own presidential candidate or exerting more influence by forming a bloc of African American voters.

The keyword in the previous sentence is *or*. From the outset the absence of a unified vision regarding the mission of this new party repeatedly undermined its effectiveness, which in turn discouraged many highly regarded African American leaders from committing to the effort. While Taylor was highly regarded, he was not the first pick of the convention. In fact he was *fifth*—and before getting to him, they'd even picked a white guy.

First to be nominated was Alexander Walters, an activist bishop in the AME Church who had served on various commissions and in other political capacities.[1] He declined the offer. The convention then set its sights on J. Milton Turner, who was the first African American in the nation's diplomatic corps when President Grant appointed him ambassador to Liberia.[2] He too said no thanks. The delegates in St. Louis then voted to back the candidacy of Theodore Roosevelt. Or not, as the next day they rescinded that vote and opted instead to nominate William T. Scott. He accepted.[3]

"Candidate for President Arrested" read the headline in Minnesota's *St. Paul Globe* on July 14, 1904, two days after the reports of Scott's nomination. The article reported, "William T. Scott, candidate for president of the United States on the National Liberty Party (colored) ticket, was arrested today on account of an unpaid fine. . . . Several months ago, Scott, who runs a saloon and summer garden, was convicted of conducting a disorderly place."[4]

Scott was removed from the ticket and replaced with George Edwin Taylor, whose rise had been as impressive, albeit less exuberant, than that of the more charismatic Scott. Nevertheless several of the details surrounding Scott's removal provide us with a view of racism being camouflaged in that era. Despite the widespread acceptance back then of racist ridicule in depictions of African Americans in literature and by whites in blackface on stage, many Americans sought to cloak their racism from others (and, perhaps, themselves) in ways that would soon be aimed at the Taylor campaign.

"It is extremely painful to learn that the presidential candidate of the National Liberty Party, who is the conductor of a beer garden in East St. Louis, has been arrested for keeping a disorderly place," one Pennsylvania news report began with seeming sincerity. It then pulled the rug out from under that concern when it went on to make a play on words regarding alcohol: "This is a free country and allows almost anyone to run for president, but the National Liberty Party appears to have *reached the limit*."[5]

Similarly from an Arizona newspaper: "The National Liberty Party (colored) has selected Payne and Scott as its standard bearers, although one of its candidates is a little handicapped by reason of being in jail at East St. Louis for failure to pay [a] fine for running a disorderly house."[6] The phrase "disorderly house" was often a form of camouflage. Today it may sound like a euphemism for "whorehouse," but the term encompassed much more. A "disorderly house" was a place where any illegal activities were believed to occur habitually—a term so broad that, in time, courts ruled it unduly vague and therefore susceptible to arbitrary and capricious enforcement.[7] Which is also to say, a useful tool for racists.

Camouflage of a different stripe was embedded in the report of Scott's arrest that appeared in a St. Louis newspaper when it stated, "It is an insult to the Negro of the state of Illinois and of the United States by placing such an objectionable Negro at the head of such a movement." After citing this statement in his biography of Scott, Bruce Mouser (the biographer also of Taylor) asked, "'Objectionable Negro'?"[8] The phrase was not random at the time. In *A Guide into the South* (1910), the word *objectionable* occurs six times—five in the context of African Americans, the sixth in reference to a spring at a particular resort having a "not objectionable scent." Similarly "objectionable Negro" was frequently used in other books and newspapers at the time.[9] But hold onto your hats. The St. Louis newspaper that hurled this term at Scott was that city's African American newspaper, the *Palladium*.

All of these issues beset the National Liberty Party's convention, culminating in its ultimately nominating Taylor. These are the same complexities that cause us to question whether Taylor was a "fringe" candidate or a third party candidate. For beneath these semantics is the key question: Was Taylor's candidacy widely viewed with ridicule?

Clearly, even in 1904 many white Americans spoke of Taylor's presidential bid with respect. Days after his nomination, the *Omaha Bee* ran an article recounting the education he cobbled together while growing up in Wisconsin, his entry as a youth into the newspaper trade as a printer's assistant and subsequent rise through the ranks of that white newspaper to become its city editor, moving on to create his own newspaper in Iowa, and later becoming a successful farmer and active Democrat.[10] Press material announcing Taylor's candidacy and providing a more detailed account of his life appeared verbatim as newspaper articles in numerous northern states.[11]

In Taylor's hometown of Ottumwa, Iowa, both of the newspapers—one aligned with Democratic Party views, the other with Republican—printed in full Taylor's "Letter of Acceptance," that era's version of the speech nominees deliver today at their party's convention. In it Taylor spoke of the poll taxes and literacy tests used to block African Americans from voting. He then pivoted from pointing at southern Democrats to pointing at northern Republicans:

> The present president [Theodore Roosevelt] and the Republican congress, together with the Supreme Court, dodge behind the ghost of Jefferson Davis . . . while to the politically crucified negro of the South they say "peace, be still, run with patience in the race that is set before you." The only difference I am able to discern between the [southern] Democrats and the present administration Republicans, as to the subject of disfranchisement, is that the former are scrupulously honest in expressing their determination . . . while

the latter are most unscrupulously dishonest, trying to run with the hounds, but sop with the coons.[12]

Taylor's still-pungent words did not fall on deaf ears throughout the country. But that's because no other newspaper printed his words, though several, in reporting on his candidacy, summed up his thoughts in words of their own.[13] In Ottumwa the newspaper editors knew Taylor personally. Elsewhere he was known racially. From that distinction arises the proverbial, albeit genuinely felt catch-phrase of subconscious denial of prejudice, "Some of my best friends are [FILL IN THE BLANK]." Taylor's candidacy provides a unique view of that distinction in action.

In one instance, however, Taylor was handed a nationwide megaphone in the form of a weekly magazine called the *Independent,* which published an article he wrote shortly before the election. Once again he cited what all Americans knew, that African Americans were being systematically excluded from voting in the South, but this time he replaced witticisms such as *racing with hounds while sopping with coons* with something more powerful: muscle. "No other race of our strength would have quietly submitted to what we have . . . without rebellion, a revolution, an uprising," he wrote. "We, too, propose a rebellion, a revolution, an uprising, but not by physical force, but by the ballot—through the National Liberty Party."[14]

But Taylor's views on racism transcended race. He saw the efforts to marginalize African Americans in the larger context of maintaining power by diminishing the power of others. While skeptical of the Socialist Party and aware of the racism among many Populists, Taylor took the opportunity in this magazine article to urge other groups facing forms of persecution to recognize their common ground: "Whenever the [African American] race and their co-laborers shall array themselves in one grand independent political phalanx, the very foundations of the two dominant political parties will be shaken, and the leaders of both will be brought to a realization of the danger which threatens their organization, and the rights of the people will again be considered by them instead of those of special classes as is the present rule."[15]

If the truth and intelligence of his statements did not inoculate Taylor against ridicule, add to them the fact that he also spoke to his expectations as a candidate for president—expectations that were far from those of a fool. "The campaign will be of an educational nature, and confined largely to the distribution of literature," the *Ottumwa Weekly Democrat* reported in a follow-up article on Taylor's candidacy.[16] The previously mentioned newspaper reports that summed up his acceptance letter included Taylor's fondest presidential hope, that his candidacy "may hold the balance of power which will decide who shall be president."

All told, there was nothing ridiculous in Taylor's candidacy. Except, for some number of Americans, his race.

"Taylor is nothing more than a tool used by the Democratic Party to cut into the Negro vote of the Republicans," declared H. R. Wright, an attorney and Republican activist.[17] But grab hold of your hats again: Wright was African American. Moreover he was one of many African Americans who looked askance at Taylor and the entire effort to form a separate party based mainly on race. In reporting on the planned convention to create the National Liberty Party, an African American newspaper in Minnesota smirked, "We know nothing of the affair, but suppose some schemers are trying to catch suckers, of which it is said one is born every minute."[18] Here again Taylor's candidacy reveals racial views at the time to be far from simple.

Needless to say, there was no shortage of smirks from whites. "All Reformers are funny, but none of them are quite as funny as the Reformers of the National Liberty Party," California's *Modesto Evening News* chortled. Iowa's *Cedar Falls Gazette* sniffed, "We are not yet ready to turn the government over to them, and the fact that they are clamoring for this state of affairs is proof positive that they are incapable . . . and wholly unable to control what they seek."[19]

Just as an absence of facts camouflaged the ridicule heaped on Scott following his arrest on the unsubstantiated claims in the charge that he operated a "disorderly place," so too were details deleted when the *Iowa State Bystander* stood by and said, "And lastly, the National Liberty Party, headed by one Geo. E. Taylor of this state as its sponsor and candidate for president with no plat-

form and but few principles in [his] letter of acceptance."[20] In point
of fact Taylor's party had adopted a platform, one that was just as
extensive as those of the Democrats and Republicans, all of which
was detailed in Taylor's letter of acceptance. In addition to advocating federal intervention to dismantle racially aimed restric-
tions on voting, Taylor cited the platform calling for the enactment
of pensions for veterans of the Mexican-American War and the
Civil War and for former slaves. It also called for a federal prohibition on polygamy (this issue aimed at that era's Mormons in
Utah), independence for the Philippines, the elimination of tar-
iffs on imports, the establishment of a national arbitration board
to resolve disputes between labor and management, and the use
of a national referendum when Congress so deems. But—hat-grab
time again—the *Bystander* was an African American newspaper.

Undoubtedly there was outright racist ridicule based on stereotypes of African Americans. Such remarks, however, appear
to have gone from car to car without settling on a printed page
where more equality-minded Americans could spot it and swat
it. Nevertheless Taylor's candidacy lifts the camouflage used to
cloak such stereotypes.

"Colored Man Fails to File His Nomination Papers" headlined
an article in Iowa's *Marshalltown Times-Republican*. Similarly his
hometown *Ottumwa Weekly Courier* told readers Taylor "neglected
to file the necessary papers and his name and that of his party will
be missing from the ticket voted in Iowa."[21] These depictions of
Taylor as inept, at best, and in way over his head, at worst, cloaked
quite a few facts from readers.

By the time the newly formed National Liberty Party nominated Taylor, there was barely enough time, if that, to organize at
state and local levels, learn the requirements of those states for filing to be on the ballot, completing the paperwork for each, and
coming up with filing fees and related costs for each state.[22] Further thwarting those efforts was the continuing uncertainty as to
the mission of the party, exemplified by Taylor's running mate,
W. C. Payne, endorsing Roosevelt eight weeks into the campaign,
such as it was.

There was yet another wrinkle in the shape of racial views at the time. Ohio's *Stark County Democrat* declared, "If Mr. Turner's [meaning Taylor's] colored brethren don't stand by the National Liberty Party better than they stood by the Negro Protective Party in Ohio some years ago, he will scarcely get a thousand votes in the United States."[23] Getting Taylor's name wrong was most likely an honest mistake, and "colored brethren" may or may not have been intended to convey ridicule. But predicting the number of votes Taylor turned out to be spot on, given that some 13,500,000 votes were cast in that year's presidential election. Taylor received approximately 2,000 votes—a difference of less than .001 percent from that newspaper's prediction.[24]

"George E. Taylor, candidate of the National Liberty Party for president in the past campaign, has announced his intention to try again. Nailed the 'colors' to the mast, as it were," Iowa's *Times-Republican* punned shortly after the election.[25] But it was not to be. The National Liberty Party collapsed and disappeared.

In time Ottumwa's unit of the Democratic Party accepted Taylor back, and in return for his efforts on behalf of the party's gubernatorial candidate in 1907, he was provided with the salary—and job, ostensibly, given that he was now fifty years old—of a police officer.[26] In response to which, the season was opened for ridicule. "From nominee for the office of president of the United States to night policeman in Smoky Row, in the 'red light' district, Ottumwa, is the unique change which time has wrought for George E. Taylor," Iowa's *Oxford Mirror* reported. But the news was not confined to Taylor's home state; articles appeared in papers ranging from North Dakota's *Bismarck Daily Tribune* to the *Washington Post*—that seemingly even-keeled news vessel telling its readers, "Ottumwa [Iowa] enjoys the distinction of having as a member of its police force a man who, during the last national campaign, made the race for the office of President of the United States. George E. Taylor, who was nominated for President by the National Liberty Party . . . has just been appointed to the position of night patrolman by Mayor-elect T. J. Phillips. . . . The Liberty Party is composed of colored voters."[27]

Was it because Taylor was African American that newspapers

across the nation, including the *Washington Post*, chimed in on this incident of small-town graft? You decide.

Indeed "you decide" was the underlying dynamic in much of the racist ridicule aimed at Taylor and the National Liberty Party. After all, African Americans have never been the only ones victimized by an absence of key details in press attacks. Nor have they ever been the only object of the adjective "objectionable." And, theoretically at least, literacy tests and other requirements for voting did not only apply to them. Likewise laws regarding a disorderly place. Nor, to take the flip-side from a contemporary example, does the right to carry a firearm in public theoretically apply only to whites. But would you want to be a law-abiding black man with a gun holstered to your hip?

In Taylor's candidacy we see how the shape of racial views in his era bore more facets than we may have thought. In addition it brings greater perspective and more dimensions to the changes that led to the election of Barack Obama as president of the United States. Yet it also brings very clearly into view an aspect of racism that has not changed: the use of camouflage that hides prejudice in ways that say *You decide.*

PART 2

Running onto the New Field
of Radio and Television

Will Rogers

Anti-Bunk Party

WHEN INDUSTRIALIZATION CREATED RADIO, IT ALSO created a new stage for political candidates. Professional comedians quickly recognized it as one upon which they too could clown as candidates for president. The speed with which comedians took to the airwaves to run for president was nothing short of remarkable. NBC tested the first coast-to-coast broadcast that hooked together a network of local stations in 1926; CBS followed suit the very next year, and just a year after that Will Rogers, the nation's preeminent political humorist in that era, took to those airwaves as a presidential candidate against the Democrat's 1928 nominee, Governor Al Smith of New York, and the Republican's Herbert Hoover.

Rogers ran as the nominee of the Anti-Bunk Party. Acknowledging that, after being nominated, it was customary for the candidate to register modesty, Rogers commenced his campaign by declaring he didn't feel that way at all. "After all," he told voters, "it's only the office of Candidate that I am accepting. You know it don't take near as good a man to be Candidate as it does to hold office. That's why we wisely defeat more than we elect."[1]

But Rogers did not make this acceptance speech on radio; he made it in *Life* magazine—at the time a satirical magazine, prior to its reinvention as the hugely successful forum for photojournalism. At the outset Rogers's campaign was less a reflection of radio than of the 1848 bid for the White House generated by the similarly satirical magazine, *The John-Donkey*. In this instance *Life* magazine launched the campaign when it solicited, or at least claimed to be soliciting, suggestions from readers for a "bunkless" candidate, casting aside political party prejudices. In the issue that followed, an article titled "Will Rogers for President" claimed that the famous humorist was the overwhelming response they had received.[2] *Life* wholeheartedly agreed, noting, "If elected, he would be the first president in sixty-two years who was funny intentionally." A funny line in itself, and one that provides a sense of how admired Rogers was, assuming it to be a (mathematically faulty) comparison to Abraham Lincoln—arrived at by subtracting 62 from 1928 and assuming they were not referring to Andrew Johnson, who has not come down in history for his wit. While Lincoln is most remembered for his Emancipation Proclamation, he was also known for his many humorous (some said annoying) anecdotes.

After accepting the nomination, Rogers gave the equivalent of twenty-two stump speeches in the pages of *Life*, which the magazine featured under banner headlines trumpeting a series of anti-bunk virtues:

Our Candidate Spurns the Ballyhoo

Our Candidate Won't Meet the Voters

Our Candidate Has No Religion

Our Candidate Won't Sling Mud

Our Candidate Is Not Optimistic

America loved it. After all, who wouldn't love a candidate that vowed to eliminate such things as slogans? "Slogans," Rogers declaimed, "have been more harmful to this country than Bo-Weevil, Luncheon Clubs, Sand Fleas, Detours, Conventions, and Golf Pants." Regarding the controversy over the prohibition of alcohol, in force at the time, Rogers told voters, "The Republicans will try and get by on the old gag, 'We are for law enforcement,' which . . . don't mean anything more than an Aviators' convention going on record as being in favor of 'Tail Winds.'" Going on to predict the Democrats would dodge the issue by nominating a presidential candidate on one side of the issue and a vice presidential candidate on the other side, Rogers made his "no bunk" position crystal clear: "Wine for the rich, beer for the poor, and moonshine liquor for the Prohibitionist."

Under the *Life* headline "Our Candidate Insults the Voters,"

Rogers noted a remark by an up-and-coming figure in the Democratic Party named Franklin Roosevelt. Young Roosevelt declared that the Republican Party's claim that it was the party of prosperity was false and that Americans were too smart to be misled again by such bunk. In response to which Rogers said, "Of all the bunk handed out during a campaign, the biggest one of all is to try and compliment the knowledge of the voter and tell him he can't be fooled like he used to be."[3]

The public ate it up. So much so that radio came a-calling. Rogers, no stranger to radio (or film or vaudeville), answered the call. Having already hosted the largest network hook-up of stations to date (an event so momentous it received front-page coverage in the *New York Times* that filled an entire page in its continuation), Rogers knew the power of radio and knew ways to put that power to work. As in that historic January 4, 1928, network program, which featured a variety of celebrity appearances, Rogers's radio campaign for the presidency featured a line-up of endorsement performances by the likes of the popular song-and-dance comedian Eddie Cantor, the columnist Walter Winchell, and the highly intellectual newspaper humorist Robert Benchley. As Election Day neared, numerous newspapers reported that the grand finale of the Rogers campaign would be a "torchlight parade" featuring the nation's most recent aviation hero, Amelia Earhart, proclaiming her endorsement of Rogers.

The torchlight parade took place in a CBS radio studio.

The news media wanted as much of this campaign as it could get. It spread to Rogers's regular letters to the *New York Times* that appeared in syndication nationwide and into the numerous public appearances he made for other purposes.

While all this was good business for Rogers, there was also a serious side to his humor—one that, in that 1928 election, went beyond bunk: freedom of religion. For the first time in the nation's history, a major political party had nominated a Catholic for president, that candidate being Al Smith, and that fact explaining the meaning not only of *Life*'s banner "Our Candidate Won't Sling Mud" but of the next week's more explicit banner, "Our Candidate Has No Religion."

"Well, the campaign is degenerating," Rogers wrote in the first of these two addresses. With his aw shucks manner bolstered by occasional aw shucks spelling and grammar he told voters, "It started in by 'Whispering.' . . . At first we was all hearing so many whispers that it begin to look like everybody that spoke to you had lost their voice. We laid it to bad colds for awhile, then we discovered that everybody couldent have Phenomonia at once. . . . [Later] it was the idea of whispering that made everybody sore, so they quit whispering and started saying worse things at the top of their voice."[4]

In his own way, Rogers too was testing the waters with whispers, but it wasn't until his next address in *Life* that he gave it full voice. "I told you last week that the 'Whispering' would stop," he began, "and they would start 'Shouting' instead." He too, this time, went on to yodel what most troubled him: "A woman in Virginia sent out a Scenario saying that the Catholics would not make good Postmasters, that the mail would be read in Rome before delivery. . . . Then the only white Republican in Alabama [back then still solidly anti-Lincoln Democrats] felt called upon to instruct what few constituents he had that could read, that in case of Al's election the Protestants would be called on to meet a Lion in a catch-as-catch-can combat for the jollification of Tammany Hall and the visiting Cardinals."[5] Rogers then used humor to lasso as many readers as he could regarding this serious issue, proudly asserting that his own Anti-Bunk Party "not only kept clear of Church, but also of State matters."

In regard to his own candidacy, Rogers himself appears to have engaged in a backroom deal to create whispering before shouting. Prior to *Life* asking its readers to suggest a bunkless presidential candidate, a letter to the editor of the *Baltimore Sun* urged "the conscription of Will Rogers" for president.[6] While the letter writer, one L. J. Quinby, was clearly writing in jest, unknown to Baltimoreans was that Quinby was a professional writer who lived in Hollywood.[7] Three weeks later the local Democratic Party in the county where Rogers grew up voted to honor their hometown celebrity by offering his name as a presidential candidate. Somehow this seemingly benign local event triggered national news coverage.[8]

Rogers responded by declaring, "I do not contemplate becoming involved in a political conflict of any nature during the Autumn of 1928."[9] Which, as it turned out, was bunk—albeit comic bunk. After all, he did accept the satiric nomination of *Life* magazine. The events that preceded his acceptance, however, provide reason to suspect that Rogers and the magazine had themselves engaged in a whispering campaign. But Rogers opted not to drop his rope over this bunk and drag it into the daylight—understandably; after all, he was a performer.

If indeed Rogers's antibunk campaign was itself bunk, the significance is not an indictment of Rogers. The significance is in recognizing the symbiotic relationship between politics and performance. And in recognizing the curtain that is used to hide that relationship from public view. Rogers couldn't say so outright; it would ruin the humor. But he often had an ironic twinkle in his eye, particularly when he said such things as "I do not contemplate becoming involved in a political conflict of any nature during the Autumn of 1928."

So effective was that curtain in this instance, some seriously began to ask whether or not Will Rogers should be elected president. This despite the fact that, starting with his acceptance address, Rogers repeatedly stressed the first and foremost point in his party platform: "If elected, I absolutely and positively agree to resign."[10]

"While the candidacy of Will Rogers is providing the laughs in the presidential campaign," Wisconsin's *Fond du Lac Reporter* predicted, "it may also corral more votes than some folks anticipate"—a not so humorous prospect that *Life* liked so much it printed it in a piece that also included Connecticut's *Bridgeport Post* opining, "Nobody can see through the politicians at Washington more clearly than Rogers. Nobody holds them in less awe. As President, he certainly would not be afraid of the Senate; the Senate would be afraid of him. Every time one of the Senate windbags began to gas, Rogers would utter a piercing remark of perhaps ten words and deflate him."[11]

No less a figure than the automobile magnate Henry Ford (who himself periodically tested the waters for a presidential bid) declared, "The joke of Will Rogers's candidacy for President is that it is no joke. It is a serious attempt to restore American common sense to American politics. . . . There is however, one item in his platform with which I cannot agree—'If elected, I will resign.' . . . The real reason for electing him is to see what kind of a President he will make."[12]

Not all the endorsements from famous Americans were so bold; indeed, most were as tongue-in-cheek as the political promises of the candidate himself. When, for instance, Amelia Earhart (with whom Rogers shared a passion for aviation) spoke on his behalf at the grand torchlight parade on radio, she shifted from a light-hearted endorsement of her friend to serious remarks about her own ideas regarding the development of air travel.[13]

Even at the height of Rogers's ballyhoo of laughter against bunk there were occasional journalistic turds in the punchbowl. "A candidate for President on the no-bunk ticket, Will Rogers deals in just about as much bunk as the average politicians," Iowa's *Waterloo Times-Tribune* insightfully, if drearily, observed in an editorial. Which *Life*, in fairness and self-insightfulness, included in its periodic roundup of what newspapers were saying of their candidate, albeit under the headline "An Insult." Similarly *Life* had previously included, from Oregon's *Corvallis Gazette*, "LIFE has started a boom for Will Rogers for President to head a 'bunkless' party. On such a party platform, Will would get about one per cent of the votes . . . because bunk appeals to the majority more than anything else."[14]

The *Corvallis Gazette* got it right, in that it said "about." Of the 36,808,961 votes that were cast in the 1928 election, Rogers received some percentage of the 323 votes cast nationwide (less than .001 percent) for candidates other than Herbert Hoover, Al Smith, or those representing third parties on that year's ballots.[15]

Gracie Allen

Surprise Party

THE FRONT PAGE OF CRESTON, IOWA'S MAY 18, 1940, *NEWS Advertiser* bore the banner headline "Belgium's Cities Are Falling." Its equally depressing sub-headline read: "Nazis Push to 60 Miles from Paris." Just below these massive words, a small news item was squeezed in among the columns of devastating reports from Europe. "The nation has a new presidential candidate today," it noted, "Gracie Allen, nominated by the Surprise Party at a convention as goofy as Gracie's patter." Comic relief doesn't get much clearer than that. But Allen's campaign ended up entailing much more than comic relief.

Gracie Allen was one of America's most popular comedians. She and her husband, George Burns, had been headliners in vaudeville, then became radio stars, and would go on to become television stars. For those unfamiliar with what this newspaper meant by Allen's goofy patter, here's a sample from a broadcast in which she is telling Burns about waiting in line at a department store exchange counter for the clerk to return from lunch:

Allen: There was a lady and her husband in front of me. And I said to her, "I hope that girl comes back from lunch soon." And she said, "So do I. I have to make an exchange for my husband; this hat's too small."

Burns: And you said . . .

Allen: "Why change your husband? Why not get him a larger hat?"[1]

In her mock campaign for president, Allen brought that same verbal chaos to a nation fearfully watching the world turn into actual and frightening chaos. Declaring that she was seeking the nomination of the Surprise Party, she delighted reporters and their readers with her views on foreign relations ("They're all right with me, only when they come they've got to bring their own bedding") and the Neutrality Bill ("If we owe it, let's pay it").[2]

The idea of running for president in a mock campaign did not originate with Allen or Burns. It began with the writers of their radio show as a running gag they could use for a few episodes in February 1940. The public loved it, so much that one syndicated columnist expressed his own qualms about comedians as clown candidates when he wrote, "Now comes Gracie Allen with a real screwball stunt which calls for her running for the presidency of the United States." But, he had to admit, "if anybody can do the trick in good taste it will be Gracie."[3]

The gag expanded as other radio stars had Allen "unexpectedly" appear during their shows to solicit their support for her presidential bid, parrying their questions and doubts, such those of Fibber McGee and Molly, who told her they'd heard *rumors* about Allen and the White House. "They're not true," she snapped, "I don't intend to take in any roomers."[4]

What began as a radio gag turned into a road-show campaign when the Union Pacific Railroad spotted an opportunity for publicity. The previous year, the railroad had partnered with Omaha, Nebraska, and Paramount Pictures to promote the film *Union Pacific* (dramatizing its struggles when becoming part of the nation's first transcontinental railroad) by sponsoring a Golden Spike Days festival. Setting aside the fact that the "golden spike" that joined the eastern and western branches to create the transcontinental railroad is in Utah (specifically Middleofnowhere, Utah), the event was so successful the railroad wanted to sponsor a sequel. Representatives of the Union Pacific approached Allen about doing a whistle-stop tour with thirty-four stops for stump speeches as it traveled from Los Angles to Omaha, where a grand celebration would again take place, this one culminating with a mock convention of her Surprise Party to nominate her as its candidate.

Tempting as the offer was, Allen had qualms. "She didn't think she could do it," Burns recalled. "Gracie disliked making speeches, even to small groups."[5] While she may well have disliked making speeches, these would not have been speeches per se but rather comic monologues in the form of speeches. Even though she was the one who got the laughs in their act, those laughs were connected to Burns as the straight man, for his feeding her the setups and for the couple's impeccable sense of mutual timing. Going solo would be risking an entirely different act from the one with which the public was familiar. To a comedian, flopping is every bit as devastating as losing an election is to a politician.

Moreover their act had never been political. Nor had either of them ever personally been much interested in politics. The closest they'd come was their patriotism. When, during the worst years of the Depression, the federal government asked them to do some routines promoting the National Recovery Act, they promptly did. One such broadcast had Burns trying to explain to Allen the benefits of this new program's minimum-wage provision:

Burns: Look here, Gracie. This means that women will be getting men's wages.

Allen: Don't be silly, George. My sister Bessie has been married to three men and never got their wages.

Clearly their writers knew how to pull off political gags for Allen and, simply as a matter of craft, could turn those gags into monologues posing as mock speeches. As to her uncertainty regarding their reception, if publicity could generate large enough crowds at the stops along the way and the monologues did work, it could be a boffo bonanza.

And was it ever.

Even before the whistle-stop tour commenced, the National Women's Press Club invited Allen to attend an annual dinner in Washington as a guest of honor along with the likes of Eleanor Roosevelt. "Mrs. Roosevelt has nothing to worry about if Gracie is elected President," one columnist wrote regarding the invitation. "Miss Allen has already sent out a statement saying she wanted Mrs. Roosevelt to remain in the White House because George cannot write 'My Day'" (Eleanor Roosevelt's own syndicated column that she wrote as first lady).[6] At the event Allen charmed Mrs.

Roosevelt—and, as important, the women's press corps—with remarks such as her promise that, if elected, she would change DC to AC so her clock would work.[7]

Meanwhile Burns and Allen's publicity people were obtaining eight hundred signatures in Los Angeles supporting her presidential bid. While those signing undoubtedly did so to play along, not everyone was amused. Yet another syndicated columnist declared that those who signed "were really writing a sad comment on the irresponsibility of the American voter."[8] Similarly, albeit conversely, what made Allen's campaign sad for one of the most famous of that era's columnists, Walter Winchell, was not what it said about voters but what it said about politicians. "Gracie Allen must be heartsick," he told his readers, "listening to some of the White House candidates—realizing that her clown candidacy will never get as many laughs as theirs."[9] Viewed either way, right off the bat there was more to her candidacy than comic relief; there was commentary. And there was commentary because her fringe candidacy resonated with, and amplified, (dis)chords barely heard in a political landscape trembling amid so many nations at war.

By the time Allen's campaign train rolled up to its first stop in Riverside, California, on May 9, Burns estimated some three thousand people were waiting for her. Even if exaggerated it was quite a throng. Her speech there and at all the stops along the way left them laughing since, as the publicity mill kept grinding, large crowds greeted her even at the smallest towns in their scheduled stops. By the time the train reached Salt Lake City, the mayor was there to greet her for a parade in which thousands lined the streets.[10] In Omaha some seventy-five thousand people had assembled for the grand parade of its second Golden Spike Days festival, with Allen in the reviewing stand alongside Mayor Dan Butler and, in front of her, network radio microphones. When the mayor told her to call him Dan, she recoiled, telling him, "Everyone knows you can't say Dan on the radio." She did, however, offer him the job of secretary of the interior "so we can have x-ray pictures taken together."[11]

The Surprise Party nominating convention took place in Omaha's mammoth Ak-Sar-Ben Arena, its exotic name being more corny than mystical: Nebraska spelled backward. Some ten thousand "delegates" gathered to hear Allen declare, "You are probably just as anxious as I am to find out what I stand for." She then pounded away at her campaign platform. "I propose to extend the Civil Service to all branches of the government, because I think a little politeness goes a long way, don't you? . . . To take care of Emergency Relief, I plan to build thousands of new gas stations. . . . But Social Progress, no. Social Progress is not one of my goals. This country is not a social-climber."[12]

Allen was nominated by acclamation.

Along the way to Omaha, something more had become part of her candidacy. Increasingly she was campaigning, in her way, on behalf of women. By the time she reached Omaha she told those gathered at her convention that she was "a better man for the job than many who aren't even a woman. . . . The reason we need a woman in the presidential chair is to pave the way for other political jobs for women, such as lady senators and lady congressmen. Anybody knows that a woman is much better than a man when it comes to introducing bills into the house."[13]

Growing more comfortable in the role of mock candidate, Allen tooted women's rights more clearly (and less comically) in her book, *How to Become President*, which appeared in stores right after her nomination. In the book she did not need vocal and instantaneous laughs in the way a comedian does in performance. This format enabled her to assert, "Let me tell you that women are getting very tired of running a poor second to the Forgotten Man. And with all the practice we've had around the house, the time is ripe for a woman to sweep the country."[14]

More notable was a remark she made without a punchline: "The Constitution doesn't say anything about 'he' or 'him'; it refers only to the 'the person to be voted for.' And if women aren't persons, what goes on here?" Most notable, however, was what she wrote after mentioning Eleanor Roosevelt: "Now that I think of it, have you ever considered what a great President Mrs. Roosevelt would make? It's not just her charm and personality. She has intellect, tact, humor, a keen sense of her responsibilities to—but wait a minute! Who am I campaigning for, Mrs. Roosevelt or me?"[15] While there was a punchline in this instance, it was a punch in her own nose aimed to leave them not only laughing but also thinking.

For the most part, however, *How to Become President* was apolitical and aimed at giving her readers a hoot. As its title suggests, she urged all Americans to consider that they too could be president, and accordingly she provided advice: "Of course, it goes without saying that every candidate must be . . . awake to the needs of the people whether they know what they need or not. You should also come from a good family, because while breeding isn't everything, it is said to be lots of fun."[16]

After making her big splash in Omaha on May 18, followed closely by her book, Burns and Allen soon returned to their apolitical radio hijinks. In mid-June one columnist asked, "Whatever did become of the Gracie Allen for President movement, anyhow?"[17]

The answer came two weeks later, when she announced she was withdrawing from the race and that she'd instructed her publisher to send the proceeds from her book to the Red Cross. "Fun is fun," she told the press, "but the sacred right of franchise under the American Constitution is nothing to be trifled with. I've carried the joke far enough. . . . We are on the eve of selecting a president in the gravest period in our history." She would, she said in closing, throw her party's support to "whoever is elected."[18] A classic Gracie Allen laugh line. And simultaneously a patriotic statement.

It was also a rare moment in which Allen spoke in the voice of the highly intelligent woman who created her daffy stage character. Why, then, did she build her career in comedy on self-ridicule with lines such as "You are probably just as anxious as I am to find out what I stand for." Here is where Allen's "campaign" reveals its most profound significance. Successful women comics at the time of her campaign, and right on through to TV's *I Love Lucy* in the 1950s, nearly all relied on self-deprecating humor (Mae West being an exception that proved the rule).[19] The comic mayhem of Allen's and Lucille Ball's humor remained under the onstage control of their husbands. In the signature closing to Burns and Allen's act, Burns said, "Say goodnight, Gracie." And she immediately complied.

Scholars have engaged in a lively discussion about self-deprecating humor, particularly in regard to female comedians. Take a gander at a few of the titles from academic journals: "Self-Deprecatory Humor and the Female Comic: Self-Destruction or Comedic Construction?"; "Comedy and Femininity in Early Twentieth Century Film"; "Situation Comedy, Feminism and Freud: Discourses of Gracie and Lucy."[20] Although they have disagreed regarding self-deprecating humor, all have recognized that it contains a powerful paradox. On the one hand, one presents oneself as ridiculous; on the other hand, making a successful career by presenting oneself as ridiculous is not ridiculous.

In this regard, consider Burns's role during Allen's comic campaign. "In Las Vegas we rode in a long torchlight parade—they made me drive an oxcart," he recalled. "In the parade held in Salt Lake City they made me drive a midget racing car. During the torchlight parade in Cheyenne I had to drive a stagecoach."[21] Let's lift his modesty; no local yokel made Burns do anything. Rather, with Allen performing solo and empowered, he helped sell the act by clowning as the disempowered husband.

Most significant, however, Allen occasionally delivered lines such as this: "A platform is something a candidate stands for and the voters fall for."[22] That laugh was not a self-ridiculing punchline; that was a punch at the public. In getting that laugh, Allen took a step into the empowered realm of hurling humor at others.

Just as quickly, however, she stepped back from that realm by announcing the end of her comic campaign. As we will see, however, for another famous female comic, Roseanne Barr, it will be her starting point in 2012. For Gracie Allen in 1940, it was a goal.

John Maxwell

Vegetarian Party

"FINE REPORTER I AM. I'M ASHAMED TO SAY I JUST FOUND out the Vegetarian Party was running its own candidates for president and vice president in the fall election," a syndicated columnist confessed shortly before the 1948 election, then speculated, "And the more you think about it, it seems they've got a good chance." Notably the columnist was none other than Gracie Allen, who wrote a humor column from 1945 to 1949. In this instance her readers were undoubtedly licking their chops for vegetarian jokes and, true to form, she dished them out. The nation, she observed, was "chockful of vegetarians—especially the people who got that way whether they liked it or not, due to high meat prices." She went on to point out, "A vegetarian president who could see in the dark because he ate lots of carrots would certainly be useful for dealing with the Russians. And it would probably be the first time there was spinach in the White House since the days of Presidents U. S. Grant and Benjamin Harrison, who both sported a good crop on their chins."[1]

As often with humor, it emanates from serious issues—and not only the Soviet Union but meat prices as well were serious business in 1948, the year John Maxwell ran for president as the nominee of the Vegetarian Party. Odd as it may seem today, the Soviet Union too appears to have exerted an influence on his campaign. And even spinach and beards were a more prominent aspect of attitudes in that era than they are today.

Societies of vegetarians date back at least as far as 1850 in the United States and for just as long have been associated with having political missions. An editorial from that year downplayed concern over poverty in America when it snooted, "While much may be done to improve the conditions of the 'landless poor' by judicious individual and national effort, we still think that the country will not be seriously agitated by this question much before the Vegetarian Society succeeds in making it a *sine qua non* with candidates for Congress that they abstain from beef."[2]

Fast-forward to 1948 and the platform of the Vegetarian Party on which Maxwell, an eighty-five-year-old proprietor of a vegetarian restaurant, ran for president. While the platform did not call for congressional candidates to disavow eating meat, it did call for a prohibition on raising livestock for meat. As for the seemingly separate issue of poverty, the party called for federally funded public housing, a massive program of public works (including creation of interstate highways), a broader and more generous social security system, and a federal program to encourage the formation of food cooperatives to provide an alternative to privately owned grocery stores. Both in the 1850 news item and the 1948 platform of the Vegetarian Party, produce and poverty were intertwined. Maxwell's fringe candidacy amplified why the two were in harmony.

While the interstate highway system, the Department of Housing and Urban Development, and expansion of social security were all enacted during the next two decades, not enacted were the food co-ops or, needless to say, the prohibition on meat production. Nor were any of the Vegetarian Party's additional ideas aimed at financing those projects. These proposals included the party's call for giving Congress rather than the Federal Reserve control over the monetary supply and for taxes to be based on *gross* income rather than *net* income, thereby eliminating all tax deductions and credits.

What's vegetarianism got to do with such stuff? Or with, I should also mention, the Vegetarian Party's call for government ownership of radio and television broadcasting systems.

And electric utilities.

And the telephone system.

And all natural resources.[3]

Suppose we put the question this way: What would you call this party in 1948, with fear of the Soviet Union causing the Red Scare to get into full swing?

Not that they weren't vegetarians. Indeed they were so vegetarian that a nationally reported dust-up occurred during the election when the party's leaders repudiated George Bernard Shaw, the world-famous playwright who had long proclaimed his vegetarianism, as being insufficiently vegetarian by virtue of having once been treated for pernicious anemia with cod liver oil. "His goose is cooked," Maxwell's running made, Symon Gould, declared—demonstrating that being vegetarian doesn't mean you don't have snarly teeth. Or a sense of humor.[4]

What being vegetarian *did* mean for the members of the Vegetarian Party intertwined healthful and moral living. Both elements can be seen in a news item on Maxwell's candidacy: "'Thou shalt not kill.' So the Vegetarian Party thinks it has a moral issue. . . . It's all right if he doesn't make a law to compel us to eat more carrots and spinach."[5]

Gracie Allen's gag about Maxwell's candidacy and spinach provides a view of America's social landscape at this time as, in both of these instances, the humor relied upon spinach being viewed askance as an unpleasant "health food" (which kids were encouraged to eat because it gave Popeye super strength). When Allen went on to link spinach to past presidents with beards, the joke relied on beards being considered old-fashioned as well as a sign of nonconformity during this cold war era when allegiance was widely demanded. "Whiskers don't look so queer on poets as they do on basketball players," one columnist noted in 1949 in a piece devoted to views of beards.[6]

Allen's line about the United States being "chockful of vegetarians—especially the people who got that way whether they liked it or not, due to high meat prices," held the key as to why, in that particular year, vegetarians formed a political party for the purpose of nominating a candidate for president. For the past five years, the availability and cost of meat were often front-page news in the United States. In 1943 meat rationing went into effect as part of the war effort. One of those who sought to ease concern over the reduced availability of meat was Maxwell. He received considerable news coverage for linking patriotic meat rationing with the health benefits of a vegetarian diet.[7] One year after the war the meat supply was again front-page news with the onset of a nationwide strike by meatpackers. Once again Maxwell took the opportunity to gain adherents to vegetarianism, this time receiving even more news coverage than he had during the war.[8] Following settlement of the strike, meat repeatedly resurfaced in the news as the price of beef commenced to rise, due to higher labor costs but also higher demand from a larger population as our military returned home and, not long after, the number of children dramatically increased.[9]

With the availability and cost of meat so frequently in the spotlight, Maxwell and many other vegetarians saw an opportunity to mount the national stage in the 1948 presidential election. Notably Maxwell himself was not the driving force behind the creation of the Vegetarian Party; the man at that helm was Symond Gould, his running mate. Nor was Gould's ending up in the number two slot the result of political infighting, as neither Gould nor Maxwell had visions of winning the White House. Gould told the delegates at their convention in New York that their mission was to gain increased attention. And while their view of the importance of a vegetarian diet was central to that mission, Gould spoke to the moral components of vegetarianism when, in that speech, he held out hope for possibly three million votes that "would come from prohibitionists, anti-vivisectionists [those opposed to the sacrifice of animals in product testing and other research] and anti–cigarette smoking groups." He then employed a particularly interesting phrase in saying, "We will also attract other groups of people of similar high moral principal."[10]

Sounds a little like the High Moral Party created by Live Forever Jones. Where Jones asserted that adhering to a highly moral life could enable one to live forever, Maxwell similarly (though infinitely more reasonably) claimed, "There's no question about it, vegetarianism does lead to longevity."[11] A reporter for the Associated Press conceded that Maxwell did not look as old as he was; indeed he wrote that Maxwell would have looked thirty years younger than his actual age if he shaved off his beard.[12] Because he was so healthy and alert at his age, Maxwell was an ideal candidate to spread the word about the benefits of vegetarianism. As to the beard, to the extent that it made him look older, so much the better, though the downside was the extent to which it made him look like a nonconformist.

Maxwell was well suited to be the party's standard-bearer because he was more widely known than any of its other leaders. He had appeared in news reports concerning the availability of meat from 1943 to 1948, and in the 1930s he was frequently mentioned in the press for his involvement in a movement called the Townsend Plan. Little remembered today, a physician named Francis Townsend commenced an effort in the early years of the Great Depression to enact federal pensions for elderly Americans. The creation of Townsend Clubs spread like wildfire. In Chicago, where Maxwell was well-known for having one of the largest vegetarian restaurants in the nation, he formed and led the Downtown Townsend Club and began to acquire a national name as a speaker and close adviser to Townsend. When the Social Security Act of 1935 failed to measure up to the legislation sought by Townsend and his followers, the movement continued, with Maxwell often appearing as an advocate for an expansion of the program. For a time Maxwell also hosted a radio show in Chicago and, prior to that, was a columnist for the *Milwaukee Leader* when he lived in that city. With the degree of name recognition he'd acquired through these activities, Maxwell was able to attract coverage as a presidential candidate in *Time* magazine, a full page with photo in *Life* magazine, and nationwide air-time on CBS radio.[13]

While Live Forever Jones was clearly far more idiosyncratic than John Maxwell, both campaigns amplified an attitude that had not changed and that periodically becomes political—a belief that healthfulness and righteousness go hand in hand. During the 1948 campaign, however, Maxwell had to concede that vegetarianism did not necessarily result in righteousness. Adolf Hitler, after all, had been a vegetarian. Still, the duality can be traced back to biblical times, as Leviticus intertwines dietary and religious tenets. Similarly Muslims, Hindus, Seventh Day Adventists, Mormons, and numerous other religions conjoin the two, just as, on the secular side, a coach at my high school would cite and then translate a maxim from Ancient Rome: *Mens sana in corpore sano*—a healthy mind in a healthy body.

The 1868 candidacy of Live Forever Jones and, eighty years later, the 1948 candidacy of John Maxwell bring into focus the persistence and power of this belief. *Sharp* focus, for their candidacies also provide perspective on just how powerful it was.

Or wasn't.

Never powerful enough to elect a president. Not even enough to avoid considerable ridicule.

One local columnist in Illinois went hog wild—or perhaps the more apt pun would be completely corny—when he penned a mock speech in which Maxwell says: "We do not meat today to lambast the other parties, and neither do we want to turnip our noses at the opposition although we think some of our hecklers artichoke. . . . Some of the things that have been said about the way our country is being run are parsley true and parsley false. . . . We believe it to be a berry good suggestion that we all peach in and win the Cucumber election."[14]

In one instance ridicule of Maxwell's candidacy even turned up in the classified ads. Amid the listings of houses for sale it read:

THE VEGETARIAN PARTY

The other day a fellow wanted me to join the Vegetarian Party and try to elect a non–meat eating president. It sounded pretty sensible at first. Remove meat from the budget and high food prices would fall; people would be calmer and less animated. . . . But then I thought things might not be so smooth for a vegetarian nation in a meat eating world . . . so I didn't join the party. In fact, to make sure . . . I ate a hamburger right away; and it made me so animated I dug out all these real estate bargains.[15]

A shrewd use of filler for days when the page ran short of ads.

From the moment of Maxwell's nomination, the press began slinging zingers. "Lettuce-Nibblers Will Put Up Doctor for President" a headline in a Wisconsin newspaper declared, competing with "Meat Tee-totaler Candidate for Party" in an Iowa paper. A Missouri newspaper wondered if the Vegetarian Party "would be against muttonheads in public office and all form of pork-barrel legislation."[16]

Curiously (but answerably) the press mentioned but did not make fun of *Dr.* Maxwell's claim to be a "naturopath physician." Similarly (and getting us closer to answerably), only rarely did the press mention that Maxwell was born in England, which disqualified him from becoming president.[17] Neither of these facts is funny. And for the press, the value of fringe candidates is that they can be made funny. Which more than just rhymes with money.

And that is yet another way fringe candidates, whether they like it or not, help shape this nation's political landscape. Through mockery of fringe candidates the media adds to its coffers and all who engage in such ridicule contribute to enforcing society's prevailing norms.

No record exists of the number of votes Maxwell received. Probably less than the number of newspapers that couldn't resist one last poke, running an Associated Press report that began, "The Vegetarian Party's presidential candidate, Dr. John Maxwell of Chicago, made sure of one vote in today's election—his own."[18] Maxwell, who sought only to bring attention to his issues, anticipated the outcome, taking it not only in stride but with humor. "We'll try again next year," he told the press. "I'm young yet and will only be ninety in the next election."[19]

As it turned out, by then aging was beginning to snare him. He relocated to the warmer climes of California, where he passed away—though not until 1963, at the age of one hundred. Having outlived so many who had known of his achievements and having no offspring, Maxwell was buried in a grave that remained unmarked for the next fifty years. When a professor of history brought this oversight to the attention of the press, even in death one newspaper could not resist a parting shot. "Lettuce Adorn Vegetarian Presidential Candidate's Final Plot" its headline read.[20]

As for the Vegetarian Party, it moved on to another candidate in the 1958 election. This time around, however, the campaign

received less attention, in part because an internal conflict inter-
fered with its message. In the 1960 election the party received
only scant notice, as many of the programs it originally advocated
were now either in place or had become part of the platform of
the mainstream candidates.

Homer Tomlinson

"King of the World" Candidate

"WEARING A MANY-COLORED ROBE AND HIS $16 GOLD-LEAF crown, he goes about carrying a portable throne in one hand and a 'banner of peace' in the other, and the world on his shoulder—in the form of an inflatable globe." Thus one West Virginia newspaper described Homer Tomlinson, "the most confident presidential aspirant these days . . . who expects to be elected by miracles . . . [and] regards himself as a serious contender."[1] Readers of the article may have wondered why Tomlinson sought the presidency since, as the paper pointed out, he already considered himself "King of All Nations."

Clearly we can dismiss this individual as, sadly, psychotic.

Or was he?

Tomlinson, a perennial candidate from 1952 to 1968, was the leader of a no-nonsense church that frowned upon the use of lipstick, bobbed hairstyles, and wedding ceremonies while parachuting. Actually, not so much the last one.[2]

"Miss Ann Hayward . . . and Arno Rudolphi . . . were joined in marriage by Homer A. Tomlinson of the Church of God, Jamaica, Queens, as all three sat suspended in mid-air parachutes," the *New York Times* reported in what may be the most unusual wedding announcement in that newspaper's distinguished history. The event took place in 1940 at the New York World's Fair and drew national attention. "At a signal from the minister," an Ohio paper reported, "the wedding party was dropped to the ground."[3]

Maybe Tomlinson was starting to lose (or had already lost) his grip—or maybe he was applying his professional skills. Prior to becoming a minister, he had worked in advertising and public relations in the 1920s—the era in which publicity stunts were becoming professionalized. A fox hunt on Fifth Avenue and a hoax reception for the queen of Romania were among such antics on behalf of particular clients or causes in New York during this time.[4] Consequently, whether or not Tomlinson was psychotic was a question which, like that wedding ceremony, hung in the air for some time.

What was never a question, however, is that his presidential bids were viewed with ridicule. "Tomlinson Is Confident of Election by Miracle" was typical of the headlines in coverage of his candidacy—those headlines running the gamut from "Church of God Overseer to Run for President" to "What Homer Wants Is to Be King of U.S."[5] The chronology of that gamut, however, provides an insight into a subtle distinction in American attitudes toward religion that Tomlinson's fringe campaigns amplified. Of the three headlines just cited, ridicule is absent in "Church of God Overseer to Run for President," from Tomlinson's 1950 campaign. The other two, which barely suppress their mirth at Tomlinson's confidence in being elected by a miracle or his seeking to become America's king, were from his 1960 campaign. The key to the distinction took place in between those years, when, in 1954, a wire service article reported, "Bishop Homer A. Tomlinson, robed and crowned for the occasion, today proclaimed himself 'King of the World.'"[6]

Spiritual beliefs can be easy targets for ridicule. Seas getting parted, water turned into wine—the list could easily go on. The point at which ridicule commenced regarding the Tomlinson presidential campaigns reveals the extent to which most Americans respect the religious beliefs of others. That respect ends at the point where miraculous claims are made for *present-day* events.

For some, that point was reached in Tomlinson's first campaign, in 1952, which is to say, prior to proclaiming himself King of the World in 1954. Right from the get-go, the *Washington Post* told readers, "Tomlinson appears pretty confident of his chances of election . . . based upon a prophecy in the Book of Daniel, which says that one of these days dominion of the whole earth will be given to the people of the saints of the Most High"—continuing with the tipping point—"though we cannot find anything that indicates specifically that it will happen in November 1952." That this claim does not begin to match the enormity of the claim that one is God's designated King of the World likely accounts for the *Post* then hedging its humor by adding, "Still, there are plenty of people who believe the Bible is a safer guide than . . . the Gallup Poll."[7]

During Tomlinson's 1952 campaign such jabs remained rare; most of the news coverage kept a straight face. "In Seeking Presidency, Bishop Will Fast 21 Days" headlined a Maryland news report upon Tomlinson's announcing his candidacy. Under the headline "Bishop Runs for President," a Texas newspaper suppressed any mirth in reporting, "Tomlinson will begin his campaign with a 21-day fast starting at midnight Sunday, after which he will make a 42-state tour." Possibly on the verge, however, a Mississippi newspaper told readers, "He is taking only water and orange juice and black coffee, without sugar."[8] Did readers need to know how he takes his coffee, or was the reporter stirring in a teaspoon of absurdity?

Whether Tomlinson's fast was a period of spiritual cleansing and reflection or an aspect of insanity, it got him a lot of publicity—not as much as the Republican's nominee, Gen. Dwight D. Eisenhower, or the Democrat's choice, Illinois governor Adlai Stevenson, but far more than any of the seventeen other candidates who managed to get press coverage that year.[9]

With Tomlinson's 1954 announcement of his kingship, ridicule predominated, continuing through his 1956 and 1960 presidential campaigns, for which he toured the nation in kingly garb and a throne fashioned from an aluminum lawn chair. Typical media coverage: "The self-proclaimed 'King of The World' today crowned himself King of Iowa . . . on the steps of the statehouse, with an audience of two reporters, a photographer and a church representative." This report came from a journalist whose story went nationwide via United Press International. The other journalist present, whose story went national via the Associated Press, reported, "He carried with him a 28-inch plastic globe of the world which he inflated with the kingly breath before assuming the throne. The new king's world almost blew away in the stiff breeze, but he caught it in time to avert catastrophe."[10]

Tomlinson did not confine his royal appearances to campaign events. After his 1954 self-coronation before congregants gathered in a Tennessee tobacco barn, he set out for London, where he drew attention to his reign in Hyde Park, then moved on to Paris, where the press reported on that city's gendarmes prohibiting him from staging a ceremony in Napoleon's tomb. In 1958 Tomlinson drew worldwide attention when he popped up in the Soviet Union, enthroned just outside the Kremlin, announcing his kingship to passersby. The Russians were so puzzled the authorities let him be.[11] Clearly a cuckoo Amerikanski.

Except not entirely clearly. During his 1960 run for the White House, he admitted to one interviewer, "There may be some objection to my wearing robes and a crown. I know my wife objects."[12] Pretty lucid comment, not to mention amusing and endearing, for someone suspected of suffering from psychosis.

To another reporter, however, he said of his garb, "Would you rather I come as a soldier, gun in hand? This uniform I have is a robe of righteousness. It signifies a peaceful approach."[13]

Well, no. The garb of a king does not signify peace nor, necessarily, righteousness; it signifies power. And the choice of campaigning in either kingly garb or military garb is a false dichotomy; he could also campaign, if he thought about it, in a suit and tie. Or, for that matter, sackcloth and ashes.

Apparently he did think about it. When Tomlinson again donned robe and crown for his 1964 presidential bid, his running mate, fellow bishop W. R. Rogers, campaigned in sackcloth and ashes, quite possibly indicating: message received.[14] Which, if indeed the message was received by Tomlinson, casts further doubt on his living in a world all his own.

Moreover, even though kingly garb does not signify peace, turning swords in plowshares, as written in Isaiah, does. And Tomlinson did—literally, working with a blacksmith—in his 1952 campaign. As with his earlier parachute wedding and later with his kingship, the event drew nationwide press attention.[15] Undeniably Tomlinson knew how to publicize.

That Tomlinson may have been crazy like a fox is further suggested by his reaction to being mocked. At a 1960 campaign stop in Arkansas to proclaim himself king of that state, a man stepped up with his pet monkey and crowned her Queen of Arkansas.

"Tomlinson took the jibe good naturedly," the press reported.[16] Indeed journalists who interviewed Tomlinson never reported his being anything other than unexpectedly good-natured. In 1960 an Arkansas columnist told his readers that Tomlinson "turned out to be a most agreeable gentleman with a finely developed sense of humor—a quality I hadn't expected to find in a man who considers himself King of the World."[17]

In 1966 the highly regarded journalist, William Whitworth, interviewed Tomlinson for an extensive profile in the *New Yorker*. Describing his first impression, he wrote, "I was expecting to be greeted by a bodyguard or a State Overseer, or someone of the sort, but presently I saw in the distance a blue 1958 Chevrolet with a familiar figure at the wheel. The round, pink-face, the warm smile, and the large nose were clearly those of Bishop Tomlinson himself."[18] Of his parting impression, Whitworth wrote with greater affection, due in no small part to the self-awareness Tomlinson had displayed during the interview and now at their farewell, when the self-proclaimed King of the World said:

> "They've accused me of being a publicity hound. But I've never done any of this from a sense of pride. You have to be meek. Because people can really laugh at you." The Bishop sat in silence for a few seconds, and then, as I opened the door and got out, he abruptly became his old merry self. He leaned over to the window on my side of the car and said, "But I don't care. It's the work that matters. After all, what's Homer?" He burst into laughter, and he was still smiling as he drove away.[19]

In the 1964 presidential election (the one that preceded Whitworth's 1966 interview) depictions of Tomlinson had already begun to shift away from ridicule—and did so for the same reason they had previously shifted toward it. "Bishop Homer A. Tomlinson has given up his title as King of the World," the Associated Press reported in 1963, "to promote what he called a 'golden age' free of strife."[20] Tomlinson additionally strove in that campaign to widen his base beyond his own congregants by changing the name of his party from Church of God (which had stirred resentment from

Church of God congregations not affiliated with his) to the Theo-cratic Party.[21]

These actions didn't entirely insulate Tomlinson from ridicule, but the mockery did shift from explicit insults to implicit innuendos, as when the Associated Press reported, "Seven adults and eight children attended the national convention of the Theocratic Party Saturday night."[22] But even these kinds of wisecracks became rare; the preponderance of the news coverage reverted to its pre-kingship mode of simply reporting facts, as typified by such headlines as "Theocratic Party Plans Clergy Cabinet," "Theocratic Party Favors 10 Per Cent Income Tax," and "Theocratic Candidates Campaign."[23]

While separating religiously based prophecy and miracles from present-day events fended off depictions of Tomlinson as a kook, his faith-based campaign still left him vulnerable to criticism for being out of touch with the realities of the day. In the 1968 election, for example, he renewed his 1964 pledge to return the world to a strife-free Garden of Eden through the implementation of religious faith. A Minnesota editorial, reprinted in newspapers elsewhere, commented: "The prospect is pleasing until one contemplates what a modern-day garden might be like. There would be rides for the kids, of course. And cotton candy and popcorn vendors. There would be a tall metal-spike fence around it. And an 18-hole golf course nearby. The gates would lock at 10 p.m., but nobody would dare venture into the garden after dark anyway. And finally, as sure as the bishop makes little green apples, the highway engineers would run a freeway right down the middle."[24] Though no longer suggesting Tomlinson was out of his mind, the prevailing view now was that he was out of touch with the times.

Quite likely Tomlinson sensed it as well. During that campaign he had urged his supporters to back the reelection of Lyndon Johnson. But those who attended the Theocratic Party convention nominated Tomlinson instead. Not attending the convention was Tomlinson himself, who was in ill health.[25] The press—now far more familiar with Tomlinson—reported, "The clever, stocky old clergyman, a one-time Madison Avenue advertising man with a flair for religious showmanship, doesn't expect to win, but he says the campaign 'will give me a pulpit for citing our goals.'"[26] Not at all a statement one would expect from a psychotic.

Tomlinson's 1968 candidacy—as he also seems very lucidly to have sensed—would be his last. He passed away one month after the election.

Even before changing the name of his political party to the Theocratic Party, Homer Tomlinson had advocated turning the United States into a theocracy. His 1952 platform consisted of the Ten Commandments along with two additional commandments: "This is My Beloved Son; hear ye him" and "Love one another."[27] In his 1960 campaign he declared that he would "change the United States government from a democracy to a theocracy."[28] And he told voters how he would effect this change: "America is ready for a king. These things run in cycles and we are ready now."[29]

In this quest Tomlinson was addressing a deeper question that has caused conflicts throughout the history of the United States. Who is the ultimate authority: the government or God? It is a conflict that scholars have found embedded even in Genesis and Exodus.[30] In the United States the question has been particularly troubling since the Constitution's prohibition of an official religion confines God to less than certain authority. Tomlinson's fringe candidacy reveals the extent to which Americans have resolved this constitutional uncertainty—that extent being, to borrow a phrase from a news report on Tomlinson's campaign, "slightly less successful than a dog fight."[31]

Gabriel Green

Universal Flying Saucer Party

ANNOUNCING HIS CANDIDACY FOR PRESIDENT IN THE 1960 election, Gabriel Green told those present at his press conference that he had been instructed to run "by people from outer space. His advisers," the *Los Angeles Times* reported, "were from the Alpha Centauri system."[1] While Homer Tomlinson may have been pulling publicity stunts that made him look nuts, this Green guy for sure was off his rocker—or rocket. Or, as with "King of the World" Tomlinson, is that too easy an answer?

Certainly one can call Gabriel Green a kook or a clown, as most Americans did at the time. Nevertheless this candidate of the self-created Universal Flying Saucer Party reveals how fringe candidates bring into focus the shape we're in. In this instance it's a shape very similar to one the United States had been in before and, alas, may someday be in again.

Green grew up in Whittier, California—ironically the same town as another 1960 presidential candidate, Richard Nixon. While they did not know each other, Nixon being eleven years older, Green said he had taken a typing course from the future president's mother. Then again, he also said, "On several occasions I have talked to people from other planets."[2]

Green first attracted press attention in 1956, when he formed a club whose members claimed to have seen UFOs. A wire service report that appeared in multiple newspapers told the nation, "The group [is] headed by president Gabriel Green . . . a 31-year-old photographer for the Los Angeles city school system," then added a dash of ridicule by noting he was "a bachelor who still lives with his parents."[3] Back then there were so many claims of UFO sightings that, by 1956, newspapers reported them very selectively. The reason the press chose to report on Green's club was the group's prediction, based on messages they said they received from space people, that a flying saucer would appear in the skies over Los Angles at 10:30 p.m. on November 7, 1956. To which the wire service report couldn't resist adding, "Whether the Martians will disembark and be photographed with Jayne Mansfield [a Hollywood sex goddess] at Ciro's, he [Green] does not know."

For all its wisecracks, the report also included three statements that were, even if inadvertently, significant. It observed that the belief in UFOs had "become virtually another popular religion." It quoted Green as saying that the reason aliens from outer spaces were coming to earth was to "help people solve their problems." And it speculated that Green was "enjoying local fame with his project, which might explain it."

As to the last, that didn't explain it. Green lived until 2001, yet at no time other than 1960 did he seek the spotlight. Why only then? We can't climb into Green's head, but we can climb back to the years leading up to the 1960 election to recollect what was going on at the time that led to his candidacy with its "Space Age Platform," as he called it.

In 1945 the world learned of the atomic bomb. While very few fully grasped the physics that resulted in a heretofore inconceivable blast, given the devastation it wrought in Hiroshima and Nagasaki—and the Japanese surrender that followed—everyone believed in its power. No sooner had World War II ended than the cold war began. Four months after the end of the war with Japan, a wire service report informed Americans, "Army tells plans for new rocket weapon, space ships." Eighteen months later newspapers were reporting, as headlined in the *Chicago Tribune*, "supersonic flying saucers sighted by Idaho pilot." "Supersonic" meaning faster than the speed of sound, which was particularly eerie since human aviation had not yet achieved such speed.[4]

Unbelievable—except that many would have considered it unbelievable to detonate a bomb far more powerful than any previously conceived by splitting an atom. In this instance, however, scientists and the military scoffed. "Lt. Col. Harold R. Turner, an army rocket expert, ventured the opinion Saturday that Kenneth Arnold's [the Idaho pilot] flying saucers were merely jet planes," a wire service report stated three days after the sighting was first reported. But the report went on to state that "almost a dozen persons sprang up about the country to say they had seen the mysterious discs also."[5] This created a question that, as time went on, would increasingly shape the nation's political landscape: *Can we believe the government?*

The front page of one Texas newspaper not only published that report but also a wire service report that stated, "A crackdown on communism and persons deemed 'bad risks' from the national security standpoint today cost ten State Department employees their jobs." Similarly two wire service stories that ran on the same page of a Maryland newspaper on December 22, 1947, told the nation, "U.S. plane has flown faster than speed of sound," and "'flying saucers' may be Russian."[6]

In November 1949 the syndicated columnist Drew Pearson added to the nation's shock and awe when he wrote, "Although the United States now has an A-bomb many times more powerful than that dropped on Hiroshima, nevertheless it is true, as Senator [Louis A.] Johnson says, that scientists are working on a bomb more devastating than anything so far conceived by the mind of man. This is the hydrogen bomb."[7] Soon Americans were reading of "such advanced weapons as guided missiles" and that "the conquest of outer space has begun, with the first man-made satellite [the Soviet Union's *Sputnik*] circling the earth every hour and 36 minutes," followed not long after by the more startling headline "Russians Launch Rocket at Moon."[8]

These reports about Russian rocketry now aiming for the moon, about increasingly powerful atomic bombs, about communist infiltration, and about flying saucers were appearing in greater numbers every year. By 1950 more than 150 suspected communists were listed in the book *Red Channels* and subsequently blacklisted from employment in film, television, and radio; by 1955 twice that many people had reported to the U.S. Air Force what they believed to be sightings of flying saucers.[9] Stir all this together and by 1959 you get:

The Amalgamated Flying Saucers Clubs of America announced
yesterday that the Russian moon rocket never reached its desti-
nation. A statement issued under the name of Gabriel Green said
information received at 10:15 AM disclosed that intelligent beings
manning space craft from other planets destroyed the moon rocket
190,000 miles from earth. Green said the moon rocket was destroyed
because the nose cone contained active disease and virus bacte-
ria intentionally placed there by the Russians. "The space people
have indicated," Green said, "that they cannot allow any vehicle
of a destructive nature to contaminate outer space or the surface
of any other planetary bodies."[10]

And that same year you get this tidbit, under the heading "So
They Say": "The space people tell us that before we are ready to
be received back into the universal confederation of planets, certain social and economic reforms on our planet are necessary." It's
signed "Gabriel Green, director of Amalgamated Flying Saucer
Clubs of America."[11] And ultimately you get, "Gabriel Green, 35,
self-styled choice of the 'space people,' has declared his candidacy
for the presidency. . . . His campaign would be based on his system of 'prior choice economics' which he explained thus, 'Everything is or should be the sum total of all that has gone before.'"[12]

Quite likely the reason Green did not elaborate on what he
meant by "prior choice economics" being based on "the sum total
of all that has gone before" is that others had already detailed how
economics could be restructured based on its historical arc. Karl
Marx and Frederick Engels posited such a view in the *Communist Manifesto* when they wrote, "The means of production and
of exchange on whose foundation the bourgeoisie built itself up
were generated in feudal society. . . . The weapons with which the
bourgeoisie felled feudalism to the ground are now turned against
the bourgeoisie itself . . . [by] the modern working-class—the proletariat. . . . The proletariat [also] goes through various stages of
development."[13]

Yikes. Better to attribute the view to space people than those
guys. Especially during the cold war.

Not everyone, however, missed the connection. In a 1960 *Harp-*

er's magazine article, Hal Draper wrote, "Mr. Green told me his program was not entirely incompatible with Socialism; but Socialism is a dirty word here." The article further revealed that a good deal of Green's campaign strategy was actually very down to earth. "You've got to give something for everybody," Green commented when speaking of "means to the end."[14]

While Green gave few details during his campaign about "prior choice economics," he did allude to it in ways earthlings had heard before, when a newspaper ad he ran spoke of "true freedom where there is oppression and economic slavery"—economic slavery being a phrase familiar to anticapitalists. As to the other touchy issue—space people in flying saucers—that same literature contained a similarly soft-pedaled statement in Green's pledge of a "true Stairway to the Stars instead of missile-fizzles and launching pad blues." It did not, however, mention space people providing the expertise to overcome America's many failed efforts to launch a rocket. And, reflecting the era, the same document alluded to the cold war and the fears it engendered of World War III in a list headed "IF YOU WANT," which included "Survival instead of annihilation" and "A better tomorrow instead of no tomorrow."[15]

Green may have been a kook, but he was not necessarily crazy. UFOs were being reported by airline pilots and police officers—at considerable risk to their careers—along with too many otherwise totally stable individuals to dismiss all these people as even temporarily mentally unbalanced (though they may have been mistaken).[16] Even another presidential candidate claimed to have seen UFOs—a 1976 contender named Jimmy Carter.[17]

On the flip side, most of the pledges Green made in that same campaign ad could have come from any mainstream candidate. Also under "IF YOU WANT" Green listed, "Results instead of promises," "Ideas instead of double-talk," "Leadership instead of rule by political opportunists . . . and pressure groups." Normally banal, but weird when espoused by the candidate of the Universal Flying Saucer Party. What in God's name is going on here?

Here, in God's name, is a weird hint. James R. Lewis, a professor of religious studies, revealed a connection between flying saucer believers and cosmological politics in words from the Book of

Exodus: "There were thunders and lightnings, and a thick cloud upon the mount . . . so that all the people that was in the camp trembled . . . and Mount Sinai was altogether on a smoke, because the LORD descended upon it in fire."[18] Lewis was not suggesting that God descended upon Mount Sinai in a flying saucer, nor that angels were piloting the UFOs so many people reported seeing in the years following World War II. What he and scholars such as Gordon Melton, John Saliba, and Ted Peters have suggested is that, as with many of those in this era who believed UFOs were present, others had long before similarly claimed they had acquired special knowledge by contact with heavenly beings.

Also among scholars who addressed this recurrence of visitations from the heavens was the noted psychoanalyst Carl Jung. Writing in 1959, Jung maintained that the UFO phenomenon then taking place was the result of "emotional tension having its cause in a situation of collective distress . . . [that] undoubtedly exists today, in so far as the whole world is suffering under the strain of Russian policies and their still unpredictable consequences." As Jung went on, he shed light both on Green's quest for the presidency and on Green's political platform: "Such psychic tension issues in the unconscious a call for a Messiah to deliver us from our impending catastrophe."[19]

The clearest sign that Green was not nuts is the fact that he withdrew from the presidential race one week before Election Day, stating, "Not enough Americans have yet seen flying saucers or talked to outer space people to vote" for him.[20]

Green again threw his hat, complete with its fully extended antennas, into the ring in 1972. His beliefs about space people had not changed, but the way he campaigned did—and did so in ways that amplified changes difficult to detect amid predominant views.

While fears remained regarding a nuclear war annihilating the planet, those fears had begun to lessen in 1972 with that year's signing of the Anti-Ballistic Missile Treaty by the United States and the Soviet Union. The groundwork from which the treaty sprouted became more fertile with the decline in the Red Scare that had gripped the United States in the 1950s.

Consequently Green could speak more freely, without fear of

being branded a commie. As he did when one newspaper reported, "In place of money, Green said, the extra-terrestrial economics would substitute a worldwide system of credits."[21] Marx had similarly predicted money would become obsolete as communism became the dominant worldview: "Since money, as the existing and active concept of value, confounds and exchanges everything, it is the universal confusion and exchange of all things, an inverted world, the confusion and exchange of all natural and human qualities."[22]

On the other hand, by 1972 those in a fever over flying saucers had increasingly commingled with other spiritualistic groups, resulting in Green's running as the nominee of the Universal Party, founded in 1963 by Kirby J. Hensley, a Pentecostal minister, believer in UFOs, and staunch libertarian. The party's 1972 platform called for "the establishment of Libertarian Government" and for "a Constitution for the United Nations of the World." It went on to urge this one-world government to enact a "universal law . . . for all contact and social interaction with other Life Forms and Species in the Universe."[23]

While the Universal Party was a sufficiently bigger tent to draw in Green, it nevertheless remained on the fringe. The convention that nominated Green for president was attended by about thirty self-appointed delegates.[24] And despite the broader interests of the Universal Party, ridicule continued to hover over Green's campaign. One West Virginia columnist wrote, "I would hesitate to guess how well the Green candidacy would do in West Virginia. Since we don't trust anybody from out of state, Lord knows how we'd feel about somebody from out of planet."[25]

Likewise Green hesitated to guess how well he'd do. When asked if he expected to win he replied, "Certainly not in 1972. The purpose of any campaign is to educate people to the new ideas to bring about changes."[26] Which not only shows this flying saucer candidate had his feet on the ground but describes a key significance of fringe candidates for president.

In 1996 a reporter for a Riverside, California, newspaper interviewed the seventy-one-year-old former flying saucer candidate.

Green continued to believe that beings from outer space were periodically making contact with our planet. And while he had continued to be a featured speaker at gatherings of UFO believers, he had demonstrated no need to remain the center of attention; indeed his attention had turned to the theories of George Van Tassel, who, ostensibly following instructions provided by space people, constructed an Integreton in the remote southern California town of Landers. Green spoke of his and the late Van Tassel's belief that, once the space people return to activate the Integreton, it will create an electromagnetic field to eliminate old age.[27] In a sense Live Forever Jones did live on, in this aspect of the space age campaign of Gabriel Green. And in terms of living forever, both, as we shall see, returned yet again, in the 2016 candidacy of Zoltan Istvan.

PART 3

The Earthquake of 1968 and Its Aftershocks

Louis Abolafia

World Love Party

LOUIS ABOLAFIA WAS ONE OF A GROUP OF FRINGE candidates who received widespread attention in the 1968 presidential election. That year also saw the satiric candidacy of comedian Pat Paulsen, the not at all satiric candidacy of militant African American leader Eldridge Cleaver, the serious candidacy of African American comedian Dick Gregory, and the candidacy of a pig named Pigasus. That all of these fringe candidates received considerable national attention reflects the fact that a multitude of profound concerns were in the wind at that time.

In addition to those five newcomers, Homer Tomlinson conducted his last campaign in 1968. Notably both he and Abolafia advocated a restoration of life as it was in the Garden of Eden. Abolafia's campaign poster, however, depicted him doing so as in the days of the Garden of Eden: buck naked. Outdoing all the other little-known presidential contenders that year, Abolafia threw everything *except his hat* into the ring. He held onto that in his poster, providing cover from the law. The poster featured his campaign slogan, "What have I got to hide?"

Needless to say, Tomlinson, despite invoking the Garden of Eden, would not have appeared thus fig-leafed. Nevertheless he and Abolafia shared other similarities. "A 24-year-old artist, who believes that he is being discriminated against by museums because he is not internationally famous, reached the fifth day of a hunger strike yesterday as a means of arguing his case," the *New York Times* reported in 1965, that artist being Abolafia and that report being very similar to the *Times* previously reporting that Tomlinson commenced his 1952 presidential campaign by going on a twenty-one-day fast.[1]

As Abolafia's campaign slogan stated, he did not hide the reason for his publicity-seeking acts. Prior to his hunger strike, he had smuggled one of his paintings into the Metropolitan Museum of Art and hung it on the wall. But it was spotted and taken down before becoming newsworthy. The announcement of his hunger strike was attached to the end of two other Abolafian strikes—one in which he picketed the Museum of Modern Art, again getting no news coverage, and the other picketing the newly opened, less venerable, more vulnerable, and short-lived Gallery of Modern Art. That protest managed to receive mention in the soon-to-be-defunct *New York Herald Tribune*.[2]

Being in his early twenties, Abolafia may have been youthfully impatient for artistic recognition, but he was impatient for a reason. By the age of ten he had already demonstrated such artistic talent that he received a scholarship to the Museum of Modern Art's educational project, the People's Art Center. He later graduated from Julliard, the nation's preeminent performing and visual arts college. Along the way he may well have learned that making a splash in the art world entailed more than paint.

Abolafia persevered in seeking to call attention to himself as an artist. The year after his pickets and hunger strike, he ran for governor of New York, despite, at age twenty-five, being five years younger than the age mandated by the state's constitution. But getting elected wasn't his objective. Rather he began achieving his aim when a *New York Times* article on his campaign identified him as "Louis Abolafia, an artist," in a report headlined "Gubernatorial Aspirant Throws Beret in Ring"—berets being associated with French painters. While his platform did not overtly promote his own art, it did call for more art schools, free art galleries, and subsidies for artistically talented students.[3]

Not surprisingly, then, bright and early in the campaign season for the 1968 presidential election, Abolafia announced his candidacy, this time aiming for nationwide recognition as an artist. To enter the presidential stage he produced a version of the hippie love-ins and be-ins (the distinction being unclear) that were getting widespread attention in the news media.[4] He called his event the Cosmic Love Convention. It would be, he announced to the press, "a 72-hour Freakathon for Hippies and Saints."[5]

The press bit the bait. Then, reversing the metaphor, reeled in ridicule.

"A delegate with a banana skin stuck on his nose was walking down the aisle of the Village Theater as Louis Abolafia spelled out his campaign platform for the presidency of the United States," the Associated Press reported in an article that appeared nationwide under the headline "Hippie Seeking Presidency Stages Campaign Happening." Similar headlines were "Platform of Love for U.S. President" and my personal favorite, "Help a Humble Beatnik Earn an Honest Living." (The beatnik turned out not to be Abolafia; it was the guy selling bananas in the lobby.) The wire service's photo from the event was captioned by one Pennsylvania newspaper, "Would you believe the bearded kook in the center—name of Louis Abolafia who wants people to smoke banana peels because it makes them happy—is running for President? He is. He announced his candidacy at a 72-hour 'Cosmic Love Convention for Hippies and Saints' at a theater in Greenwich Village."[6]

Amid the rock music and moving images projected on all the surfaces of the venue, Abolafia proclaimed, "I want to spread love through art. If I become president, I will set up cultural centers throughout the country. People's tastes would be improved. Eventually love would spread all over the world and wars would become impossible because everybody would love everybody else." The Associated Press report ended with the least eye-popping, but actually most significant, detail regarding Abolafia's candidacy. It noted that his campaign manager, Andrew Kent, admitted they did not expect to win. Kent, later internationally renowned for his photography, then said, "However, it's a sign that Abolafia is emerging from the underground."[7]

Emerging yes, but only to be ridiculed in the press. Brush-stroking a somewhat different picture than the Associated Press reported, the *New Yorker* included Abolafia's Cosmic Love Convention in its "Talk of the Town" section, telling its nationwide readership:

> It was supposed to continue day & night for 4 days, but when the writer arrived one morning at 10, no one was there . . . [except for] a girl campaign worker who said . . . a lot of people were worn out from the night before and she guessed that today's Love-In would start around 2 PM. Writer came back to the theatre at that time and found it full of cheerful people. Louis had arrived. He said: "In running for the Presidency I'm trying to bring about a world unity. We should be a country of giving and giving and giving. The way we're going now, we're all wrong. We could be giants; we should be 10 times above what the Renaissance was." The purpose of the Love-In, he said, was to bring all the arts together. He said he was a painter.[8]

Even New York's hip newspaper, the *Village Voice*, described Abolafia as "a professional self-publicist who has made a career of fame-gaining schemes. . . . The campaign is as phony as a nickel bag of oregano."[9]

Still, this initial blast of publicity got sufficient attention to attract interviewers from print and broadcast media. While ideal for Abolafia to create interest in him as an artist, the interviewers had their own interests for which Abolafia was ideal. For wire service correspondent Tom Tiede, Abolafia could be put on a pedestal as a representation of all that was eye-rolling about the tide of hippies unwashing across America in the latter half of the 1960s. Headlined in one newspaper "He Sees World Going to Pot," his report began, "Louis Abolafia, 25, used to be just another unknown nuisance who let his hair grow to his shoulders . . . but now, he insists, 'the whole world knows who I am.'" Indeed Tiede correctly smelled ulterior motives. But he was less interested in Abolafia's motives than his own. "Thus he's no longer an unknown nuisance; he's a notorious nuisance," Tiede continued. "By his own admission, Louis Abolafia has, through two years of concentrated mischief, become the best-known hippie in the land." Tiede went on to castigate Abolafia's "noxious" campaign poster featuring him "full-length in the buff" (no mention of the strategically placed hat) and scoffed at "the hundreds of protests he attends. Against the draft, against the war. Abolafia here and Abolafia there, continually on the search for a photographer, a reporter or a man with a microphone." (No mention of similar behavior by mainstream politicians.) "He has even begun criticizing hippyism," Tiede exclaimed, quoting Abolafia telling him, "Actually, I'm not a hippie. I just look like a hippie."[10] Citing an example of his not being a stereotypical hippie, Abolafia told Tiede about an endeavor he currently oversaw in the East Village, New York's hippie mecca, which had also become a mecca for runaway teens. Their vulnerability so troubled him that he had organized an effort to offer them shelter in drug-free apartments whose occupants joined social workers in volunteering to help see if contact could be reestablished between these youths and their parents. Or, as Tiede described it, "his hippie lost-and-found bureau." When the interview got around to the purpose of the candidate's World Love Party, Abolafia's frustration in seeking to create interest in his art appears to have slipped into Tiede's reporting when he wrote, "'The party,' he sighs, 'is mostly beauty and culture.'" A telling sigh.

Not all the interviewers were hostile, but all were as motivated by their objectives as Abolafia was by his. The syndicated columnist Sylvie Reice, for example, wrote of his views on the Vietnam War, on lowering the voting age to eighteen, and, with considerably more sympathy, on his efforts to help young runaways. The only levity she made of Abolafia's candidacy was in her opening line: "You have to be at least 35 years old to serve as President of the United States but to Louis Abolafia, a 26-year-old New York painter, that detail doesn't matter."[11] The detail about being a painter, however, mattered a lot to Abolafia, but not to Reice, for whom it was her only reference.

There was at least one interviewer who spotted the significance of Abolafia's artistic quest and saw fit to include it. The syndicated columnist Mike Jahn wrote of Abolafia's past efforts to have his art recognized and quoted him saying, "At most museums they didn't show real American artists. You had to be a member of a clique, a group."[12] Jahn, himself only twenty-five years old, would go on that same year to become the first reporter hired by the

New York Times whose full-time assignment was the rock music scene—the springboard to his becoming a highly regarded journalist and the author of nonfiction and fiction. Not surprisingly, then, because Jahn dug the arts, in his interview he understood Abolafia's campaign.

Being a visual artist, Abolafia tried to convey his candidacy's artistic quest visually. But the press still did not, or chose not, to catch on. In an Associated Press interview he sought to show himself as an artist through his clothing. "Over his turtleneck and skimpy dark suit he slings one of two black capes with gold or silver linings," the article read, clearly aware that this garb differed from that of your typical hippie. "He seems a sort of hybrid Abe Lincoln and Batman."[13]

Sigh. Lincoln-Batman? Not maybe a Degas-Rodin? Or a Warhol-Picasso?

So Abolafia tried other imagery. "Draped in a Roman-type toga and sporting a beard and shaggy hair, a presidential candidate addressed hundreds of followers Sunday in Boston Common," another wire service reported.[14] Shaggy hair and beard, no doubt about that: hippie. But toga? Rather than ask or speculate, the reporter just let it hang. An arts reporter might have caught on, recognizing Abolafia's allusion to neoclassical sculptures in the pantheon of American art depicting George Washington, Benjamin Franklin, and Alexander Hamilton in togas, thereby connecting them to the democracies of ancient Greece and Rome.[15]

This same news item contained two additional details worthy of note. It quoted Abolafia proclaiming, "Make love not war," which he did so frequently that, over time, the origin of that hallmark phrase from the antiwar era has often been attributed to him, becoming part of his legacy among later generations of hipsters and other aficionados of mid-twentieth-century dissenters. The phrase had actually been used a year earlier by one of the philosophical patriarchs of that era's dissenters, Herbert Marcuse.[16]

Of note also was the report's closing sentence: "His followers, dandelions in their hair and carrying balloons, shouted 'Fascists!' and 'Warmongers!' to anyone who dared heckle candidate Abolafia." Which seems a bit contradictory for supporters of the World Love Party.

And that is what Abolafia's fringe candidacy brings into very sharp focus.

The 1968 presidential campaign that Abolafia began the year before occurred at the peak of an era of intense and often violent social and political conflict. In 1967, 11,363 Americans died in Vietnam, a war that generated strong emotions, pro and con.[17] In April of that year tens of thousands had gathered in New York and San Francisco to protest it. In October one hundred thousand joined in Washington DC to march against it—fifty thousand of whom joined hippie leaders Abbie Hoffman and Jerry Rubin and poet Allen Ginsberg in a chant to levitate the Pentagon. That same month police clubbed University of Wisconsin students protesting the presence of recruiters from Dow Chemical, manufacturer of napalm, which burned away dense foliage (and human skin) in Vietnam. The antiwar movement intersected with the civil rights movement in 1967 when African American students at Howard University vociferously protested a talk on campus by the director of the Selective Service, which drafted young men into the army. The joining of the two movements was underscored that year when Dr. Martin Luther King Jr. spoke out for the first time in opposition to the war in Vietnam—though clearly not due to a shortage of racial concerns. In June 1967 race riots flared in Tampa and Buffalo. And the next month in Newark and Minneapolis. And Detroit. And Milwaukee. And, in August, Washington DC.

None of which came close to equaling the turmoil in 1968. Race riots erupted in nearly every urban area in the United States following King's assassination that year. His death was followed by the assassination of presidential aspirant Robert F. Kennedy, campaigning as a strong civil rights proponent and Vietnam War opponent. That year's death toll in Vietnam rose to 16,899 Americans; likewise antiwar protests and violence swelled, culminating live on national television outside the Democratic National Convention in Chicago as police and protestors battled in the streets.

With so much upheaval, logic was often lost in the tumult.

And not only among Abolafia's peace and love supporters shouting hateful words.

"Hippies claim that . . . those who devote themselves to Beauty and Art at all times, except when they're cashing their unemployment or allowance checks, should outrank those who merely produce," Al Capp, the popular cartoonist of *Li'l Abner*, wrote as the person chosen (oddly if not illogically) by the journal *Nation's Business* to review Harvard economist John Kenneth Galbraith's 1967 book, *The New Industrial State*. Ever the comic, Capp added, "The hippies, however, don't go along with those who believe that producers should be beaten up and all their productions burnt. That's the Non-Violent Movement."[18]

Capp was wrong. The leading voices for nonviolence, such as King and Ginsberg, never supported violence or vandalism. And Capp was right. Many who identified with those movements, such as Abolafia's supporters at his rally in Boston, engaged in verbal and physical violence. All this upheaval was so politically dizzying, logic often lost its balance. Which explains why, at the center of Capp's review of Galbraith's book, we find Louis Abolafia.

"You can't talk about John Kenneth Galbraith and his *New Industrial State* without talking about Louis Abolafia," Capp wrote, going on to describe Abolafia's presidential campaign poster and the length of his hair. But despite noting that the poster identified him as an artist, and despite Capp's being an artist himself, he made no mention of how that might explain Abolafia's campaign. After all, doing so would ruin the cartoon.

"Does Galbraith support Abolafia?" Capp then asked. "Let him answer in his own words," he answered, quoting from Galbraith's book, "Aesthetic achievement is beyond the reach of the industrial system—in conflict with it." The review maintained that Galbraith supported Abolafia's presidential bid by pinning this and other quotations from the book to Abolafia statements.

And here, from the original men in togas, is the essence of that logic. *All cats have ears. Socrates has ears. Therefore Socrates is a cat.* Just because certain statements by Galbraith resembled statements by Abolafia did not mean Galbraith supported Abolafia for president, any more than Socrates and cats having certain characteristics in common meant Socrates was a cat. In point of fact, Galbraith supported the Democrats' nominee, Hubert Humphrey, in the 1968 presidential election.[19] Yet so blown away was rationality that Capp's outrageous (key syllable being *rage*) review was not only reprinted in newspapers across the country but was also entered into the *Congressional Record*.[20]

Reflecting this maelstrom—or, more accurately, refracting it—Abolafia's fringe candidacy also lost its way. Whither it had blown by September 27, 1968, was visually displayed in Phoenix on page 14 of that day's *Arizona Republic*. Tucked into an article at the bottom of the page headlined "Jackson Square, New Orleans: 'Grease in Hippie Garb,'" we find mention of a shop selling hippie paraphernalia, including posters such as "a Revlon skin cream advertisement, altered with a hideously napalmed Vietnamese girl standing beside the attractive model; Louis Abolafia naked with the caption, 'I have nothing to hide.'" Meanwhile, at the top of the page, an article headlined "New Antiwar Goal" told readers, "Leaders in the antiwar movement have drawn up protest tactics for a concerted attempt to disrupt the presidential campaign." Nowhere in this article is Abolafia mentioned. It does, however, report, "They have their own candidate—a pig."

While the countercultural candidacy of that pig (soon to be discussed) reveals other aspects of the political earthquake taking place, Abolafia's absence in this report further reveals that those objectives were not his objectives. Having recognized back in July that his campaign had become peripheral, Abolafia now announced that he was ending his candidacy.[21]

But even his announcement was lost in those winds. A month later a Michigan columnist, writing about teen runaways and Abolafia's efforts on their behalf, concluded his piece, "What he's doing sounds a lot more worthwhile than all the political oratory I've heard from the other candidates. I may just vote for him."[22] Three months after Abolafia ended his campaign, the lead editorial in an Arkansas paper began, "If we were somehow forced to endorse a political candidate this election year, we suppose we'd have to settle for Louis Abolafia."[23] No matter that he had dropped out, was too young to be the president—no matter the reality of who

Louis Abolafia really was—to many in the press he was a modern-day John Donkey.

November 4, 1980. "'We are the solution for voters on the brink of terminal boredom,' said Louis Abolafia, the favorite son of the Nudist Party."[24] Still at it over a decade later.

Abandoned, however, was his self-created World Love Party. Shortly after announcing the end of his 1968 campaign, Abolafia joined in a less than loving hijacking of the newly opened Fillmore East, a long-abandoned theater from the days of New York's once immigrant-teeming Lower East Side. With the neighborhood now transforming into the East Village, rock music promoter Bill Graham had revitalized the theater, allowing it also to be used as a venue for other events. On October 23, 1968, a benefit performance was taking place to raise defense funds for arrested student protestors when, as Graham recalled:

> Halfway through the show, Louis Abolafia, the Naked candidate for president whose slogan was "I Have Nothing To Hide," came in with that element and then went on stage and said, "This is now the theater of the people." . . . People with berets positioned themselves everywhere and down the center aisle came a mimeograph machine. For the rest of the night, they would . . . run off copies and then distribute them in the street, letting people know what was going on inside the theater. . . . The actors and performers knew that it was out of control and they had lost it.[25]

Abolafia too had lost it. Not only in the chaos of that evening but of that era. To some degree he too probably knew it when, in reading the extensive coverage of this incident in the *New York Times*, he did not find himself even mentioned.[26]

Abolafia drifted to San Francisco, where he tried his luck raising money for future presidential bids by organizing what came to be a major annual event in that city's celebrated above-ground underground scene, the Exotic-Erotic Ball. But his 1976 and 1980 campaigns registered only brief blips in the press.[27] While his slogan remained "I have nothing to hide," one thing was still missing: he had nothing to show.

Where was the art?

Opportunities had abounded to include his art in his campaign events, yet he had not. As for exhibitions in galleries, his presidential campaigns clearly created name recognition, and he clearly had enough talent that, back in 1966, his paintings had been displayed in New York's prestigious Crespi Gallery on Madison Avenue.[28] Was he still painting? Was he still really an artist? Or had he, by diving headfirst into that era's presidential campaigns rather than stepping back and observing with brush and paint, emerged as dazed and confused as was that tempestuous era? His death from a drug overdose in 1995 says yes. But in truth, we don't know.

We do know this: Abolafia's hippie candidacy—in which we find not only an aspiring painter but also a future famed photographer (campaign manager Andrew Kent) and not-really-carefree runaway flower children—reveals that Louis Abolafia was not, *nor was anyone else*, a typical hippie.

Widening that view enables us to see that, in the political landscape, no one is a typical anything.

Pat Paulsen

T V Comedian—S T A G Party

"IF WE'RE GOING TO HAVE A CLOWN IN THE WHITE HOUSE, we might as well have a professional," the culture critic Digby Diehl quoted a Pat Paulsen presidential fan saying during the 1968 election. Writing for the *New York Times*, Diehl pointed out the significance of Paulsen's fringe candidacy when he continued, "This may be a tragicomic comment on the state of American politics, but it is also a tribute to the deadpan wit of a comedian who has waged the largest, most successful mock campaign in the history of presidential politics."[1]

All of which is true—and to anyone who disagrees, I cite Paulsen's trademark rejoinder, "Picky, picky, picky."

Paulsen ran as the nominee of the faux Straight Talking American Government (STAG) Party. (For those of you who came of age in a less-sexist America, "stag party" refers to a men's-only whoop-it-up.) In actuality Paulsen was the nominee of a television show, *The Smothers Brothers Comedy Hour*, his presidential stage being the CBS television network. A far cry from Louis Abolafia, an unknown artist seeking the spotlight, yet in other respects Paulsen was akin to Abolafia and to the other fringe candidates of that pivotal year. All either voiced dissent or, if not explicitly voicing it (Pigasus, for one, could only oink), implicitly conveyed dissent through performances that undermined prevailing views.

The arc of Pat Paulsen's political career/act closely paralleled that of *The Smothers Brothers Comedy Hour*. Premiering in February 1967, it followed the format of other popular variety shows: a star or costars hosting various performers, often including comic skits. Tom and Dick Smothers, two clean-cut young men who sang folk songs that went comically off the rails into sibling issues, looked like two darling, if maybe a bit mischievous, all-American boys. An example of their mischievously undermining prevailing views through performance was the appearance during the show's first month of George Burns, the husband and comedic partner of the 1940 fringe candidate Gracie Allen. Burns was enormously popular with a now middle-aged fan base of all political stripes. Among the acts in which he participated on the show was joining in with the shaggy-haired rock-n-roll stars Herman's Hermits, thereby subverting the view that the country was politically divided by a "generation gap."

The next week's show undermined a prevailing view through a more explicit performance: an editorial by "Smothers Brothers Vice President" Pat Paulsen, his executive title and dour delivery mocking the demeanor of commentators who had recently become popular in television news. Paulsen weighed in on the noncontroversial topic of auto safety, opining with "logic" that occasionally soared into intellectually intoned babble such as this: "There are only two ways to go. One way is neither right nor wrong and the other way isn't. We know that taking a firm grade is pledganous and facts will bare us out. . . . We suggest simply lowering the statistics, which implies we stop counting accidents. This is a necessity for all who trudge and all those who glog the gains of life and I think we should all ask ourselves this question: How Much?"[2] Something must have been bugging America about television (if not all) editorials; some seventeen thousand fan letters followed.[3]

Needless to say, the show continued the bit. But Paulsen's next editorial tread on more explosive turf: gun control. The issue was in the news at the time as Congress was debating a proposal that became the Gun Control Act of 1968. In March 1967 Smothers Brothers Vice President Paulsen weighed in:

> Many people today are suggesting that restrictions be placed on the purchase and ownership of firearms. . . . No one questions that these are good solid citizens . . . and we will fight to the death against their right to express their opinions. . . . I ask you, what is our most cherished right since pioneer days? The right for every man, woman and child to carry a gun. This is not a statement of

kration but has a man to meetings that even a child could understand. If you are old enough to get arrested, you're old enough to carry a gun.[4]

In performance Paulsen's editorials further ridiculed the authoritativeness of such commentators with physical comedy, such as his stiffly using fingers a moment too late to indicate his first and second points, or an emphatic tap on his executive desk hitting a saucer that caused his coffee cup to flip in the air, or, regarding gun control, pulling from his coat the revolver he carried and, at the close of his comments, accidently shooting the off-camera announcer.

The public loved it.

Indeed the public was taken by the whole show, in part because of its veering into realms of controversy. Along with editorial pokes at topics like gun control, those darling but devilish Smothers boys brought on performers such as the folk singer Pete Seeger, long blacklisted from television as a suspected communist sympathizer. Seeger sang of a training incident during World War II that resulted in a needless death—a song that resonated with what many thought were needless deaths in the Vietnam War. CBS censored the song, resulting in a rash of news reports in which Tom and Dick Smothers complained of a rash of network interference, resulting in a rash of viewers tuning in to see what all the fuss was about.

To some degree the fuss was about putting a dent in the ratings of *Bonanza*, an NBC western that had long dominated that timeslot until the Smothers Brothers got a grip on its audience share. Which, from the get-go, they did using controversy cloaked in comedy. "The first reaction to the new Smothers Brothers Show on CBS has been favorable, and the credit must go to Ernest Chambers and Saul Ilson, the producers," one wire service report stated, going on to reveal, "They realize that being up against Bonanza is something like flying a kamikaze. . . . 'You have to do something to shake the complacency of the viewers,' says Ilson. 'You have to make them say, 'Did you see The Smothers Brothers show last night?' To do that, you have to be different, maybe even controversial.'"[5]

While the show stayed in the news with disputes over CBS censorship of content ranging from the folk singer Joan Baez dedicating a song to her husband going to prison for draft evasion to a skit about (of all things) censorship, Paulsen's editorials plowed beneath such explicit surfaces. Instead he seemingly nonsensically loosened the soil of prevailing views on topics such as sex education, the war on poverty, legalized gambling, and health care legislation. Where he went into nonsensical realms, however, is where he conveyed views through performance that would have been censored had he verbally stated them, as seen in the opening of his editorial on health care. From the time federal health care was first proposed, in November 1945 (referred to as President Truman's "compulsory national health insurance" and as "socialized medicine"), to the equally contentious enactment of Medicare in 1964 (and through to, and after, the 2010 enactment of the Affordable Care Act), health care legislation has been a hot-button issue.[6] But in Paulsen's September 24, 1967, editorial we can see him burrowing beneath the reach of the censor's red pencil even as he began, "Of late, more and more people are expressing the view that doctors are charging too much for their services. Now the complaints of exorbitant fees come almost without exception from those who have been going to doctors. I say these people are sick, and why listen to them?"[7]

The nation laughed and, slapping its collective knee, slapped medical fees.

The newspaper listings of television shows for October 1, 1967, reported that the Smothers Brothers show would feature film star Jane Powell, British stage actor Noel Harrison, Tom and Dick Smothers singing "Sweetheart, Sweetheart," and Pat Paulsen entering the presidential race clad as Tarzan.

Much as with Paulsen's first editorial, the show's creators could only have dreamed the fan approval would be as huge. It wasn't. It was huger. And politically edgier. "We talked to him for nearly an hour," one columnist wrote of a Paulsen press conference that followed on the heels of announcing his candidacy. "At the end of that time, some half dozen reporters were hard-pressed to tell exactly what it was Paulsen was talking about or whether he was 'putting us on' or not."[8] *What are you talking about?* and *Are you putting us on?* precisely convey the way Paulsen and his *Smothers Brothers Comedy Hour* handlers undermined mainstream presidential bunk.

In a show that followed the press conference, Dick Smothers conducted a comic presidential preference poll among those in the studio audience. The upshot of this and other such antics soon surfaced in a news item that began, "The Smothers Brothers insist they are serious about nominating comic Pat Paulsen as a presidential candidate."[9] In that politically dizzying era, Paulsen's candidacy had heads spinning from the moment he knocked his coffee cup into the presidential ring.

Technically Paulsen had not announced that he was running; rather he parodied politicians who coyly announce that they are not announcing they are running.[10] "Clubs seem to be springing up in my behalf all over the country," he separately told the press. "But although I am unable to say anything at this time, I am glad of an opportunity so early in my campaign to deny that I am running." At which point he asked the reporters to attribute any further statements "either to a 'spokesman' or a 'close associate.'" The news media ate it up. One wire service report of these remarks stated, "A spokesman explained that the candidate would represent the 'Straight Talking American Government party,' or 'STAG party.'"[11]

Others in the media, seeing an opportunity for themselves, played along in similar ways. Radio station KRLA, for example, mock-editorialized, "Pat Paulsen formally announced that he is not a candidate for the presidency, thus placing himself in the company of other such non-candidates. It should be obvious to everyone that Pat Paulsen is out of place in such rich company." The editorial continued to slam Paulsen in this manner before concluding, "In accordance with the equal time provisions, we now present Mr. Pat Paulsen with a non-rebuttal to a KRLA non-editorial." Paulsen's mock rebuttal began by telling "the millions of Americans yelling for me to run, save your breath. Simply sign one of the petitions . . . floating around your neighborhood." And concluded by saying KRLA's listeners should "feel free to turn your dial to some other radio station that has some class."[12]

Amid nonsensical candidate platitudes such as "If elected, I promise I will win," Paulsen threw in zingers aimed at actual candidates. His campaign slogan, "We Cannot Stand Pat," was a traditional rallying cry; its humor resided in its simultaneously insulting the candidate himself. But it also jabbed at Republican candidate Richard Nixon, who frequently said, "I'll stand pat on that." (And perhaps another layer for wags who pointed out that the name of Nixon's wife was Pat.)

Meanwhile Paulsen's editorials on *The Smothers Brothers Comedy Hour* continued, now also serving, in effect, as his campaign platform—and taking on increasingly controversial issues. Three weeks into his presidential campaign, he editorialized on an issue that was triggering often violent protest, the military draft, which included his observing, "A good many people feel our present draft laws are unjust. These people are called soldiers. . . . What are the arguments against the draft? We hear that it is unfair, immoral, discourages young men from studying, ruins their careers, and their lives. Picky, picky, picky."[13]

Capitalizing on their bonanza, the producers of *The Smothers Brothers Comedy Hour* took Paulsen's candidacy on the road. They arranged for speeches, rallies, and even parades in cities across the country, accompanied by a film crew preparing a one-hour documentary special that the show aired shortly before Election Day. They arranged for the sale of campaign paraphernalia and a book, *Pat Paulsen for President*. In Los Angeles and New York they arranged campaign dinners for Paulsen's candidacy at which donors had to pay eighty-nine cents a plate, the proceeds going to the cafeterias at which they were held. Many of the biggest stars in show business attended, pausing for the news media and paparazzi before entering.[14]

Amid the hoopla Paulsen maintained both his genuine modesty and the false modesty of mainstream candidates. Of the genuine modesty, one interviewer noted, "Pat's conversation was low-key, diffident but friendly; his manner totally without pretension."[15] Likewise, except not, candidate Paulsen repeatedly assured voters and viewers, "I will always be aware of my humble station in life. A common, ordinary, simple savior of America's destiny."[16]

Paulsen's widespread appeal rested largely on his low-key delivery and the ability of the show's writers to crank out benign jabs that cloaked the occasional satirical stiletto. Paulsen's speeches, for example, often mocked political claptrap with the relatively safe joke: "I know what the average voter wants. In fact, I'd like to get a little myself." Amid such lines, however, he'd periodically deliver far sharper punchlines, such as, on the divisive Vietnam War, "A lot of people don't understand our problems there, and these people are our leaders."[17] Other lines seemed benign, but their humor actually detonated in realms of fundamental protest, as when he went Lincolnesque by declaring he would be elected "for the people, by the people, and in spite of the people."[18]

Just how finely attuned the staff writers were to their audiences can be seen by comparing Paulsen's remarks when he went to Miami during the Republican National Convention to those he made in Chicago during that year's tumultuous Democratic National Convention. With the more conservative Republicans, his comments were predominantly benign. Speaking as a candidate to delegates from his home state of Washington he said, "I was glad to hear the Washington delegation is uncommitted. I hear some of the delegations have been committed, and that's a shame. Just because they're a little oddball in their political thinking is no reason to have them committed."[19] The writers scripted him only a bit more pointedly when, after his request to address the Republican Convention was turned down, he told the press, "I'm not a vindictive person, but I am revengeful. Naturally, I didn't want to interfere with the solemnity of a political convention—the seriousness of popping balloons, tooting horns, and parading around."[20]

At the Democratic Convention, however, where police and protestors were battling in the streets and the national guard had been called in to contain the violence, Paulsen's writers ratcheted his remarks up a notch toward resonating with the protests against the Vietnam War. "Personally, I believe we should limit the ground fighting and send our troops home as soon as possible," he opined. "In fact, I see no reason to keep them here past

Friday."[21] Other remarks he made in Chicago detonated in more fundamental realms of protest, as when he proclaimed, "We must preserve the current system with its checks and balances which prevent the majority from obtaining control."[22]

The conflicts between *The Smothers Brothers Comedy Hour* and CBS continued throughout Paulsen's year-long presidential campaign. These disputes provided the news media with an ideal story, as it enabled journalists to raise the important issue of censorship while at the same time marginalizing its controversial aspects. The *New York Times*, for example, stated, "Industry observers point out that the Smothers Brothers highly publicized battle with the network over censorship might not be entirely unrelated to their ratings battle with the National Broadcasting Company's long running 'Bonanza.' There is also some evidence for believing that not everyone in high places at the network is unhappy about the publicity given the show over the censorship issue."[23]

Still, the fact that it was a great way to raise and evade a controversial issue did not make such reports wrong. Indeed Pete Seeger was back in the news when CBS permitted him to return to the show and sing the song it had previously censored.[24] The *Washington Post* cut right to the chase when its TV columnist wrote, "The Brothers and their manager simply must be aware of TV's first rule: Almost anything can be forgiven or overlooked if audience ratings are sufficiently large."[25]

The fact that the conflict made for good ratings was further evidenced when CBS permitted the conflict itself to become part of Paulsen's campaign. On the January 7, 1968, show, he editorialized:

The time has come to quit [BLEEP]ing around and talk about censorship. We of the Smothers Brothers Comedy Hour have had our share of censorship problems, but we are not against censorship because we realize there is always the danger of something being said.... Many people feel that censorship is a violation of Freedom of Speech. Bull feathers.... The Bill of Rights says nothing about Freedom of Hearing.... There is nothing in the Bill of Rights about Freedom of Seeing.... Let's face it, there have to be some realistic taboos—especially with political comment. After all, the leaders of our country were not elected to be tittered at. . . . You can't say anything bad about President Johnson because you shouldn't insult the President. But if you compliment him, who will believe it? So in conclusion, you can see that there is a place for censors, and we only wish that we could tell you where it is.

Through the lens of the fringe candidacy of Paulsen as a proxy of *The Smothers Brothers Comedy Hour* we can see the nation's political landscape shifting amid the upheavals of that era. On Election Day the Republican candidate, Richard Nixon, narrowly edged out his Democratic challenger, Hubert Humphrey. In the executive suite at CBS it is quite likely they were also eyeing the vote count for Paulsen: less than .01 percent. Or, in showbiz terms, less than his fellow comedian and fringe candidate that year, Dick Gregory, who garnered .06 percent of voter and audience share.

The results, albeit close, were in and indicated that *The Smothers Brothers Comedy Hour* was trending out. Five months later CBS canceled it.[26]

For the 1972 election Paulsen again announced he was a candidate. Seeking to recapture the spotlight as he had in 1968, he upped the ante by officially getting on the ballot in the New Hampshire primary. In so doing he nearly upended his career since he was now, in the eyes of the Federal Communications Commission, a "legally qualified candidate" and consequently was subject to the equal time provisions of the Federal Communications Act. That law was also interpreted to mean that whenever he appeared on television—even on a show like Walt Disney's *Mouse Factory* (for which he was scheduled)—the broadcaster was obligated to offer equal time to the other legally qualified candidates. Paulsen commenced a lengthy legal battle against the ruling but, in the meantime, withdrew from the race.

In the 1976 and 1980 elections Paulsen reprised his 1968 announcement that he was not a candidate, but he now limited his noncampaign, incorporating it into his stand-up comedy act.[27] Likely he saw the handwriting on the wall back in 1972, when the news coverage he got was almost exclusively in regard to the equal time provision, not his satiric campaign. Communications professor Steven Alan Carr aptly describes what Paulsen's 1968 fringe candidacy—and the network television stage that served as its headquarters—brings into focus: "Only in the context of shifting norms and collapsing boundaries did *The Smothers Brothers Comedy Hour* become publicized. Only in this context was it politicized. And only in this context could the results have been so drastic."[28]

Eldridge Cleaver

Black Panther—Peace and Freedom Party

ELDRIDGE CLEAVER, THE MINISTER OF INFORMATION FOR the militant African American organization the Black Panthers, ran for president in 1968 as the nominee of the Peace and Freedom Party. Addressing that party's founding convention in March of that year, Cleaver summed up his perspective on the plight of African Americans with a "basic definition that black people in America are a colonized people in every sense of the term and that white America is an organized Imperialist force holding black people in colonial bondage. From this definition," he continued, "what we need is a revolution."[1] In a self-published essay Cleaver more specifically declared, "In order to bring this situation about, black men know that they must pick up the gun, they must arm black people to the teeth, they must organize an army to confront the mother country with a most drastic consequence if she attempts to assert police power over the colony."[2] During that same presidential campaign the *New York Times* reported, "Cleaver hesitated to describe himself as a revolutionary."[3]

His hesitation is baffling. And understandable—since never before in the history of colonial independence movements did anyone among the subjugated people seek to be elected president or prime minister of the nation whose rule they sought to overthrow. In the preface to her biography of Cleaver, Kathleen Rout explains that she sought "to understand Cleaver by reading between the lines." Yet even in her extremely well-researched and revealing study of the man, Rout ultimately had to concede, "The enigma of Cleaver as a personality remains intriguing."[4] The significance of his presidential candidacy, however, does not reside in resolving the man's riddles but in seeing how those riddles provide us with a particularly clear view of riddles in the nation's political landscape in 1968.

Part of the reason the Peace and Freedom Party, predominantly composed of left-wing whites, nominated Black Panther Eldridge Cleaver for president was his fame as the author of *Soul on Ice*, a critically acclaimed and widely read collection of essays, written while in prison, in which Cleaver examined his violent past and the future he foresaw for his race. More significant, however, all of the pro-Cleaver elements were youthful: the Black Panthers had been formed only two years earlier; the Peace and Freedom Party was newly born; *Soul on Ice* had been published just that year; and Cleaver, barely a year out of prison, was two years too young to be president. Youth ruled—or so thought the World War II baby boom generation, not yet old enough to know better.

Yet for all the youthful exuberance and excess of Cleaver's campaign, his candidacy clung to the cusp between third party and fringe. To the extent that it was widely ridiculed, which it was, it was fringe. But to the extent his presidential bid was viewed as impossible but not laughable, it was third party—to which should be added 36,571 Americans who voted for him.[5]

By calling upon African Americans to arm themselves for mass resistance to the white establishment, Cleaver does not come off as a guy with a sense of humor. Particularly in regard to whites. Yet after his nomination he urged the Peace and Freedom Party to select Jerry Rubin as his running mate. This white, Jewish, radical antiwar activist first gained national fame when, having been subpoenaed to appear before the House Un-American Activities Committee, he testified wearing the costume of a Revolutionary War soldier. The committee members were not amused—but the news media was.[6] Amused as well, apparently, was Cleaver. And unamused as well was the majority of the Peace and Freedom Party, which rejected his suggestion.[7]

To ridicule an African American candidate for president without appearing to be (or demonstrating that one is) a racist is tricky business. One way ridicule was heaped on Cleaver's campaign was through his wanting Rubin for a running mate. Approximately

90 percent fewer newspapers reported Cleaver's announcement that he intended to run for president than those that reported his choice of Rubin.[8]

Most often, ridicule and belittlement of his candidacy were tucked into the tone of news reports and related remarks. The sentence "Eldridge Cleaver—black protagonist, white antagonist—moved through a large, loitering crowd in the Tides Bookstore in Sausalito last night, sat down and signed autographs" was deemed an appropriate opening to a front-page article under the far more newsworthy headline "Black Panther Author Tells Views on Weapons, 'Pigs.'" Also deemed newsworthy in the article was that Cleaver's wife was "lean" and "comely."[9] Another newspaper, reporting on California's Peace and Freedom delegation selecting Cleaver as its choice for the upcoming national nominating convention, told readers the meeting "resembled a picnic or love-in."[10] The television commentator and syndicated columnist James J. Kilpatrick dismissed Cleaver's candidacy as ridiculous when he wrote briefly of "the 'Peace and Freedom Party,' whatever that is."[11]

The ridicule that came closest to overt racism was aimed at Cleaver's giving a series of lectures at the University of California–Berkeley during his presidential campaign. The Republican vice presidential nominee, Spiro Agnew, declared, "Trying to learn from such criminals is like trying to clean up by taking a bath in a sewer."[12] More subtle, and more profoundly ridiculing, were news articles on Cleaver's scholarly lectures, the ridicule residing in the quotation marks around the word *scholarly.* One wire service that employed such quotation marks in its report of the talk nevertheless conceded, "Cleaver confined his remarks directly to his topic, 'The Roots of Racism,'" and the report went on to quote one of students who attended describing it as "a real surprise—it was extremely scholarly." As to the lecture's actual content, the report barely concealed its smirk when quoting Cleaver telling the students, "Black is a connotation of evil," and his going on in this vein when it reported, "Cleaver said that whereas the white dress of a bride symbolizes purity, black is for a funeral, a black beard means a pirate, a black cat means bad luck."[13]

This is scholarly?

Actually, yes. Though Cleaver was ahead of his time in this regard, connotations of whiteness and blackness would become a subject of considerable academic research in the years to come.[14]

As for Cleaver, he could dish out ridicule pretty well himself. In response to California's governor, Ronald Reagan, strenuously objecting to Cleaver's being permitted to speak at Berkeley, Cleaver challenged the governor to "a duel to the death" with whatever weapon Reagan wanted. "I will beat him to death with a marshmallow," he told a rally of some five thousand people.[15] Though it was perceived by few at the time, Cleaver did not lack a sense of humor—as also seen in his admiration of the radical prankster Rubin.

Just as there is ambiguity in challenging someone to a duel to the death with weaponry ranging from knives to marshmallows, ambiguity accompanied the threats and actual violence that were a hallmark of Cleaver's campaign for the presidency. "When I write," he declared, "I want to drive a spear into the heart of America," attaching ambiguity to that spear by using it metaphorically.[16] Nevertheless other violence surrounding his campaign was not metaphorical. Less than a month after Cleaver announced his intention to run for president, Martin Luther King Jr. was assassinated, triggering the most widespread and destructive of the riots that increasingly had been flaring in American cities. During that turmoil a shootout erupted at a house in Oakland, California, in which there were several Black Panthers, including Cleaver. Ambiguity still surrounds the cause of the gunfire. The police claimed they were fired upon after questioning the occupants of some parked cars. The Panthers maintained the police instigated the attack, pointing to the almost immediate arrival of a squadron of police vehicles with floodlights and machine guns. Ambiguity also left questions regarding an unarmed twenty-two-year-old, shot dead by police as he ran toward them from the house. Cleaver was wounded, charged with attempted murder, and returned to prison for violating parole.[17]

Being in the clink would put a crimp in anyone's campaign, but Cleaver wasn't behind bars for long. Since he had not yet been convicted of this recent charge, a California judge ruled that it had not yet been proven that he had violated parole. The prosecution appealed the ruling, thereby creating a legal cloud that hovered over Cleaver for the duration of his presidential campaign.

"Dumbfounding Ruling by a Court" headlined an editorial in one newspaper that went on to express what many Americans thought: "At lay levels far below the Olympian heights of the bench, the ordinary citizen is impelled to wonder by this judicial action . . . [given] the fact that a paroled convict has been indicted for taking part in a fight with firearms. . . . Is [the judge] saying it is permissible to advance political views with a gun in hand?"[18]

Some might argue that it was not the judge but the Second Amendment to the Constitution that renders it permissible to advance pretty much any way one wants with a gun in hand. Indeed, as previously mentioned, gun control was already a hot topic in 1967 and 1968, with legislation pending in Congress. One realm in which the right to bear arms was soon to be proscribed was in legislative bodies—in no small part because an armed cadre of Black Panthers had entered California's Legislative Assembly in May 1967, among whom was the not-yet-famous Eldridge Cleaver. The authorities charged them with all the law allowed at the time: "conspiracy to forcibly enter the chambers of the state legislature."[19] When asked during his presidential campaign for his view on gun control, Cleaver answered, "They are always trying to take guns from the black people." But ambiguity attached when he added the proviso, "Disarm the pigs first."[20]

Cleaver's use of *pigs* for police and his frequent profanity conveyed unbridled rage, a fearsome thing. But it resonated with many at the time—and not just angry ghetto dwellers and white radicals. "Eldridge Cleaver is not the only angry black man in the State of California," the psychiatrist Price Cobbs declared. Dr. Cobbs had authored a study of rage. And was African American.[21] Cleaver's rage, however, was not unbridled. He could ratchet his use of vitriol and profanity up, down, or out. All the news reports of his first lecture at Berkeley noted the absence of profanity—language that today is widely used even on network TV. Not so, however, in 1968, and Cleaver's ability to control its flow reveals that profanity functioned for him as the verbal spears he described, thrusting them to get attention and arouse fear among whites—but also to subvert prevailing views of propriety, since propriety extended not only to language but to limiting the acceptable range of racial views.

Ambiguity attached itself even to Cleaver's rage when, days before the election, he endorsed Jerry Rubin and Abbie Hoffman's Yippie Party nominee for president, Pigasus, in a speech at a Pre–Erection Day rally sponsored by that group. And ambiguity attached to that endorsement, as Cleaver was admittedly high on pot when he spoke.[22]

Two weeks after the election Cleaver's legal battles came to a head when the California Supreme Court ordered him back to prison. Instead he fled the country, taking refuge in Cuba, Algeria, and finally Paris, where, in 1972, he became a born-again Christian and began manufacturing a line of men's wear. He returned to the United States and to prison in 1977, but through the assistance of his new comrades in the evangelical community, he was released on bail in 1978 and was able to complete his sentence with community service.

Looking back, the rage, ambiguities, and violence that surrounded Cleaver's campaign for president, along with some genuinely scholarly analysis, bursts of humor, and the terrible damage inflicted by verbal spears and actual bullets, provide us with an extraordinary view of the many nuances in race relations in 1968. Most important, however, we can see that the price we pay for free speech is less than the dividends we earn in becoming a more equal nation.

Dick Gregory

TV Comedian—Freedom and Peace Party

DICK GREGORY IS OFTEN DESCRIBED, MORE CORRECTLY than not, as the first African American stand-up comedian to succeed in venues previously unavailable to predecessors such as Nipsey Russell and Moms Mabley. Thanks to his frequent appearances on television, Gregory was famous when he sought the nomination of the Peace and Freedom Party in the 1968 presidential election. After that nomination went to Eldridge Cleaver—who was too young to be president, under a legal cloud involving his return to prison, and too militant for some in the party—a group broke away from the Peace and Freedom Party and formed the Freedom and Peace Party. And (what journalist could resist?) the ridicule commenced.

"It should be noted that the Peace and Freedom Party is not the same as the Freedom and Peace party," the *Albuquerque Journal* informed its readers before snapping off a series of one-liners. "It's still not too late for other groups to stake a claim to peace and freedom, or vice-versa. There could be the Peace with Freedom party, the Freedom or Peace party, and to widen the appeal even further, the Peace, Freedom and Motherhood Party."[1]

Being a comedian Gregory risked further ridicule by running as a serious candidate. Some reports sought to glom onto his famed humor with headlines such as "Low Comedy." In that particle article, ridicule was heaped on Gregory out of resentment that a comedian would run as a serious candidate for president—resentment possibly augmented by the racist position that an African American comedian should know his place. "Dick used to be a great comedian," it opined. "From a talent for making others look ridiculous he has switched to a facility for making himself look ridiculous."[2]

Through Gregory's candidacy we can also see that the political landscape among African Americans was as nuanced even in that era of intense racial turmoil as it was when George Edwin Walker ran for president in 1904. The pseudonymous African American columnist Diggs Datrooth characterized Gregory as a "comedian-turned-crusader" who was "never one to let an opportunity pass to state his position on a national issue." Similarly a columnist for the African American–owned *New York Amsterdam News* told her readers, "Comedian Dick Gregory . . . really can't be a serious candidate for the presidency." On the other hand, such major voices among African Americans as James Farmer, Roy Innis, and Dr. Alvin Poussaint applauded Gregory's candidacy, even knowing his chances were nil and despite their intentions to vote for the Democratic nominee Hubert Humphrey—while other leading voices, such as Whitney Young, thought Gregory's candidacy wrong-headed.[3]

Ridicule also resided in headlines such as "Dick Gregory Is Not So Funny Now." It emanated from Gregory's involvement in equal rights protests that, as early as 1963, led Americans to associate him less with appearances as a comedian and more with news reports such as "Police Seize 48 in Protest at Chicago: Dick Gregory Is among Group Arrested at Building Site" and "Gregory on Hunger Strike."[4] Indeed by 1968 Gregory had virtually suspended his show business career. But despite the way many Americans now perceived him, he never suspended his humor. As for example on the campaign trail:

I have no doubt that [if elected] I would have the most trouble with colored folks. One of my first programs would be to wipe out the poverty program and set up a fifty-five billion dollar a year White Folks Rest Program. I'd take all those white folks off their good jobs and put them on my Rest Program. And I'd give my black brother a good job for the first time in his life. I guarantee that after six months of doing this, colored folks would be marching on me at the White House, saying, "What's wrong with you? Lettin' these white folks lay around not working, getting relief checks, havin' all them babies."[5]

However, Gregory's campaign was not conducted for laughs. His speeches and campaign book, *Write Me In!*, were primarily devoted to exposing racism but also included his views on the Vietnam War, tax loopholes, foreign aid, gun control, and the environment.[6] Like Cleaver's campaign, it progressed along the cusp of fringe and third party.

In some instances, spotting belittlement of Gregory was tricky (as also with Cleaver) due to the offender's efforts not to be appear racist. Thus belittlement often resided in absences. The African American–owned newspaper *Chicago Daily Defender* cited one such instance when it called out the white-owned *Chicago American* for not including Gregory in an article profiling that year's presidential candidates. "Gregory's absence," it declared, "was an indication of the paper's lack of belief that the comedian-philosopher is sincerely determined to be President of the United States."[7]

Ridicule via absence also resided in the discrepancy between "Dick Gregory Is Not So Funny Now" and the actual content in that *New York Times Sunday Magazine* feature. Written by Eliot Asinof, a highly regarded author of fiction and nonfiction, it presented not only the serious aspects of Gregory's campaign but also a remarkably vivid depiction of Gregory's strategic use of humor. Describing a speech Gregory gave to a packed auditorium at the elite Massachusetts Institute of Technology, Asinof wrote of its opening:

> He stands there for a long moment in the anticipatory silence, looking them over. Finally, he walks to the front of the huge stage and takes an even closer look. "Why, you're *normal*. You're just a bunch of cats like anywhere else. . . . Man, it's M.I.T. and I expected robots!" They roar with laughter and he is off and running. Like Bob Hope at a Vietnam airbase, he unravels a string of jokes. . . . Then suddenly . . . he regards them all again, his entire style changing like an actor playing a whole new role. Even before he says a word, the audience senses the difference.

Not only was Dick Gregory still funny; he was more *Dick Gregory funny* than ever. Two milestones in his life accounted for his more individual comedy. Indeed these two milestones led him to run for president.

Gregory spoke of the first in a 1965 interview titled (mistakenly and belittlingly) "Dick Gregory Not Feeling Too Funny." In it he told of growing up "the skinniest kid on the block" who "learned to quip when the other children picked on him." In his teens he realized that with this device, "once you get a man to laugh with you, it's hard for him to laugh at you."[8] In humor Gregory had found an antidote to ridicule. Hence the opening sequence in his remarks at MIT.

That racism resided in mistakenly viewing Gregory as no longer funny was revealed by Gregory himself when he spoke of things that made Americans (in the parlance of the day) uptight. In campaign speeches aimed at whites, he frequently declared:

America is the number one racist country on the face of the earth, bar none. Now, a lot of times when a black man says that, white folks get uptight. Well, if anybody got uptight just now, that's the racism in your own head. I did not say American white folks were the number one racists on the face of the earth, I said America; and one day when we realize that black and white folks in this country are Americans, then maybe when you hear that statement you will realize that means black folks and white folks.[9]

Further evidence that racism resides deep in the psyche, often filtering perceptions without our even realizing it, are the numerous headlines belittling the full extent of Gregory's abilities by declaring he was no longer funny.

Similarly, deep in the psyche was the second milestone, this one in Gregory's professional growth. It occurred following his initial success as a stand-up comic in the latter half of the 1950s. Much of his material back then dealt with nonracial topics or turned on noncontroversial aspects of race. He would then slip in a zinger: "Every time a delegation of Negroes flies to Washington to discuss civil rights, Eisenhower flies to Augusta, Georgia. 'Come see me at the golf club,' he says—'if you can get in.'"[10]

As with many successful comedians, Gregory did not write all of his material. Among the top comedy writers he approached back then was Robert Orben, who told him, "You need material that is especially suited for you. Before that can happen, you've got to find your voice. . . . At that point where you can tell me who Dick Gregory is, then I'll write for you. Otherwise, I'll be floundering along with you."[11] It was by participating in the civil rights movement, both witnessing and being a victim of the mass arrests and the violent attacks upon those protesting segregation and other racial injustices, that he found his voice. That voice did not, however, lose its humor. Rather it acquired an additional dimension.

Ever the professional, Gregory saved his biggest punch line, as it were, for his campaign's finale. In October his party began distributing campaign literature that mimicked the one dollar bill. In lieu of the image of George Washington was a picture of Dick Gregory, bearded and bemused with his hat tipped back, beneath which it declared itself to be a "One Vote" bill. On the reverse side a dove of peace and the scales of justice replaced the images on actual dollar bills, with text inserted at the bottom, where no comparable text appeared on the actual one dollar bill:

TAKE THIS

ONE OPPORTUNITY

TO EXPRESS YOUR FREE CHOICE. THIS COUNTRY

IS REDEEMABLE. TAKE THIS TO THE POLL WITH YOU AND

VOTE FOR

DICK GREGORY PRESIDENT DAVID FROST VICE PRESIDENT

Among Gregory's reasons for issuing his dollar bill: "I wanted some campaign literature that if you threw it down, somebody would pick it up."[12]

And picked up it was—by the federal government. "The Secret Service has seized Dick Gregory-for-president campaign pamphlets on grounds they look too much like dollar bills," United Press International reported, along with all the wire services, in articles that appeared in newspapers nationwide. According to some owners of laundromats and similar self-service sites, the One Vote bill was turning up in machines that gave change for genuine dollar bills.[13]

The seizure and news reports that followed were manna from heaven for Gregory. "What kind of machine can't tell a nigger from George Washington?" he asked. While most white-owned newspapers left out that statement, they did include his comment that the literature was seized "because it is definitely dangerous to the political machines."[14] The incident was even reported on *The* CBS *Evening News*, with Walter Cronkite, the nation's preeminent news anchor, ending the report by noting that they had tried using one in the company cafeteria's dollar bill changer, which rejected it. Clearly Gregory had the last laugh, as all this publicity far exceeded that which the One Vote bill would have otherwise gotten.

Yet even that laugh went largely unheard. More than any of the other fringe candidates in 1968, Gregory's candidacy demonstrates how the turbulence of the era included a vast inability among Americans to hear each other. Think about Gregory's statement regarding America as the most racist nation in the world; think about his One Vote bill declaring, "THIS COUNTRY IS REDEEMABLE"; then think about this, from a review of his campaign book *Write Me In!*: "In his sly way, Gregory has made a devil out of the white man and a saint out of the colored man. . . . He never misses an opportunity to downgrade the white man. . . . If what Gregory says is true, then the world has truly gone insane and there is no hope left—and the chance of any man, white or black, changing it doesn't exist."[15]

More than forty-seven thousand Americans registered their disagreement with that assessment by voting for Gregory.[16] Countless others (literally, as no measure is available) also disagreed but did not vote for him. Still, while a considerable number of Americans did hear his message—not just its warnings but its moral plea and abiding humor—as many or more did not. In the realm of presidential candidacies, it would take the continued efforts of twenty-one subsequent African Americans seeking the presidency via major parties, third parties, or as noted fringe candidates before the stage was set for Barack Obama to take the Oath of Office on January 20, 2009.[17]

Pigasus

Yippie Candidate

PIGASUS WAS THE 1968 PRESIDENTIAL NOMINEE OF THE
Youth International Party. And he was a 155-pound pig—though
accounts vary regarding his weight, as they do regarding many
of the incidents involving the Yippies, whose leaders had a keen
appreciation for the power of myth. Indeed by naming their nominee Pigasus, the Yippies punningly combined *Pegasus*, the heroic
winged stallion from Greek mythology, with *pig*, a slur coined in the
late 1960s for police officers and others among the powers-that-be.

The significance of Pigasus resides in those who nominated
him: the Youth International Party, which itself was more mythical than material and went by its acronym nickname, Yippie. Like
the name Pigasus, the nickname was also a pun. It combined the
era's countercultural phenomenon of the *hippie*—a name derived
from *hip*, in the sense of cutting-edge and in the know—with the
corny old-time exclamation of glee, *yippie!* The name conveyed
a mind-set that, by extension, implied a worldview, the pun thus
becoming something of a poem in a single word. Theirs may have
been "a tale told by an idiot, full of sound and fury," but they had
a bit of Shakespeare's genius in them too.

The Yippies originated at a 1967–68 New York's Eve party at the
apartment of Abbie Hoffman. Previously an activist for a variety
of progressive causes, Hoffman had become disillusioned with
established paths of protest and had begun to pursue a route more
akin to that of another fringe candidate making a White House
bid in 1968, Homer "King of the World" Tomlinson. Like Tomlinson, Hoffman had an intuitive grasp of theatrics—or (as also many
suspected of Tomlinson) was mentally ill. Even among supporters
of Pigasus, one longtime associate of Hoffman's attending the pig's

nomination confided to the veteran *New York Times* reporter Tom Buckley that Hoffman might be a "paranoid-schizophrenic." While Buckley found Hoffman to be "unquestionably eloquent," he too felt "even a well-disposed listener senses a certain lack of balance."[1]

Among all fringe candidates, how fully they commit themselves to such a futile effort suggests, to a commensurate degree, a lack of balance. Far more important, however, this aspect of fringe candidates reveals that, for conventional candidates, seeking the presidency entails a delicate balancing act. Whether we realize it or not, how well a candidate can balance his or her public and private egos is an essential element of what, in political campaigns, is called "character."

In the more bemused sense of the term, Hoffman was quite a character. He first came to public attention in 1967, when he and his cohorts entered the visitors' gallery overlooking the New York Stock Exchange and commenced fluttering wads of one-dollar bills down to the trading floor. The incident made national news since, for some reason, the press arrived with the group, despite Hoffman's claim (and Tomlinsonian skill in public relations) that his group had not told them in advance.[2] The security staff, having sensed something was up, had prohibited the press from entering the gallery. Ultimately, however, this strong-arm tactic backfired. One newspaper reported, "Stockbrokers, clerks and runners . . . stared at the visitors' gallery. A few smiled and blew kisses, but most jeered, shouted, pointed fingers and shook their fists. Some clerks ran to pick up the bills."[3] Another stated, "Startled clerks, runners and stockbrokers . . . cheered and scrambled when the bills landed."[4] Hoffman aptly summed up the experience: "It was a perfect mythical event, since every reporter, not being allowed to actually witness the scene, had to make up his own fantasy."[5]

With the 1968 presidential election on the horizon, Hoffman next focused his news-making and myth-making skills on undermining the Democrats' presumptive nominee, President Lyndon Johnson, whom Hoffman abhorred for escalating the war in Vietnam. (Although Senator Eugene McCarthy had recently announced his intention to seek the party's nomination as an antiwar candidate, few believed he had a chance against the incumbent president.) At the New Year's Eve party that Hoffman and his wife, Anita, hosted, they got to talking tactics with the similarly prankish Jerry Rubin and journalist and author Paul Krassner.[6] What most appealed to the group was the notion of a political party that, in the words of Hoffman's biographer, Jonah Raskin, was "both mythical and mysterious, a paper party with make-believe leaders and an imaginary membership. It was a put-on and a prank, a colossal fiction that soon became a disturbing reality to police chiefs, mayors, and military officers."[7]

Raskin himself later became a Yippie, and did so, in a sense, mythically. While driving in the Bronx with Hoffman and Rubin, he suggested that they issue a Yippie manifesto aimed at college students, to attract their support by giving the appearance of having an organizational apparatus. Taken by the idea, Hoffman and Rubin then and there conferred upon him the title of minister of education. When Raskin asked if his position would require approval, Hoffman and Rubin laughed, realizing Raskin still didn't fully get it. But he soon did. "When my book about culture and empire was reviewed in the press," he wrote, "I was described solemnly in the *Times Literary Supplement* as the Minister of Education for the Youth International Party."[8]

Between the creation of the Yippies and the Democratic National Convention in August, the intense turmoil of that year both set the stage and determined its location, as it were, for the nomination of Pigasus. A sampling of front-page banner headlines from the *Des Moines Register*, a newspaper in the middle of the nation, provides a sense of how most Americans experienced those months:

Strong McCarthy Showing
(March 13 report on the New Hampshire primary, the first to take place, in which the nation was startled that McCarthy nearly defeated Johnson)

Kennedy Jars Iowa Democrats
(March 17 report that Senator Robert F. Kennedy announced he too would oppose his party's incumbent president and seek the nomination)

Johnson: "I Will Not Run"

(April 1 report that Johnson would not seek reelection)

Martin Luther King Slain

(April 5 report on the assassination of the nation's preeminent civil rights leader)

Troops Ordered to Washington

(April 6 report on race riots erupting in cities across the country)

Unity Theme for Humphrey

(April 28 report on Vice President Hubert Humphrey officially declaring himself a candidate for the Democratic Party nomination)

Student Clash at Columbia

(April 30 report on Columbia University students protesting racism and the war in Vietnam by taking over the administration building)

Robert Kennedy Near Death

(June 6 report of what, even as this edition hit the streets, became the assassination of presidential contender Kennedy)

When the Democrats gathered in Chicago in August for their convention, the syndicated columnist John Chamberlain wrote of the impact of these events, "You don't know whether to laugh or cry at the kids who have been pouring into this city to disrupt the Democratic convention. . . . It seemed ridiculous to suppose that the Yippies, with their lapses into low comedy, could ever move in the same league as Trotsky. The Yippies had just their pig, Pigasus, a 200-pound beast which they had brought to Chicago to run for President." But Chamberlain recognized that the "menace they pose is symptomatic of what the Democrats are up against. . . . The old coalition is disintegrating. Democrats in the South have been becoming Wallacites on the one hand and Republicans on the other," referring to George Wallace, a former Democrat and Alabama governor, running as a third party candidate advocating racial segregation. "The Negroes are in a pox-on-both-your-houses mood. The McCarthy doves threaten to move off into a fourth party. . . . The richer union members have become suburbanites and hence open to the lure of Republicans."[9]

Fractures were also splitting the antiwar and civil rights groups. Unable to reach consensus on tactics, many urged their supporters not to join the protests being planned for Chicago. Still, many protesters did converge on the city, primarily those who identified with the Students for a Democratic Society (SDS), as well as those attracted to the subversive theatrics of the Yippies, and a large number who arrived earnestly concerned but left dazed and confused—literally in many cases, given the violence that ensued. "Everything runs on emotions here," one such protester said. "It's emotion versus intellect, I guess. It's so confusing."[10]

Amid this maelstrom police held back some 250 protesters who gathered outside the Civic Center in Chicago to see the Yippie candidate for president arrive in a battered station wagon and to witness the nomination of Pigasus by Rubin, joined by the pig's provider, Hugh Romney (soon to be known as Wavy Gravy), a founder of a New Mexico commune called the Hog Farm—and, as they say in law enforcement, "a person of interest" (soon to be discussed in more detail).[11]

The candidate and his handlers were taken into custody before Pigasus could be placed in nomination. The handlers were charged with bringing livestock into the downtown Loop, for which they faced fines; the pig was charged with being a pig, for which he was sent to the local Humane Society (and probably, subsequently, eaten).

While the theatrics surrounding the nomination of Pigasus assured considerable media attention, the headline of one newspaper article put the event in perspective when it declared, "Yippies Are Sideshow in Chicago."[12] Indeed many in the media were aware that the nomination of Pigasus was style over substance. The *Washington Post* columnist Nicholas von Hoffman complained to his readers, "The representatives of the media . . . had been sent to interview a pig because their assignment editors were afraid the competition might score a beat on them." Although von Hoffman was among the most left-wing commentators in the mainstream media, he nevertheless scorned the fact that "Lincoln Park, where the Yippies and the crazies are supposed to be camping out, is overrun with newsmen poking under bushes looking for outrageous quotes." He cited as an example "Jerry Rubin, one of the Yippies' raggedy publicity geniuses. 'We want to give you a chance to talk to our candidate,' he said, 'and to restate our demand that Pigasus be given Secret Service protection and brought to the White House for his foreign policy briefing.'"[13]

Even when making this statement Rubin knew the press knew that he knew what they both were doing. Privately, and later publicly, Rubin gleefully admitted, "Yippies would use the Democratic Party and the Chicago theater to build our stage and make the myth; we'd steal the media away from the Democrats and create the specter of Yippies overthrowing America."[14]

Other journalists undoubtedly shared von Hoffman's contempt for reporting entertaining events as if they were political news. Not wanting to tempt the fates, however, this perspective rarely governed their reporting on Pigasus. The vast majority of articles on the pig's candidacy participated in the Yippie parody with tongue-in-cheek depictions of the pig as if he were a serious, albeit controversial candidate—as, for example, an unidentified Pigasus supporter (very likely Hugh Romney) saying, "He was born in the slums of a pig-sty, he is many colors, and he is going to be slaughtered."[15]

Even after Pigasus had been replaced with a stand-in, no less than the nation's most august media forum, the *New York Times*, could not entirely resist such delicious news. After characterizing a later campaign rally for (a new) Pigasus as a "satire of the American political campaign," it played along by reporting that "the march included several young men dressed in dark business suits and sunglasses of the type that Secret Service men wear. . . . Abbie Hoffman, a Yippie leader wearing a shirt that resembled an American flag, said Pigasus would begin a tour of Europe this week."[16]

On the eve of Election Day a widely published wire service report on alternatives to the Democrats' Humphrey, the Republicans' Nixon, and third party contender Wallace included two paragraphs that combined the candidacies of Eldridge Cleaver and Dick Gregory, and four paragraphs on Pigasus.[17]

After the election Pigasus's two foremost campaign aides, Hoffman and Rubin, continued to "steal the media away" from the government. When on trial with other protest leaders charged with conspiracy to incite a riot in Chicago, Hoffman and Rubin mocked the judge's authority by appearing one day wearing black robes identical to his. This "thea'trick" (as one scholar later termed their techniques) earned them news coverage that ranged from Montana's *Billings Gazette* (and included a posed wire service photo of the two, smiling back to back in their robes) to a headline in the *New York Times*, "Two of Chicago 7 Don Black Robes."[18]

Hoffman and Rubin similarly stole the show from the House Un-American Activities Committee (HUAC) during its investigation of the violence at the Democratic convention. When summoned to appear before this panel, which during the 1950s Red Scare was the potentially career-ending bane of progressives, Hoffman showed up wearing his American flag shirt and was promptly arrested for desecrating the flag. He continued to turn the incident into theater by proclaiming, "I regret that I have but one shirt to give for my country." A federal appeals court ultimately overturned the verdict.[19]

Rubin, for his part, avoided controversy over his shirt by not wearing one when he and Hoffman appeared before HUAC, opting instead to accessorize his bare chest with love beads, jingle bells, a belt of bullets slung over his shoulder and a toy rifle. Though he had to leave his ammo outside the committee room, the authorities engaged in no other headline-grabbing actions against his attire. So the duo had to ad lib, which Hoffman did by jumping up from his seat during the hearing, pointing to a member of the Capitol Police and exclaiming, "Mr. Chairman, that man has a loaded gun! They took ours away, but your team kept theirs."[20]

While HUAC had already lost the authority it had commanded during the Red Scare, the antics of Hoffman and Rubin tapped the final nail in its coffin. Shortly after Nixon's inauguration as the winner of the 1968 election (he first rose to prominence as a member of HUAC), the committee sought to rebrand itself as the

House Committee on Internal Security. No one bought it. In 1975 Congress eliminated the committee.

After President Nixon found a rationale to end the Vietnam War in 1975, Hoffman and Rubin proceeded along separate paths. For a time both continued to make public appearances. In 1978 Rubin married a former debutante and moved into a high-end Upper East Side apartment in Manhattan. He then formed a nonprofit that organized "how to" events, later worked for a Wall Street brokerage firm, then moved to Los Angeles and formed a company that provided a networking service for individuals seeking to make business connections. He died in 1994 at age fifty-six, after being hit by a car when jaywalking.

Hoffman went underground in 1974 to avoid facing charges of selling cocaine—lots of cocaine. If convicted (and the sting operation had him nailed), he faced fifteen years to life in prison. After plastic surgery, he fled to upstate New York, where he successfully masqueraded as Barry Freed. In 1980, realizing the animus against him had largely abated, Hoffman theatrically reappeared on network television with the celebrity interviewer Barbara Walters. Surrendering to the authorities the following day, he pleaded guilty and was sentenced to three years in prison, most of which he served on a work-release basis. Over the ensuing years Hoffman staggered between seeking a role for himself in current political protests and seeking to self-medicate his increasingly profound psychological problems with illicit drugs. On April 12, 1989, now fifty-two years old, Hoffman committed suicide by drinking a glass of Scotch in which he had dissolved 150 capsules of phenobarbital.[21]

Even though the upheavals of 1968 were erupting at the left wing of what had been the Democratic Party's longtime coalition, the events sent shivers through the Republican Party as well. In 1969 both parties enacted changes in their nominating procedures that shifted considerably more weight to the primary elections.[22] The upshot, of course, was that the nomination of presidential candidates became more democratic, thereby reducing the risk that any group within the party would feel left out. The long-shot risk, however, was that party leaders might find it virtually impossible to make deals in order to preclude nominating a candidate who was anathema to them.

Not unrelated to the consequences of these changes in party rules is a broader view expressed in 2014 by Professor Elodie Chazalon (coiner of the term *thea'trick*). "It is hard to state positively that the year 1968 is a crucial one in U.S. history," she wrote. "Nevertheless, 1968 obviously marked the blooming of forms of resistance and ways of doing politics. Such a 'cross-pollination' and blurring of the boundaries . . . show that 1968 stands, if not as the most innovative year in terms of social progress, as a training ground . . . emphasizing poaching and trickery as core elements."[23]

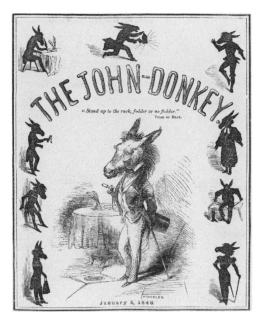

1. Cartoon candidate John Donkey ran for president by satirizing the nation's politicians, who, by 1848, were increasingly turning into jackasses with oratorical hot air. Prints and Photographs Division, Library of Congress.

2. George Francis Train ran for president in 1872. A highly successful businessman, Train nevertheless exaggerated his achievements and made amazing claims that were entirely false—but, for some reason, he lost. Prints and Photographs Division, Library of Congress.

3. and 4. (*left and below*) In 1872 Victoria Woodhull became the first woman to run for president—before women were allowed to vote (though nothing said they couldn't run for office). Figure 3 shows how she appeared in life; figure 4 shows how she appeared in *Harper's* magazine. Portrait: Courtesy of Special Collections, Fine Arts Library, Harvard University. Cartoon: Prints and Photographs Division, Library of Congress.

5. George Edwin Taylor ran for president in 1904, the first African American to do so. Racists cloaked their opposition in humor. Not using humor were numerous African Americans who opposed his decision to run. Eartha M. M. White Collection, University of North Florida, Thomas G. Carpenter Library, Special Collections and Archives.

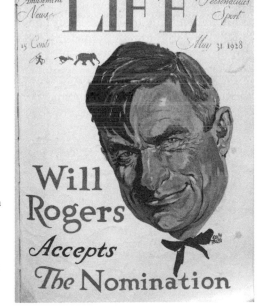

6. Humorist Will Rogers ran for president in 1928 on an antibunk campaign. Under the cover of *Life* magazine, his own campaign had a fair share of bunk. Library of Congress.

7. Comedian Gracie Allen ran a comic campaign for president in 1940 as the candidate of the Surprise Party. Though known for her daffy humor, she got in quite a few punchlines in support of women. Getty Images.

8. The 1848 campaign of Vegetarian Party nominee John Maxwell entailed more than "meats" the eye, including links to the 1848 campaign of Live Forever Jones and to socialism. Getty Images.

9. Homer Tomlinson, who ran for president from 1952 to 1968, claimed to be King of the World. Clearly this man was mentally ill. Or was he? Getty Images.

10. Gabriel Green's 1960 nomination by the Universal Flying Saucer Party was propelled by cold war fears causing hope for aliens as saviors. Courtesy of the author.

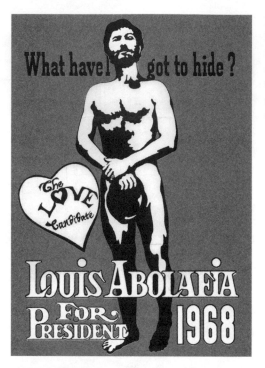

11. In his birthday suit and hat in hand, Louis Abolafia turned heads in his 1968 campaign, but few looked at the issues he really wanted them to see. Wikimedia Commons.

12. Comedian Pat Paulsen's 1968 candidacy was a popular recurring segment on *The Smothers Brothers Comedy Hour*. Behind the scenes it was part of a struggle over who controls content on television. Getty Images.

13. Though Dick Gregory was a famous comedian, his 1968 bid for president was not part of his act—though parts of it were funny, such as this campaign handout, his "One Vote" bill. Getty Images.

14. Naked Cowboy (aka Robert Burck), who ran for president in 2012, ended up revealing more about traditional candidates than he did of himself. Getty Images.

15. In this 1992 campaign poster mirroring a photo of Black Panther leader Huey Newton, professional drag queen Joan Jett Blakk sought to break down more than the gender barriers dividing humanity. © Marc Geller.

16. Vermin Supreme's recurring candidacies may seem absurd, but the absurdities are filled with meaning.

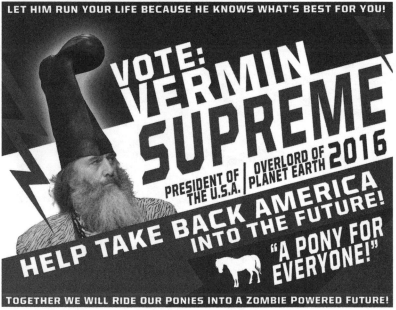

Aftershocks

Nobody for President

FOR MORE THAN A DECADE AFTER THE 1968 ELECTION, only one fringe candidate received widespread public atten tion. During these years there were, as always, many third party candidates—that is, those neither running for laughs nor widely ridiculed. In 1976, for instance, third party candidates represented the Libertarian Party, Communist Party, Socialist Party, Socialist Workers Party, Socialist Labor Party, United States Labor Party, People's Party, Prohibition Party, Restoration Party, American Party, American Independent Party, and United American Party, along with former Democratic Party contender Eugene McCarthy running as an independent and self-described "housewife" Ellen McCormack running independently as an anti-abortion candidate. But the only campaign that triggered widespread amusement was that of, rather tellingly, "Nobody for President."

As with Pigasus, the significance of Nobody's candidacy resided in who was responsible for it. Which brings us back to Pigasus and the Hog Farm commune from which his candidacy arose. The driving force behind Nobody was none other than Hugh Romney, known more widely at this point by his *nom de clown*, Wavy Gravy. Because of his prior role in the 1968 candidacy of Pigasus, Wavy Gravy's 1972 to 1988 presidential campaigns for Nobody provide us with a particularly clear view of political transitions taking place during this era.

As the chief aide in Nobody's campaign, Wavy Gravy held the self-designated title of Nobody's Fool. Indeed in every ironic respect, Wavy Gravy was nobody's fool. Born in 1936, he entered the army in 1954 and, after his two-year stint, attended Brown University on the GI Bill, majoring in Theater Arts. Afterward he continued to hone his performance skills at New York's prestigious Neighbor-hood Playhouse while earning his income working as the enter-tainment director at Greenwich Village's Gaslight Cafe.[1] Trying his hand as a stand-up comic, Romney was drawn to California in the 1960s, as were many of the artists and activists called Beats in the 1950s who went on to become part of what, in the 1960s, came to the called the counterculture. It was during these years that Romney put into practice the training he'd received in clown-ing. After having been clubbed by police in protests, he decided to attend future demonstrations as a clown. "Whoever heard of a cop beating up a clown?" he explained.[2]

While Wavy Gravy would later be called the Clown Prince of the Under-the-Counter Culture, he was never a headliner on the countercultural stage.[3] Still, he was often on that stage—sometimes literally—in various capacities. His associations included Abbie Hoffman, Bob Dylan, the comedian Lenny Bruce, and the celeb-rity falsetto with a ukulele Tiny Tim.[4] For a time he was one of Ken Kesey's "Merry Pranksters," the subject of Tom Wolfe's long-popular book, *The Electric Kool-Aid Acid Test*, in which Rom-ney is repeatedly mentioned. Branching off from the Pranksters, he shared living accommodations with a number of others who increasingly earned money collectively by producing light shows and, in return for free rent on a California farm, tending hogs. Coalescing into the Hog Farm commune, they relocated to New Mexico, continuing to produce light shows but dropping the gig with the hogs.[5]

Still known as Hugh Romney, his first shot onstage in a major arena came in August 1969, when he and what were now some one hundred members of the Hog Farm commune were assigned to help maintain security at the Woodstock Music Festival. Rom-ney made announcements from the stage over the three days of this event at which 300,000 had gathered, far in excess of expec-tations or accommodations for food and sanitation. His perfor-mance skills contributed to one state police official stating, "I can hardly believe that there haven't been even small incidents of mis-behavior by the young people."[6] Moreover, as a police lieutenant remarked, "There hasn't been anybody yelling pig at the cops."[7]

And this with the guy who ran a pig for president now onstage as the voice of good behavior.

Two weeks later Romney and those with whom he communed were called into service again, this time to help maintain the peace among more than 120,000 who gathered at the Texas International Pop Festival held outside Dallas. This time Romney not only got his name in the news but also got his adopted name. Exhausted from the intense, nonstop work, he was napping on the stage during a break in the music when, in his words, "I felt this hand on my shoulder, and a deep voice said, 'You Wavy Gravy?' I looked up and it's B. B. King! I said, 'Yes, sir. Yes, sir.' I was getting ready to get up, but then he said, 'Well, Wavy Gravy, I can work around you.'"[8]

Nobody for President comes from a long line of such presidential candidates, dating back at least as far as 1872, when Indiana's *Clay Country Enterprise* took a poke at a rival paper in noting, "The Terre Haute Journal has declared itself in favor of nobody for president. Who is he?"[9]

Actually it's an excellent question. When people support nobody for president, they present us with, in effect, a blank to be filled by others with whatever it is that might cause them to feel disconnected from the political process. Because such reasons can range from dissatisfaction with current presidential choices to feeling alienated from the society to fundamental opposition to our form of government, Nobody can be a widely but deceptively popular choice.[10]

Nobody can also appear in various guises. Over the years the most popular form has been Mickey Mouse, dating back to 1932, when he was first mentioned as a possible presidential candidate as part of a publicity campaign by the Walt Disney Company.[11] No actual campaign, however, ensued. Still, when such candidates attract national attention, they provide some measure of the extent to which Americans feel dissatisfied with the political process. Mickey, alas, has been stymied from making this contribution by Disney's famously ferocious lawyers baring their teeth at promoters of Mickey Mouse for president.[12] Unhampered, however, were the four presidential campaigns of Nobody.

In February 1975 Wavy Gravy made a brief reference to running Nobody for president as the candidate of what he called the Birthday Party, but when Nobody surfaced again in July 1976 during the Democratic National Convention in New York City, he was the candidate of Wavy Gravy's 1968 comrades, the Yippies. Apparently Wavy Gravy hoped Nobody would be the next Pigasus, as he was among those onstage at the band shell in Central Park to nominate Nobody before seven hundred people gathered for a Yippie rally. One day later, however, Wavy Gravy, in clown getup, was unable to attract a crowd outside the convention site.[13]

The campaign went from bad to worse when it headed next to the Republican National Convention in Kansas City, Missouri. "Well, fellow Americans, the Yippies are here again," wrote the syndicated columnist Georgie Anne Geyer. Known for her conservative political views, Geyer may have been harsh, but she was not wrong when observing, "How the mighty have fallen. When the Yippies were formed . . . they had Abbie Hoffman and Jerry Rubin. . . . And today?" Among the examples she offered in answer was a "funny and sad young man in blue cheerleader's uniform named 'Wavy Gravy,' who also works as a clown, and who led a circle of Yippies, clasping hands tightly while they did breathing exercises." Geyer then asked, "And what kind of society did the Yippies, who led much of the opposition to Vietnam, want today?" That question she put to Dana Beale, then and for years to come a leader among what remained of the Yippies. "Five years ago, I would have had a lot of pat phrases," Beale replied. "I don't know any more."[14]

Wavy Gravy may not have known either, but evidently he did know that, in his friend Bob Dylan's words, "the times they are a-changin'"—and the Yippies they are a-not. He repossessed Nobody's campaign, retooled it, and in October restarted it from what had become the nation's countercultural Mecca, San Francisco. "Nobody Kicks Off Campaign" headlined an Associated Press report from that city that began, "They held a presidential campaign rally in front of City Hall—and Nobody showed up. But that was fine with Wavy Gravy and the rest of the crowd from the Nobody for President campaign, who kicked off a national tour."

The report described how Wavy Gravy, identifying his role as Nobody's Fool, attracted a crowd with oratorical flourishes such as, "Nobody loves the poor!"; "Nobody will lower your taxes!"; and the capstone, "Nobody's perfect!!" By then a couple hundred onlookers were revved up for the arrival of the candidate's motorcade, which turned out to consist of one battered sports car with a bunting-festooned chair mounted in the trunk, upon which Nobody sat. With the help of Nobody's Fool producing a set of plastic wind-up teeth, the candidate then answered questions about current political issues by chattering. The rally ended on a parody of soaring optimism when Nobody's Fool declared that this year Nobody really had a shot at winning, since "forty percent of eligible voters in the last election voted for nobody."[15]

For all its rag-tag hippie-dippy trappings, it was a highly professional show. And ready to go on the road. Traveling in an old bus advertising "Nobody for President," Wavy Gravy and his crew next headed to the Hog Farm's home state of New Mexico, seeking and getting a welcoming reception such as, in Albuquerque, an Associated Press report headlined "Wavy Gravy Brings Nobody's Drive to State."[16] They then proceeded to the nearest college campus where the students were most likely to share their appreciation for zaniness, the University of Texas at Austin, the city that would adopt the slogan "Keep Austin Weird." Six hundred people showed up, more than enough to keep the wire service humming.[17]

Just as attention was starting to build, however, the campaign ran out of time. It was already the end of October by the time they were in Austin. With the election just days away, they had to close the show for four years. But they hit the hustings again in the 1980 presidential election, again getting national attention with return rallies in Albuquerque and Austin, and similarly enthusiastic receptions at politically and comically conscious campuses such as the University of Wisconsin and the University of Michigan, and an Election Day finale in Washington DC, directly across from the White House.

While Wavy Gravy's success in attracting widespread attention to Nobody for president reveals his awareness that the revolutionary antics of the Yippies had played out, it also reveals his further insight that the antics now had to be more broad-based in their appeal. For that reason he played up the fill-in-the-blank aspect of Nobody for president. And as the widespread news coverage of Nobody's candidacy reveals, Wavy Gravy was aware of yet another shift in America's political landscape at the time. Many of the news reports included his urging, on the behalf of Nobody, that "None of the Above" be included on presidential ballots. Wavy Gravy was not alone in this call; besides discontented leftists, Nevada's Young Republicans urged the same in 1975. Likewise in 1976, conservative legislators in Kentucky and California sought (unsuccessfully) to enact the ballot choice.[18] Wavy Gravy, truly Nobody's Fool, knew the political breadth of the nation's political discontent in the aftermath of the previous decade's turmoil. He has "always been in the middle between the left and the right," he told an interviewer in 1974, "always trying to communicate that edge to the other side."[19]

Nevertheless when the Nobody for President bandwagon headed out again in the 1984 election, the press paid far less attention. In part the joke had been made. But also the political landscape had continued to change. It was now "morning again in America," as a commercial for the reelection of Ronald Reagan exhaled in satisfaction. Indeed it was. The war in Vietnam and the antiwar protests were now sufficiently in the past, as was the violence that had so often exploded during the civil rights movement. Likewise the memories of the domestic scandals of Watergate under President Nixon and the international humiliation of the Iranian hostage crisis under President Carter had sufficiently wilted. Even if President Reagan was still the film and television actor he began as, he played the role of president with consummate skill, and a great many in the nation applauded the character he brought to it. Ironically perhaps, Wavy Gravy's being a professional performer—seeing behind the curtain and being outraged—may be why he failed to discern in America's increasingly television-dominated view of the world a new view emerging among voters.

Even if his instincts failed him in 1984, Wavy Gravy snapped out of it and found once again a way to retool Nobody's campaign for the 1988 election, which would be his last hurrah. Retreating in one respect to his base, he teamed up with the rock group

Vicious Hippies and booked the show at those college campuses where he knew he'd get the best reception. On the other hand—and revealing his awareness of the recent political shift that gifted the nation with Reagan—Wavy Gravy ended the show by pointing to Hog Farm assistants with voter registration forms and declared, "If Nobody votes, Nobody wins."[20]

Joan Jett Blakk

Queer Nation Candidate

AMONG THE AFTERSHOCKS THAT FOLLOWED THE POLITICAL earthquake of 1968, newly widened fissures provided openings for fringe candidates to tread that became paths for later mainstream candidates who were African American or feminist or identified with the lesbian, gay, bisexual, transgender, or queer communities (LGBTQ). The first such fringe candidate to receive widespread attention was Joan Jett Blakk, who campaigned in a way that sought to amuse a wide variety of Americans while conveying views representing *all* of those groups. A feat not easily managed.

Joan Jett Blakk was (and as of this writing still is) the show-biz name of Terence Smith, an African American drag performer whose professional alter ego is a staunchly feminist woman of no particular race. His stage name itself is akin to cross-dressing by being an example of cross-naming. Smith adopted and adapted the name of the lead singer from the popular cutting-edge rock group Joan Jett and the Blackhearts, displaying his skill at loosening the screws of racial connections, as it were, by dubbing his drag persona Blakk rather than Black.

Similarly in performance, when Joan Jett Blakk spot-on lip-synched songs such as Patsy Cline's "Tell Me Now / Get It Over," it was for more than laughs; it was also, stunningly, as if Blakk was inhabited by the soul of that late great southern white country singer. Likewise when, recostumed and recoiffed to render Renata Tebaldi pouring her heart into the aria "Ebben, Ne Andro Lontana," Blakk brought that diva's soul to the stage—powerfully demonstrating how profoundly human connections cross sexual and racial differences.

Such connections obviously—and for Blakk seriocomically—are rarely perceived at first glance. "We got a chance to really terrify a lot of suburban families," she laughed when speaking about her 1991 campaign for mayor of Chicago. "Before they knew it there was a whole—what do you call a group of drag queens?—a gaggle?—a gaggle of drag queens right before them handing out paraphernalia and they thought, with all that commotion, it was something quite serious." And yet it was in fact comically serious. "We got people to notice us," Blakk said, summing up that campaign. "We got people to notice that drag does not have to be just standing at a microphone pretending to sing a Dionne Warwick song."[1]

Unlike the many fringe candidates who nominate themselves, Joan Jett Blakk was asked to run by Queer Nation, a national LGBTQ activist group founded in 1990. The organization's Chicago branch first turned to her in 1991, hoping she would help them gain visibility by running in that year's mayoral race. They chose Blakk because she was already well known for her astonishing performances onstage. Though reluctant at first, being a member of Queer Nation she agreed to give the political stage a try.

Being nothing if not adaptable, candidate Blakk quickly made news in ways that amused a broad spectrum of Chicagoans, appearing in the press following a spur-of-the-moment response to a cop in a coffee shop. "We were creating quite a commotion and this policeman came up and said, 'I don't understand; what's going on here?'" Blakk recounted. When told they were there with mayoral candidate Joan Jett Blakk, the police officer dared her to go out to the squad car and kiss his partner. Though the candidate protested, "He's got a gun; I'm in a dress," the group included a photographer and the point of the campaign was, after all, visibility. "I went out and . . . handed him a flyer and before he knew it I had kissed him and I said, 'Thank you! Vote for me; I'll set you free.'"[2] As the camera flashed and later, when the photo appeared in the press, Chicagoans laughed.

The success of Blakk's losing bid for mayor resulted in Queer Nation turning to her to run for president in 1992, the year in which

President George H. W. Bush, a Republican, faced challenges to his reelection from Democratic Party nominee (and winner of the election) Bill Clinton, and H. Ross Perot, a widely popular businessman running as an independent.

Once again Blakk succeeded in attracting the media spotlight by managing to elude security at the Democratic National Convention and gain entrance, with a film crew, to the convention floor. With that razzle-dazzle as backdrop, Blakk filmed her announcement as a candidate. Catching the attention of the news media, ever vigilant for amusing visuals, Blakk was conducting a full-fledged press conference moments later—until, seeing men in identical suits approaching, the nominee and her entourage quickly split. The event led to so much media attention that, at the Republican National Convention that followed, Pat Buchanan, a conservative and anti–gay rights contender for nomination, brandished Blakk's appearance at the Democrats' convention in his speech to the delegates.[3]

Using the brow-raising campaign slogan "Lick Bush in '92," Blakk took the show on the road.[4] In Milwaukee she waved to voters as part of that city's Gay and Lesbian Pride Day parade, seated in a convertible decked out with the slogan "Let's Take the 'L' Out of Flag Day."[5] In campaign speeches she tickled listeners with one-liners such as "I'm the only candidate who can successfully skirt all the issues," then delivered zingers, as in this reference to Ronald Reagan: "We've had a bad actor for president; why not a good drag queen?"[6]

Not every aspect of Blakk's campaign aimed to seduce views through humor. She again made national news by choosing as her vice presidential running mate Miriam Ben-Shalom, who herself had been in the media spotlight when she was prohibited from reenlisting in the army because she was openly gay.[7] Reflecting on her campaign when interviewed on National Public Radio, Blakk set laughs aside to explain:

> Any time people have to fight for civil rights, it's the same thing, no matter who's struggling with it—blacks, or women, or gays, or American Indians. . . . What I'm about as an activist is certainly

my visibility as a gay person, because that's the—one of the main
problems facing gay people is invisibility. . . . If people don't see
that there are gay people everywhere, then things like the killing
of Allen Schindler [a gay sailor murdered by two shipmates] . . .
people really wouldn't think of doing that kind of thing.[8]

While many Americans were amused in ways that increased
the degree to which they perceived Blakk as a person rather than
a freak, not all found the humor endearing.

In addition to Pat Buchanan speaking out against Blakk's campaign, so too did the highly acclaimed (and gay) writer and cultural commentator Bruce Bawer in his book *A Place at the Table:
The Gay Individual in American Society*. Bawer criticized Blakk
for being a presidential candidate "who presents himself as a representative of the gay population [and] insists on playing the fool,
the absurd outsider; the whole idea of gay politics, after all, should
be to stop heterosexuals from thinking of gays as the most 'other'
thing around."[9] Bawer's complaint represents what is, far and away,
the most important insight we gain from the fringe candidacy of
Joan Jett Blakk: the fact that the LGBTQ community is no more
monolithic in its views than any other group of human beings.

PART 4

Clowns and Quixotes Stampede
the Internet and Cable TV

Vermin Supreme

"Why Not the Worst?"

VERMIN SUPREME HAS RUN FOR PRESIDENT IN EVERY election from 1992 to, as of this writing, 2016. Despite the repetition, public attention to his clown candidacy has yet to diminish—rather it has skyrocketed. This fact alone suggests that his fringe campaigns for president contain considerable significance.

Some of those elements surface simply by sampling his media coverage in 1992 with that of 2016. In 1992 National Public Radio (NPR) dispatched correspondent Linda Wertheimer and guest humorist Dave Barry to the New Hampshire primary. During a conversation with Barry on that network's *All Things Considered*, Wertheimer turned to "the non-major candidates," as she called them. "I hate to characterize them," she said, "but there are some candidates—we had—we had a man in here today who—who told us his name was Vermin." Scooping up her fumbling with this oddball, humorist Barry stepped in to field it: "Vermin Supreme. . . . I ran into him at a shopping mall yesterday, which is really where you run into all of them. But Vermin Supreme came up and he was wearing—I don't know if—what—he was wearing it when he . . ." Now Wertheimer handled the bobble, "Yeah, he was wearing it." Back to Barry, "Wearing a boot on his head. . . . And it was making a statement, I think. . . . He said it was—he said, 'Why not the worst?' That was his—the campaign theme he was on when I was there." "How do we get out of this?" Wertheimer asked moments later, to which Barry said, "You mean the—how do we—how do we reform the entire campaign process and make it decent and responsive and focus on the issues instead of sleazeball tabloid stuff?" "Well, no," she replied, "actually, I was thinking how do we end this interview?"[1]

Newcomer Vermin Supreme's campaign for president was attention-getting but incomprehensible in 1992. By 1992 "tabloid stuff" was not a problem, even for the highly regarded newscasts of NPR, let alone other news outlets that reported his candidacy—though only, as on NPR, as part of a larger story, never in the headline or opening.

By comparison, here's a sampling of headlines from 2016:

Consider Supreme Candidacy
(*Foster's Daily Democrat*, Dover NH, February 1, 2016, online edition)

A Guy Named Vermin Takes on Establishment in New Hampshire Primary
(*Biloxi [MS] Sun-Herald*, February 2, 2016, online edition)

Ted Cruz Meets Rival Vermin Supreme, Rejects Toothbrush Plank
(*Dallas Morning News*, February 8, 2016, online edition)

Vermin Supreme—A Choice We Can Live With
(*Daily Progress*, Charlottesville VA, June 22, 2016, online edition)

Vermin Supreme Is What America Needs
(*Sand Mountain Reporter*, Albertville AL, June 29, 2016, online edition)

Notable in this selection is not only Vermin Supreme's now being a headliner among fringe candidates but that each of these news reports appeared online. "I'm probably a thousand times more well-known than I was previously," he told an interviewer in 2012, succinctly stating the reason as "this whole viral thing," referring to the explosion of publicity he'd acquired through the internet.[2] In 1992 Americans were just beginning to gain access to the internet. By the end of the decade that access had expanded exponentially. This new form of communication proved a boon to fringe presidential candidates.

It also radically altered the landscape on which America's political discourse takes place.

While the 2016 headlines for Vermin Supreme remained tongue-in-cheek, they raised the question: Who is Vermin Supreme? Partial answer, again regarding the internet: *Who Is Vermin Supreme?* is the title of a 2014 documentary film, which received production funding online via a Kickstarter campaign.[3]

Vermin Supreme's actual name is Vermin Supreme. At some point in his fringe candidate career he took steps to make it his legal name, most likely to add a barrier to his noncandidate life, which he has consistently kept private. Of the little that is known of his background is that his reputation for comic protest dates back to high school, circa the late 1970s (circa because he's kept his age private too via conflicting claims). After some fellow students were arrested for possession of marijuana, the young prankster silkscreened and sold T-shirts emblazoned with "Big Pig Is Watching You" and a pig in police uniform wearing a badge embossed with "Keep Off the Grass."[4]

While attending or having dropped out of art school in Baltimore (he has made both claims, but in either case he's likely referring to that city's prestigious Peabody Institute, given the talent he demonstrated in high school), he had a life-changing experience when a 1986 cross-country march for nuclear disarmament arrived in Baltimore en route from Los Angeles to Washington.[5] It was, he later recalled, a "glorious mobile city," tied down by nothing and collectively governed. "As soon as I saw that, I went to a thrift store, I bought a cheap sleeping bag, I bought a change of clothes, and I joined this march." And became devoted to "non-hierarchical organizations."[6]

From that springboard Vermin Supreme made his first splash as a fringe candidate the following year in Baltimore's mayoral election. "The Name Is Mr. Vermin and Politics Is His Game" was a headline in the *Baltimore Sun*.[7] Already he had grown his signature full beard but had not yet taken to wearing a boot on his head; rather he wore a tam-o'-shanter and kilt. Unlike his later campaigns, his fringe bid for mayor addressed the same issues raised by the mainstream candidates: housing, education, transportation, taxes. In each instance his platform's view was "No comment." Still, we

can spot a bit of his presidential campaigns to come in his platform also raising the issues of "life, liberty, the pursuit of happi-
ness, truth, justice, and the American Way," on which his position
was, likewise, "No comment."[8]

The key element in this initial campaign, however, was his declaring, as he would continue to do for the next two decades, "All politicians are vermin. And I am the Vermin Supreme. Therefore,
I am without question the most qualified." In keeping with this
view he declared, "I would, of course, buy your votes if I could
afford it. . . . I am not above graft." In addition, and also during
the decades that followed, he made impossible promises, as politicians often do, but his were absurdly impossible, such as his vow
to "do something about the weather." He offered satirical solutions
too, also as he would continue to do, such as his plan to solve the
problem of weather in Baltimore by placing a dome over the city.[9]

And there's this tidbit: Vermin Supreme's first foray into fringe
candidacy resulted in the *Baltimore Sun* reporter Sandy Banisky
writing, "Look, he sounds like a fun guy. And honest. And a good
dresser. But he lost. Maybe in the presidential campaign . . ." she
semi-concluded, letting the sentence trail where it may.[10]

At this early stage Vermin Supreme can be seen as following
in the footsteps of Wavy Gravy. Both began by promoting the
image of a pig as representing the authorities but soon moved
away from such insults and, in both cases, commenced presenting themselves as clowns. Wavy Gravy adopted the costume to
avoid police beatings; Vermin Supreme "watched as too many
peace marches devolved into violence," in the words of the journalist and author Pagan Kennedy. "So he decided that he would
show up at some demonstrations as a clown . . . helping to keep
the peace."[11] Early on, for example, a wire service report from Los
Angles began, "More than 3,500 bellowing, marching protesters
jammed downtown streets Sunday, putting police on edge." Near
the end of the article it mentioned, "A man decked out in glitter-
ing red, white, and blue, with a rainbow wig . . . drew a grinning
crowd of admirers from the march as he harangued the helmeted
officers through a bullhorn. 'Attention Los Angeles Police Department,' said the man, who claims his legal name is Vermin Supreme,

'Everything is under control. Your services are no longer needed. Please return to your homes now.'[12] Laughs erupted; violence did not. Nor were there any arrests.

But Vermin Supreme's clowning extended beyond throwing pies in the face of potential violence. "He has spent years figuring out how to transform a group-thinking throng back into a bunch of individuals," Kennedy observed. At a 2004 rally for Democratic presidential nominee John Kerry, the crowd awaiting him began chanting, "Ker-REEE, Ker-REEE," acquiring (in Kennedy's aptly chosen words) "that mob-zombie expression on their faces." Vermin Supreme raised a megaphone and interrupted, "Where does John Kerry stand on mandatory tooth brushing? Is he soft on plaque?" Covering his 2004 campaign for the *Boston Globe*, Kennedy witnessed an increasing number in the crowd stopping to listen to this peculiar man, noting, "Suddenly they're no longer members of the Kerry gang; they're just their ordinary selves again."[13]

Vermin Supreme followed in the footsteps of Wavy Gravy in another respect, but in this instance their paths diverged. Both promoted, in effect, Nobody for President. While Wavy Gravy did so directly as campaign chairman for Nobody, Vermin Supreme did so as a proxy for Nobody, much as Mickey Mouse or John Donkey served as "Nobody for President" proxies. "A vote for Vermin Supreme," he often proclaimed when bringing a speech to a close, "is a vote completely thrown away."[14] Wavy Gravy's campaign for Nobody, however, veered elsewhere over the years. As previously seen, his speeches during Nobody's final campaign in 1988 often ended with the slogan "If Nobody Votes, Nobody Wins."

While the message conveyed in Wavy Gravy's campaigns for Nobody changed, it always remained comprehensible. Not so, for many, the issues raised by Vermin Supreme. From a distance, however, connections can be seen that indicate the direction in which he was pointing—albeit not an explicitly stated point. Vermin Supreme repeatedly campaigned for mandatory tooth brushing, the issue he brandished at Kerry's supporters when they began going "zombie." Indeed zombies were also a key element in his repeated campaign proposal to convert the nation to renewable energy. The plan called for giant turbines that, like hamster wheels, turned when zombies inside the turbines chased brains being dangled in front of them. Continuing his satiric tradition of impossible promises, Vermin Supreme's most frequent campaign promise was a free pony for every American, part of his larger proposal to provide "a stable economy."[15]

"He wants to topple the politicians from their pedestals," Kennedy observed.[16] His clown campaigns have aimed to do that through what one might call *performative anarchy*—performances that use certain absurdities to loosen our connections to political leaders. While, early on, Vermin Supreme occasionally called himself an anarchist, he soon turned to describing himself as a "friendly tyrant." Tyranny and friendship, being mutually exclusive, make a good fit for performative anarchy. So too did his mimicking modern presidential aspirants authoring books, which he himself did in 2016, when he published *I Pony: Blueprint for a New America*. Rather than presenting a factual vision *for* the candidate's presidency, it presented a fictional one *of* his presidency. (And, by the way, some very fine artwork.) Most accurate, however, was Vermin Supreme's saying in 2012, "I still don't have an ultimate goal."[17] His campaigns are more about process than project.

"I should spend our time on Vermin Supreme?" the network news correspondent and coanchor Sam Donaldson once asked angrily. "Not a chance."[18] Donaldson, however, was of the generation spawned by the patriarch of television news, the esteemed journalist Edward R. Murrow. The very fact that the question of covering Vermin Supreme was put to Donaldson reflects changes that had commenced in network news in the 1970s, when its executives saw the need to compete with the growing availability of cable television. For example, in 1977 at Donaldson's network, ABC, executives expanded the role of Roone Arledge, their innovative and successful producer of sports broadcasts, to include producing the news. Fast-forward to 2016. During that year's presidential election, a series of segments on ABC News, "Your Voice / Your Vote," each of which opened with dramatic music and power-flashing graphics, devoted one of those broadcasts to Vermin Supreme.[19]

Notably—perhaps significantly (time will tell)—many in the

news media are very aware of the ways in which style and content in journalism has changed. During the protests in Los Angeles, for instance, the *Pittsburgh Post* reporter Gene Collier interviewed Vermin Supreme. "He had just begun to de-mystify himself when the heckling started," Collier wrote. "It wasn't the police being heckled. It wasn't Vermin. It was me. 'The real story's over there!' a young woman was squawking. 'Excuse me! The news? The real story's over there!' . . . 'I'll decide what the story is, ma'am,' I said. 'Can't you see this man has a Nerf ball where his nose should be?'" Why would Collier call attention to his journalistic choices in a not very flattering way? We can see by jumping further into his interview, where Collier comments on Vermin Supreme's views, "Uh-huh. Maybe I should have listened to the media critic."[20] Clearly Collier was conflicted as to which story to report to what extent— particularly given the need to compete in a media market that now included news (or what passed for it) on cable networks and the internet.

Not only journalists were aware of this competition; so too was Vermin Supreme. "The media is my willing partner in subversion," he told interviewers, regarding which Kennedy observed, "Journalists will follow a guy with a boot [on his head] the way a trout will go after a shiny plastic worm. The boot promises a good story. Vermin Supreme knows this. He has packaged himself as a made to order wacky sidebar for newspapers to run during campaign season. . . . In the past few years, our country has turned a corner. The political sideshow has moved to center stage."[21] But hold on. Have the likes of Vermin Supreme *actually* impacted our political process?

"I think he's brought a lot of light to the stupidity that we put up with in a lot of presidents we've elected," Joe Savarino, from the band Avadhootz, told a university newspaper reporter. "He's about reworking the system in a way that we all know needs to happen."[22]

Okay, but this is (1) from a college newspaper, quoting (2) a musician, who plays in a band called (3) Avadhootz.

Let's head to the solid South. "I've heard from many registered voters that they don't like the presumptive nominee of either party," Marla McKenna, managing editor of Charlottesville, Virginia's

Daily Progress, wrote during the 2016 election. "I'm here to tell you there's hope, my friends. . . . Look no further than Vermin Supreme, the man with the boot on his head." In keeping with the notion that Nobody (or a proxy for Nobody) is a blank to be filled by all forms of dissatisfaction, McKenna went on to say, "You're probably wondering if it's a right boot or a left boot. . . . Whatever it is, it appears to be perfect for tromping through the political muck. Mr. Supreme stands for nothing, so you don't need to worry about whether his views align with your own."[23]

She was clearly kidding. Not kidding, however, was columnist Mike Argento in York, Pennsylvania's *Daily Record*. During the 2016 run-up to the New Hampshire primary, he was dead earnest when comparing Donald Trump to Vermin Supreme:

> Let's take a look at two presidential candidates. One has . . . rhetoric [which] has escalated from the merely outrageous to stupefying insanity. . . . He has made outrageous promises about restoring America to greatness, although his proposals seem a little light in the fact-based realm. . . . The other candidate has also made outrageous promises. . . . He has pledged to give every American a pony and pass a law making tooth-brushing mandatory. . . . This candidate has described himself as "a friendly fascist" and "a tyrant you can trust."[24]

In that primary Vermin Supreme received nearly twice as many votes as former Virginia governor Jim Gilmore.

The degree to which Vermin Supreme's campaigns have attracted interest—and votes when on the ballot, as he was in New Hampshire—is an indication of the degree to which the urge to pull out the tent stakes of the whole political show exists in the hearts and, alas, the minds of Americans at that time.

Jonathon "The Impaler" Sharkey

Vampires Witches and Pagans Party

FIRST, A DISCLAIMER ON BEHALF OF AMERICA'S VAMPIRES, witches, and pagans, whose organizations publicly announced they did not support the political campaigns of Jonathon Sharkey, nor were they in any way associated with his self-created Vampires Witches and Pagans Party.[1] This fact, however, went unmentioned in the considerable amount of news media attention showered on Sharkey as a fringe candidate. After all, parsing the views of those groups was nowhere near as entertaining as interviewing a vampire candidate. Though for most Americans, the fact that such differences exist would be news to them. It was to me.

Sharkey announced his presidential candidacy for the 2008 election during the time he was running for governor of Minnesota in 2006, intertwining the two campaigns. "When we get ahold of [Osama] bin Laden," he declared of the 9/11 mastermind, "I'm going to impale him where the twin towers used to stand." A former professional wrestler (under the name Rocky Flash), Sharkey employed the rhetoric of that form of entertainment in this and other campaign promises, such as, "When I become president, everyone who has been tried and found guilty of inhumane treatment against Iraqis, I'm going to pardon them." In regard to Afghanistan, where bin Laden trained terrorists, Sharkey declared, "When I become president, to make sure future generations don't have to worry about being attacked by Muslims, I'm going to eradicate the whole country—I don't care; our country comes first."[2]

In fairness, Sharkey's campaign was not limited to foreign policy; he also addressed issues that came under the purview of state government. His platform's thirteen-point program for Minnesota included stiffer sentences for drug dealers, child molesters, rapists, and repeated drunk drivers—specifically "impalement in front of the State Capitol."[3]

Had Sharkey won the election, he would not have been the first professional wrestler elected governor of Minnesota. That distinction went to retired wrestler Jesse Ventura, who was elected governor in 1999. Ventura, however, had previously demonstrated his governmental abilities as mayor of Brooklyn Park, a suburb of Minneapolis–St. Paul with nearly eighty thousand residents. Moreover his political career was devoid of professional wrestling's enraged rhetoric.

It was, however, such chest-thumping braggadocio that, even in Minnesota (land of *knee-slams* and *hammer-locks*? I thought it was *the land of lakes*), made Sharkey stand out. "Looking for something really, really different in a political candidate this year?" the *Minneapolis Star Tribune* asked its readers in 2006.[4] Apparently yes—and not just in Minnesota. Over in Montana the *Billings Gazette* took note of Sharkey's candidacy, saying of him (in jest, but humor is not without a kernel of belief):

> He'll get more done as governor in two years than most governors do in eight. Among his bold ideas: "Any terrorist who is caught in Minnesota while I am governor will find out what the true meaning of my nickname, 'The Impaler,' means. Right in front of our State Capitol. Then the Feds can take the terrorist's body from the impaling stake. If the U.S. Department of Justice wants to charge me with brutally murdering a terrorist, they may do so. I do not see an American jury convicting me."[5]

This *Billings Gazette* article then addressed rumors that Montana's governor Brian Schweitzer was considering a 2008 presidential bid by suggesting (still in jest but as per previous parenthesis) that Sharkey's "addition to the Schweitzer-for-president ticket could be just the shot of excitement and controversy that our governor needs to go all the way to the White House."

With so many newspapers paying attention to Sharkey's candidacy, producers of cable news soon started calling. And not just, as some might guess, the testosterone-flowing fellows at Fox— though that network's show *Fox & Friends* was among the first to host Sharkey for an interview.[6] Over at MSNBC, the interview was not quite as friendly, but it was nothing if not fun-filled when Sharkey appeared on *The Situation with Tucker Carlson*.[7]

But let's pause. Is all this press attention something new? In the mid-nineteenth century, as we saw, newspapers had considerable fun with the presidential bid of Leonard "Live Forever" Jones, much as in the 1950s they gleefully reported on Homer "King of the World" Tomlinson's perennial campaigns. All three of these fringe candidates, at first glance at least, seem equally nuts.

Whether or not any or all of them was, by current psychiatric standards, mentally ill, one difference remains. "Live Forever" Jones and "King of the World" Tomlinson campaigned for Christian love; Sharkey campaigned for violent retribution. That, in fact, was what attracted attention at the time he ran. Strip away the vampires, witches, and pagans part of his campaign, and what remains is rage. And in 2006 rage was seeping up through the nation's political cracks.

"When I read an article about Sharkey," one college student wrote in her university's newspaper, "I caught myself thinking, 'A vampire for governor? Is this man serious?'" She went on, "Has our country's willingness to let anyone run for office finally gone too far? But as I browsed The Impaler's Web site, I began to reevaluate my opinion. Indeed, most, if not all, of Sharkey's ideas are a bit extreme."

A bit?

"But he does have a platform," she continued, ultimately arriving at the conclusion, "Isn't the point of the democratic system to have a difference of ideas and something for everyone? . . . Although both national and local media have taken interest, neither has taken him very seriously. But maybe they should. Should only those who have 'normal' or mainstream opinions be taken seriously? . . . What would the public prefer?"[8]

Intellectually curious students were not the only ones open to contemplation of the white-hot core of Sharkey's campaign. A Louisiana columnist wrote, "I think we should give the Minnesotans their due. They have figured something out. . . . Put in someone who is so over the top, he or she will leave the national media shaking its collective head and the general populace shaking on the floor in laughter."[9] An editorial one state to the west said, "What might get Texans to warm up to Sharkey is his anti-terrorism campaign," which it then related entailed public impaling.[10] A university instructor of journalism in Missouri observed:

> Election day in the United States is . . . more about relief that the stupid thing's over no matter who won. Why? Because our candidates don't address issues anyone cares about. . . . What I wouldn't give for a Truman Democrat and a Reagan Republican duking it out for office. . . . The closest we'll come to that is a vampire. . . . I'm not sure how [Sharkey] stands on taxes, but he wants to execute convicted murderers and child molesters by impaling them on a wooden pole outside the state Capitol . . . and he wants to do it personally. I'd kinda go for that.[11]

However, Sharkey's candidacy soon hit a brick wall. With all the publicity, he came to the attention of a U.S. marshal who recognized him as wrestler Rocky Flash, wanted on two warrants in Indiana, one for flight following his arrest for the other: stalking. One month into his gubernatorial campaign Sharkey was arrested, extradited, and jailed pending trial.[12]

Six months later he was acquitted. But by then his gubernatorial campaign was left in the dust of the publicity now focused on Minnesota's two most mainstream candidates, Democrat Mike Hatch and the ultimate victor, Republican Tim Pawlenty.

Sharkey sought to make his way back into the spotlight when the nation turned its attention to the 2008 presidential election. One article on his candidacy began, "Seated in a window booth inside an Elizabeth (New Jersey) luncheonette calmly discussing social issues and foreign policy, it's easy to forget for a moment that Jonathon Sharkey is a vampire."[13]

Is a vampire? Where previous news articles dropped child molesters and repeated drunk drivers from those Sharkey sought to impale, this reporter opted not to insert *alleged* or *self-professed* before *vampire*. Picky perhaps, as it's less entertaining that way; makes it sound a tad newsy.

News, as seen here, was a decreasing priority in election coverage.

During Sharkey's presidential campaign, a low-budget film about the candidate was released, titled *Impaler*. Relatively few saw the documentary as it was mainly shown at film festivals. It did, however, get reviewed in some newspapers, ranging from the *Minneapolis Star Tribune* to the *Washington Post*.[14] Despite less than rave cinematic assessments, the film did provide an astonishing view into the life of Jonathon Sharkey. That view, however, was not the kind that wins votes. In addition to a mass of tangled relationships and some eye-widening accusations by family members, audiences also saw that, to some degree, Sharkey's rage was showmanship, able to be turned on and off at the flip of an inner switch. Or, more typically, the click from a camera.

Other than the film and a few pieces in the news, Sharkey's presidential campaign never regained the traction it had prior to his arrest. In part his renewed effort floundered because he did not raise the stakes, as it were, either by adding new proposals or altering those involving impalement. Internet bloggers and news outlets had now been-there-done-that. Sharkey did receive a small flurry of attention a month before the election. Unfortunately for him, it followed his being arrested again. This time the charge was threatening the life President George W. Bush, whom Sharkey had repeatedly declared he would impale.[15]

Jonathon Sharkey no longer had a bit part on the presidential stage. But even though he exited, his rage remained. So too did his prototype. Its characteristics were inadvertently but aptly described by U.S. Marshall Jason Wojdylo, the man who recognized him as the fugitive Rocky Flash. In 2007 Wojdylo said of his quarry, "Jonathon often has this idea that he was untouchable. And from my point of view it was unfortunate that the media . . . were giving him the forum that he so much desires. . . . It's a snowball effect. You give him a little bit and he . . . believes, in his mind I think, that he's becoming more powerful."[16] True, but not true enough. The fact is, Sharkey—and those who tromped in his tracks—*were* becoming more powerful.

Stephen Colbert

"Americans for a Better Tomorrow, Tomorrow"

EXCEPT FOR PAT PAULSEN, NO OTHER FRINGE CANDIDATE, clown or Quixote, ever received as much attention as Stephen Colbert, host of the satiric television show *The Colbert Report* ("frenchenciously" pronounced, should anyone from Mars or the thirtieth century be reading this, *colbère repore*). Colbert competed in the 2008 presidential primary in his home state of South Carolina. In the 2012 election he made overtures about running again, financially endorsed this time by a satiric, but nonetheless actual, political action committee (PAC) he created known as Americans for a Better Tomorrow, Tomorrow.

On the surface Colbert's 2008 candidacy appeared to be that of yet another comedian using a presidential election as a stage for his act. "In the great American tradition of the late Pat Paulsen," one South Carolina newspaper commented, "Colbert's entry into the race in this state . . . was highlighted by this pledge to the voters. 'I defy any other candidate to pander more to the people of South Carolina.'" Similar to previous presidential bids by comedians, Colbert joked that by running in his home state he would have a "favorite son" advantage—"though not my mother's favorite son; she's too fair-minded to ever show a preference." Foremost on his platform was his vow to "crush" the state of Georgia, taking offense at its nickname, the Peach State. "Our peaches are more numerous than Georgia's," he declared, stirring up parodied passions by adding that South Carolina's peaches are "more juiciful."[1]

Right from the start, however, Colbert's campaign for the presidency showed signs of going one step beyond those of prior bids by comedians. Where Pat Paulsen and Gracie Allen (and their writers) churned out campaign-related books during their candidacies,

Colbert and his writers more accurately satirized traditional politicians by publishing a book shortly *before* the onset of his campaign. In South Carolina's primary that year's leading contenders in the Democratic Party were New York senator and former first lady Hillary Clinton, Illinois senator Barack Obama, and former North Carolina senator John Edwards; the leading Republican Party contenders were Arizona senator John McCain, Arkansas governor Mike Huckabee, former Tennessee senator Fred Thompson, Massachusetts governor Mitt Romney, Texas congressman Ron Paul, and former New York City mayor Rudy Giuliani—all of whom published books during this period of time.[2]

Likewise Colbert. His book *I Am America (And So Can You!)* appeared in bookstores in early October 2007, two weeks before he declared himself to be a candidate for president. The satiric irony in the book's content and publication date did not go unnoticed by the media's White House watchers—abetted by Colbert and his publicists. On ABC's *Good Morning America*, he commented in an interview with Diane Sawyer, "A lot of people see this book as me testing the waters for a presidential run." Sawyer (best known as a network news anchor) played along and pressed him on that point, enabling Colbert to get laughs by summoning the false modesty of traditional politicians setting the stage to announce their candidacy by "sincerely" replying, "It's just not a question I'm ready to answer right now."[3]

On the heels of that appearance, Colbert ramped up this parody when he appeared on CNN's *Larry King Live*. "A lot of people see this book," Colbert said, "and I know you're about to ask this—a lot of people see this book as testing the waters for a run for political office." King too joined in the charade by directly asking if he was going to run for president, to which Colbert's pseudo-sincere reply this go-round was, "Well Larry, I've got to—this question comes as a complete surprise."[4]

Colbert then amped the parody even higher. It was publicized that he would have a major announcement on *The Daily Show with Jon Stewart*, Comedy Central's widely watched parody of a news broadcast. Much as traditional presidential contenders often announce their candidacy from their home state or other significant place from their past, Colbert was returning to the show that begat his faux journalist persona in 1997 and eight years later begat *The Colbert Report*, which aired in the next time slot—often with Stewart and Colbert doing a comic handover. All of these elements set the stage for Colbert's returning to *The Daily Show* for his major announcement. He entered in a red, white, and blue bicycle cart pedaled by Uncle Sam, springing from it to work the cheering audience much as traditional candidates work crowds with a multitude of quick not-quite-handshakes, after which he used a hand sanitizer, then pulled out a bale of hay and sat on it with a bottle of beer, declaring, "It's great to be back with the people," referring to himself as "an Average Joe." Clearly the moment had arrived for his much anticipated announcement. Stewart set it up, and Colbert pumped up the parody yet again by declaring, in verbiage reminiscent of John Donkey, "Tonight, I, Stephen Colbert, am officially announcing that I have decided to officially consider whether or not I will announce that I am running for President of the United States. And I will be making an announcement of that decision very soon—preferably on a more prestigious show."[5]

That show turned out to be his own, in the broadcast that followed. "After nearly fifteen minutes of soul-searching," he told his audience, "I have heard the call!" Music played, a torrent of red, white, and blue balloons fell from above, and his audience duly went wild.

While Colbert had stated that he planned to enter only the South Carolina primary, some wondered if his bid would be so limited. "Exactly how far the mock conservative pundit planned to stretch his impression of a presidential candidate wasn't clear," the Associated Press noted in its report of Colbert's announcement.[6] Indeed unlike the comic candidacies of celebrities Will Rogers, Gracie Allen, and Pat Paulsen, the candidacy of Stephen Colbert caused concern among some in the news media. One day after Colbert's announcement, the *Washington Post* media critic Howard Kurtz sounded an alarm that highlighted a key difference in the political landscape of the 2008 election from that of prior eras. "Colbert's chances may be slim," he wrote, "but in today's *infotainment* culture, he could draw precious media attention from the second-tier contenders. And he has a nightly platform to milk the spectacle for jokes, if not votes . . . [by] saying what matters is not some boring adherence to the facts but a matter's essential '*truthiness.*'"[7]

Bear in mind, Kurtz was a fan of *The Colbert Report*. He'd begun this particular column by writing, "It has become something of a television cliché: politicians launching their electoral campaigns on late-night talk shows, in a calculated attempt at hipness. But a late-night comic announcing his presidential candidacy on a late-night talk show—now that is a hall of mirrors maneuver worthy of Stephen Colbert." Nevertheless there was indeed a basis for Kurtz's concern. *Infotainment* referred to news programs in which the degree of entertainment value had come to impact so much on news value as to blur the distinction. Kurtz's *Washington Post* colleague Michael Cavna spoke in more detail and more broadly about this change in the political landscape when he wrote not only of such news programs but also of Colbert's and Stewart's satiric news shows. "The blurring of news and entertainment, comedy, and punditry . . . contributes to the shift," he observed.[8] So much had infotainment become a part of the nation's political landscape that Kurtz used what was then a recently coined word, *truthiness.* Today the *Oxford English Dictionary* defines truthiness as "the quality of seeming or being felt to be true, even if not necessarily true." And attributes its first use to Stephen Colbert.

Colbert introduced the term on the first broadcast of *The Colbert Report.* When it premiered on October 17, 2005, the program included a segment that would recur, "The Word." In this first installment Colbert's parody of popular right-wing commentators such as Bill O'Reilly and Rush Limbaugh conveyed even more profoundly than all the journalists cited above what the nation's political landscape had become—doing so via this faux pledge to his viewers:

You're looking at a straight shooter, America. . . . I will speak to you in plain, simple English. And that brings us to tonight's word. Truthiness. Now I'm sure that some of the word police . . . are gonna say, "Hey, that's not a word." Well, anyone who knows me knows that I'm no fan of dictionaries or reference books. They're elitist. Constantly telling us what is or isn't true, or what did or didn't happen. . . . I don't trust books. They're all facts; no heart. And that's exactly what's pulling our country apart today. . . . We are divided between those who think with their head and those who *know* with their *heart*. . . . The truthiness is anyone can read the news to you; I promise to *feel* the news *at* you.

Others amplified the concern over Colbert's campaign (which ironically was designed, through the use of irony, to convey the same concern). One columnist noted that Colbert's "'truthiness' is so infectious, for the first time, a television character stands to make a political dent." Another columnist furthered that concern when she warned, "Even if the campaign turns out to be a farce . . . we live in a nation where celebrity influence alone can translate effectively into political support and power, or people distrust political figures to the point they will support a fictional celebrity pundit over credible candidates."[9]

Not, however, in 2008. Colbert's run never got out of the gate. Following his announcement, the hawk-eyed Federal Communications Commission began circling his television show, preparing to swoop down with its Equal Time provisions should he be deemed a viable candidate. Likewise the Federal Election Commission questioned whether or not the show's new segment— "Stephen Colbert, Hail to the Cheese, Nacho Cheese Doritos® 2008 Presidential Campaign"—constituted a corporation illegally advocating directly for a political candidate, as opposed to legally sponsoring a satire.[10] With this aspect of Colbert's clown candidacy, particularly in comparison to those of prior comics, we can see how much more than ever before in the nation's history the line between the political and the ridiculous was genuinely blurring.

Colbert managed to dodge the second of these issues by renaming the segment "Stephen Colbert, Hail to the Cheese, Nacho Cheese Doritos® 2008 Presidential Campaign COVERAGE," with the capitalization part of the gag in making it satiric *news* rather than satiric *campaigning*—and illustrating again how blurred that distinction had become. But the next snag he encountered was not so easily eluded. Initially he had said he would run in both the Republican and Democratic primaries. There are no primaries for independents, nor did either party in South Carolina enable write-in votes on their primary ballots. The Republican Party's filing fee to get on the South Carolina primary ballot was $35,000, compared to $2,500 for the Democratic Party. While Colbert's TV persona was that of an arch-conservative Republican, the actual Colbert was not. And despite his wealth as a television star, he could not bring himself to fork over $35,000 to the Republican Party. While he was happy to pay the Democratic Party fee, they allowed only viable presidential candidates on the ballot, which its officials ruled Colbert was not since he was running in only one primary.[11]

Although Colbert's campaign was over, the concern it aroused was not. "The mainstream Beltway press could barely contain its glee as it cheered on the stunt, lavishing all sorts of media attention on Colbert and basking in the entertainment glow that his act brought to the White House campaign trail," Eric Boehlert wrote in a syndicated opinion piece. Boehlert, a one-time contributing editor to *Rolling Stone*, was no knee-jerk conservative. Still, he wrote, "I'm almost relieved that Democratic officials in South Carolina squashed the Colbert stunt by denying his attempt to get on the ballot. That's the only way the press was going to drop the story." Presciently he went on to warn, "The press has decided to cover presidential candidates as celebrities . . . [not as] how candidates might function as presidents . . . [but based on] which candidate was fun to be around."[12]

On the more highbrow side, a considerable number of academics were also looking into what Colbert's campaign revealed about America. An entire volume in the series Popular Culture and Philosophy was devoted to scholarly essays regarding that volume's title, *Stephen Colbert and Philosophy*. In the behavioral sciences some researchers designed studies to measure Colbert's impact on political views. One such study found that, counter to what might be expected, "when young adults are exposed to *The Colbert Report*'s humor, they are not led to be more critical of the far right, instead, the opposite happens."[13] Another study very differently concluded, "Conservatives were more likely to report that Colbert only pretends to be joking and genuinely meant what he said while liberals were more likely to report that Colbert used satire and was not serious when offering political statements."[14] Yet another professor, Joseph Faina at the University of Texas–Austin, concluded, "These studies are not inaccurate but I do contend they are incomplete." In an article titled "Public Journalism Is a Joke," Faina delved into the full spectrum along which news and entertainment were blurring, citing a key technological development as the cause. "Cable news 'debate' shows are the primary culprit," he wrote. "These shows could provide some opportunity for deliberation but dissolve into argumentation, the objective of which is to prevail rather than resolve . . . to parse up the social and political world into 'winners' and 'losers.'"[15]

In order to compete with so much more news programming now available via cable television and the many viewers flocking to the entertainment of no-holds-barred political shows, traditional network news producers increased their reliance on entertainment values, as evidenced by traditional journalists and news anchors such as Diane Sawyer being assigned to shows such as *Good Morning America* and by the attention the entire news media devoted to Colbert's campaign.

No one was more concerned about this trend than Colbert and his faux news mentor, Stewart. While Colbert sought to combat it in 2008 with his satiric campaign, Stewart took an opportunity to combat it directly in an appearance on one of cable television's premiere no-holds-barred debate shows, CNN's *Crossfire*. Cohosted by the conservative Tucker Carlson and the liberal Paul Begala, the October 15, 2004, broadcast opened with an announcement that the two were going to take a break from campaign politics, anticipating a fun-filled interview with the comedian Stewart. But Stewart pulled the rug out from under them moments after being introduced when he asked, "Can I say something very quickly? Why do we have to fight?" Begala and Carlson did their professional best to get back on track, but Stewart wouldn't play along. "I made a special effort to come on the show today," he said, "because . . . this show is bad. . . . It's hurting America."

Carlson inadvertently demonstrated just how much the line between news and entertainment had blurred when he argued that Stewart was equally guilty by failing to ask hardball questions in his show's interviews with political candidates. "Maybe this explains a lot," Stewart snapped back, "that the news organizations look to Comedy Central for their cues on integrity. . . . You're on CNN. The show that leads into me is puppets making crank phone calls."

In the 2012 election Colbert set his satiric sights on a change in campaign financing that resulted from the 2010 Supreme Court ruling in *Citizens United v. Federal Election Commission* that corporations, labor unions, and other organizations have the same free speech rights as people—though it upheld the prohibition of such organizations from directly contributing to or coordinating their speech with candidates for public office or political parties.[16] The ruling opened the way for a flood of money to be used by PACs to finance political messages that, by law, had to disclose the name of the PAC—but not the names of its donors. President Obama declared that the ruling "reversed a century of law that, I believe, will open the floodgates for special interests, including foreign corporations, to spend without limit in our elections." His opponent from the 2008 election, Senator John McCain, called the ruling "disgraceful, absolutely disgraceful."[17]

Colbert agreed. Hence, in the 2012 election, he formed his own PAC, Americans for a Better Tomorrow, Tomorrow. To oversee and explain the legality of Colbert's clearly ridiculous but actual PAC, he brought onto those episodes of *The Colbert Report* his lawyer, Trevor Potter, who clearly knew the ins-and-outs, having been the chairman of the Federal Election Commission. Untold amounts of money (because the law didn't require him to tell) were contributed to Colbert's PAC by unknown (because the law didn't require him to tell) donors. Suffice it to say the sums were sufficient for the PAC to run satiric ads targeted at particular candidates. One such sixty-second spot opened with an American flag waving behind a "Wall St." sign, patriotic music, and a narration that began, "Corporations—America's greatest institution. They built this country one job at a time." It soon cuts to a clip of Mitt Romney saying, "Corporations are people, my friends." The visuals suddenly become disturbing and distorted as the narrator ominously says, "But Mitt Romney has a secret. As the head of Bain Capital, he bought up companies, carved them up, and got rid of what he couldn't use. If Mitt Romney really believes [repeat of Romney clip saying, "Corporations are people, my friends"] then Mitt Romney [slight pause] is a serial killer." We then hear maniacal laughter behind an image of Romney smiling, followed by the narrator intoning, "He's Mitt the Ripper!" After its closing visuals and sound effects, the ad ends with what was now the familiar verbal fine print of such commercials: "Americans for a Better Tomorrow, Tomorrow are responsible for the content of this advertisement."[18]

In a final ridiculous but real twist demonstrating how the limitations on PACS were, in reality, ridiculous, Colbert announced that he was establishing an "exploratory committee" to decide whether or not to make a second run for president. In order to run, however, he would have to disconnect himself from his PAC since, under the Supreme Court's rulings, PACS cannot coordinate with candidates. Thus on the January 12, 2012, episode of *The Colbert Report*, with attorney Potter present and providing the necessary paperwork, Colbert officially signed over his PAC to (who else?) Jon Stewart—with whom, allegedly, he would not coordinate his campaign. All of which was as legal as it was absurd.

Colbert knew as well as any comedian that jokes work only once—and no doubt knew that deadlines had passed for entering the primaries. What little effort he made this second time around ended when, because of the deadline, he was unable to enter the South Carolina primary.

Future elections would tell what impact, if any, Colbert's satiric candidacies had in reducing the degree to which news and entertainment—and, by extension, the political and the ridiculous—had merged.

SPOILER ALERT: Two days after Colbert handed over control of his PAC to Stewart, the *Washington Post* columnist Alexandra Petri commented, "I was as startled as anyone to hear CNN declare this week that the Republican race for president is a Deeply Serious Contest with no room for jokers. Has CNN been watching the race? Does it remember when it considered Donald Trump a serious candidate?"[19]

Frank Moore

Just Makes Sense Party

JUST AS A JOKE DOES NOT CONSTITUTE A COMEDY, SO TOO going viral on the internet does not constitute widespread attention if such attention does not spread to other media. Still, some fringe candidates who attracted significant attention among internet users but failed to spark much interest elsewhere are worth noting for the significance of their campaigns seeming to be insignificant.

In the 2008 election the performance artist Frank Moore created a website for his presidential bid. Moore was a prominent performance artist, creator of the San Francisco–based show *Outrageous Beauty Review*, and recipient of that city's award for Best Performance Artist in 1992.[1] His theatrical and visual art, funded in part by the National Endowment for the Arts, was provocative enough to draw the cross-hairs of Senator Jesse Helms's efforts to torpedo that federal agency.[2]

Moore also, it bears mentioning, had cerebral palsy.

Via his website Moore sought and received assistance in recruiting people to serve as state electors—individuals pledged to him in the Electoral College, a prerequisite in many states to having one's write-in votes counted. He put forth a platform that presented proposals for foreign policy, health care, public transit, international trade linked to labor and environmental standards, drug law reform, prison reform, and greater public access to cable television. Clearly he was not clowning around.

Though he may have been performing. His running mate was a self-certified sex therapist and cable television personality, Susan Block, more popularly known as "Dr. Suzy."

Moore's campaign led to an in-depth interview on the website ArabianMonkey.com along with several postings about his campaign on other websites.[3] In other media, however, he was rarely mentioned, and then only in listing the names of additional candidates—none of which mentioned (or likely knew of) his physical disability.[4]

Given that Moore's fringe candidacy did not receive widespread attention—and that none of the attention it did receive entailed laughter—why mention him at all?

Moore's campaign stands out as an excellent example of numerous other fringe campaigns that did not receive widespread attention but nevertheless shed light on American history. In 2008 Americans were becoming accustomed to seeing people with disabilities in the workplace, at school, and in public service. Had Moore run in the 1988 presidential election, he quite likely would have received greater attention, by virtue of his campaign's amplifying voices that led to the passage of the Americans with Disabilities Act, two years later.

In this regard it is noteworthy that Moore did receive brief national attention in 1987. Also noteworthy is that laughter accompanied that attention. "Laughter is the freest vocal thing Frank Moore does," a *Philadelphia Daily News* article told readers in an interview with Moore, who was satirically defending *Playboy* magazine for featuring erotic photos of a paraplegic woman. "Why should *Playboy* exploit normal people and not disabled people?" Moore asked. The article reported, "The laughter bubbles up within him [as he mock-complained] . . . 'I was the first disabled sex symbol. I use my body as a tool, just like a sexy woman uses her body as a tool. She is just copying me.'"[5]

Lack of widespread recognition of a fringe candidacy cannot automatically be interpreted as lack of interest in an issue, just as laughter cannot automatically be interpreted as ridicule. For revealing both of those facts we have Frank Moore's fringe candidacy to thank.

Keith Russell Judd

Federal Inmate 11593-051

SHOULD YOU WONDER WHETHER FRINGE CANDIDATES really have an impact, look no further than Keith Russell Judd. From the confines of the federal prison in Texarkana, Texas, Judd's 2008 presidential candidacy resulted in Idaho's changing its election laws.

Judd grew up in New Mexico, where his father was a nationally recognized mathematician at the Los Alamos National Laboratory and where his grandfather, a nuclear physicist, was chosen to oversee the nation's research into a space-based antimissile defense system.[1] Judd's passion was music, in which he was majoring at the University of New Mexico in 1992 when his life went awry.

As Judd tells it, he took an unloaded gun to the campus to promote his band, Double Shot. A misunderstanding ensued with the campus police, which, according to Judd, was made worse by the student newspaper.[2] According to a federal court in Texas, however, what went on in New Mexico was beside the point—its point being that Judd sent a former girlfriend threatening letters seeking to extort money. Judd then exacerbated the situation by sending letters to the jurors in that 1999 trial in Texas following their verdict of guilty. From the judge's point of view, Judd had earned himself seventeen and a half years in prison.[3]

Judd's letters from prison (now monitored) suggest that he was contemplating making a change in his life. "Judd for President of the USA" frequently adorned his correspondence.[4] He wasn't just embellishing his calligraphy. In the 2000 election "Keith Russell Judd of Odessa, Texas, Independent candidate," appeared on Indiana's certified list of write-in contenders for the presidency.[5]

Actually it wasn't that much of a change for Judd. In 1993 and

1997 he had run for mayor of Albuquerque. In between he ran for governor of New Mexico.[6] Not until 2008, however, did he receive national attention. For that year's presidential election he launched a full-scale effort from prison to get on the Democratic Party's primary ballots in multiple states—particularly targeting New Hampshire, where the primary season commences. In letters to the press he claimed that New Hampshire and other states were violating his civil rights by prohibiting a prisoner from appearing on their primary ballots. His story was sufficiently interesting that a few reports appeared in the press.[7] But they were nothing compared to the avalanche of coverage that followed Judd's success in getting on the ballot in Idaho.

"Texas prison candidate cons way onto Idaho primary ballot," folks in Walla Walla, Washington, read, while Tulsa, Oklahomans likewise learned, "if elected, presidential candidate can't serve," and those New Mexicans who recollected Judd's runs for office likely chuckled over the headline "Inmate Makes 'Mockery' of Idaho Ballot."[8]

Judd's ability to get on the primary ballot in Idaho demonstrated both the benefits and risks of the post-1968 primary rule changes that made candidacy more accessible. Idaho was one of a handful of states that had dragged its feet in implementing such changes. Not until shortly before the 2008 election did it alter a requirement under which he would have had to collect more than three thousand signatures from state residents. The new law allowed a fee to be paid in lieu of the signatures.[9] Absent the hurdle of gathering signatures of residents, Judd could hop from the prison yard in Texas to the primary ballot in Idaho.

Prison bars also did not bar Judd from the internet. Once on the Idaho ballot, he promptly entered the details of his candidacy on the website VoteSmart.org, providing a window to the world from which (at the behest of his letters to the press) amused newspapers could take flight with his tale.[10]

Idaho, however, still hadn't finished dragging its feet on increasing accessibility for presidential candidates. While it was now easier to get on its primary ballot, the state's Democratic and Republican choices were still ultimately determined in party caucuses. Put simply, which is indeed how Idaho's secretary of state, Ben Ysursa, put it, "The good news is, the Democratic presidential primary has absolutely no legal significance."[11]

Which raises a question: Is that good news?

For Idaho's legislature the answer was yes. Consequently there was no folderol about democracy when the legislature voted to prevent prisoners from getting onto the primary ballots. It enacted a measure amending the law requiring signatures *or* a fee to requiring signatures *and* a fee.[12]

Agree or not, it did the trick.

Though Judd was now effectively barred from the ballot in Idaho, he popped up in West Virginia during its 2012 presidential primary. Despite odds akin to lightning striking the same place twice, Judd hit the attention-getting jackpot again. "Jailbird Shocker in W.VA. Vote" the *New York Post* hollered in that tabloid's full-throated headline style. The article itself settled into a concise recitation of the facts, though they were indeed eye-popping: "A virtually unknown convict doing time in a federal pen, took 43 percent of the vote in West Virginia's Democratic primary Tuesday, dealing an embarrassing blow to President Obama's re-election bid." By comparison, the article noted, when Judd had appeared on the 2008 primary ballot in Idaho, he came away with only 1.7 percent.[13]

Needless to say, Judd's achievement in West Virginia was reported throughout the news media, as it combined a stunning rebuff of President Obama with a highly entertaining story—a truly ideal mix for the news media to report on voter views. "No one voted for Keith Judd," one columnist wrote. "They voted against a president."[14] A letter to the editor in North Carolina said, "The people spoke loud and clear. We may not know who we're voting for but we certainly know who we're voting against."[15] Some number of West Virginians did know Judd was a prisoner. On the day of the primary the front page of that state's *Charleston Gazette* ran an article under the headline "Presidential Candidate Is Inmate at Federal Prison."

Judd's feat triggered other perspectives as well. Some echoed those in Idaho, as when one West Virginia columnist wrote, "About that embarrassing vote for a felon, should it be harder to qualify for the ballot here?"[16] A very different angle was raised by *Investor's Business Daily* in an editorial that remarked, "Conservative pundit and IBD contributor Ann Coulter once said she, like many Americans, would rather vote for Jeffrey Dahmer, known for his unusual culinary choices, over President Obama. Federal prisoner Keith Russell Judd, 49, is not quite in Dahmer's league, but for a substantial portion of West Virginia's Democrats, he is also preferable to our campaigner-in-chief."[17]

Dahmer was a convicted serial killer who engaged in necrophilia and cannibalism, and Coulter did indeed say she would vote for him over Obama.[18] But it is through Judd's fringe candidacy that we see, not in Coulter's cold-blooded remark in *Investor's Business Daily*, despite its pinstripe prose, the much wider extent in which rage was flowing.

We can see a fringe candidacy's particular ability to resonate with and amplify political views frequently not well perceived by stepping back after that year's Election Day and looking at the numbers. Primaries, after all, rarely attract as many voters as general elections. Was Judd's 43 percent an accurate reflection of attitudes in West Virginia?

Judd received upwards of 72,500 votes (43 percent) in the primary; Obama received slightly more than 96,100 votes (57 percent). Judd was not on the ballot in the November general election. This time Obama was opposed by the Republican nominee Mitt Romney, along with Gary Johnson from the Libertarian Party, Jill Stein of the Mountain (Green) Party, and several independent candidates. In this instance Obama received upwards of 238,000 votes in West Virginia. That's much more than twice as many votes, but nevertheless only 35.5 percent of the total West Virginia votes in the general election. Very clearly the percentage of votes Judd received in West Virginia's primary did not accurately reflect attitudes in the state; it amplified them. Which is the value of fringe candidates.

Roseanne Barr

First Female Serious Comedian Candidate

In her early days as a stand-up comic, Roseanne Barr had a signature closing line in her act: "People say to me, 'You're not very feminine.' Well, they can suck my dick."[1]

That in a nutshell is the star of the hugely successful television show *Roseanne*. Still, it is a tough nut to crack. In her study on women comedians, Joanne Gilbert devoted five pages to debating whether or not Barr's humor was feminist. Nor was Professor Gilbert alone in taking a crack at critiquing Barr. The significance of her career has been explored in numerous scholarly articles that highlight such elements as "feminist resistance in popular culture," the "dialectical vision" through which "her radicalism is distributed over the two axes of class and gender," the "growing strain of feminist literary theory [which] suggests that humor and comedy may be valuable as empowering 'feminist tools,'" and as "an example of a woman exploiting the image meant to confine her."[2]

While all of the journals in which these scholarly critiques appeared are in the collections of university libraries, Barr's own books are in very few of those libraries. In the nonacademic world her books have been similarly devalued, as seen in the fact that used copies are currently available for one cent (plus shipping and handling). Clearly there is a disconnection between scholarly interest and public interest in Barr. The reasons for that gap become clear when viewed through the lens of her 2012 bid for the presidency.

For starters, it's significant that the reasons were clear to Barr herself. Nine years before her candidacy she told an interviewer, "I made up my mind when I got into show business that I was always going to be honest and wouldn't try to hide anything. . . . I'm a comic. I'm not the fucking president." She knew that to be president one had to keep mum on some thoughts and express others less than honestly to pander to public opinion. Hence when candidate Barr was asked in a 2012 interview what percentage of their income the wealthiest Americans should be taxed, she answered, "I think we should have a fair tax. I think that all of this stuff is a big dialog that we need to have."[3] No mainstream candidate could have dodged the question better. After all, who's against fair taxes? To the extent that Barr was indeed serious in her quest for the presidency, her answer was the same bunk derided by those previous fringe candidates who, unlike this comedian, ran clown campaigns.

"Roseanne Barr is running for President—and it's no joke," commenced an Associated Press report that appeared in newspapers nationwide.[4] The unnamed journalist who wrote that lead line was following in the footsteps of those who, in the (misperceived) absence of humor in comedian Dick Gregory's 1968 presidential bid, filled in their own punch lines. This reporter was one of a chorus of colleagues who vied for laughs when Barr revealed she was serious in her candidacy. "Raising the Barr of Election Insanity" punfully headlined a report in West Virginia's *Charleston Gazette*. Though less snappy, Fort Lauderdale's *Sun Sentinel* more presciently pointed to post-1968 changes in nomination rules when it told readers, "The joke may be on Florida voters. Roseanne Barr, the comedian and 1990s sitcom star, will be one of twelve presidential candidates on the November ballot, thanks to Florida's weakened ballot access rules."[5]

For her part, however, Barr did not so closely follow in the footsteps of Gregory's campaign. Sharpening our focus on the nation's changing political landscape in 2012, Barr merged Gregory's serious campaign with the satiric presidential campaign of Will Rogers. She echoed Rogers's antibunk platform when she cited as one plank of her platform, "Outlaw—how do we say this politely?— outlaw bull. Yes, that's it. Outlaw bull."[6] But as seen in the "bull" that wafted from Barr's answer about taxes, she wanted it both ways. Here too her campaign resembled that of Rogers in that, to the degree both sought to present themselves as candidates, call it bull or call it bunk, but it was swept under the rug just as it was with mainstream candidates.

Barr was well aware of the contradiction (and, quite likely, so too was Rogers). When, as with mainstream candidates in this era, she published a book shortly before her 2012 campaign, she alluded to such inconsistencies in its introduction. "I reserve the right as a comic," she declared, ". . . to say things that should probably not be taken literally enough to make a nut job like you (you know who you are) feel justified in attacking me."[7] In this respect she was following in the footsteps of Gracie Allen, who took a swipe at voter baloney when she declared, "The Surprise Party is conceived and desecrated . . . upon the principle that everybody is just as good as anybody else, even though they aren't quite as smart."[8] But by replacing daffy with daring, Barr paved Allen's path with the added power women had wrested in the decades that followed Allen's 1940 campaign. "I'm the only serious comedian in this race," Barr declared something Allen would not have said—and she went on to explain, "What I really want [is that] both parties be more responsive and compassionate to the American people's needs. I'm running to make that point."[9] Running to make a point is different, and more doable, than running to get elected. And more difficult than running for laughs.

Barr was well qualified to make that point. Married in her late teens to a man who struggled with alcoholism, the two of them struggled for the next sixteen years to provide for their growing family. Living in a trailer home, she worked at a variety of minimum-wage jobs, all the while becoming imbued with feminist views very much in the discourse back then, in the 1970s and 1980s. Highly extroverted, she began to speak out. Yet she could not escape the feeling that feminist leaders needed to be, to borrow from her 2012 campaign statement, "more responsive and compassionate" to the needs of women struggling—with or without husbands pitching in—to meet the needs of their families or simply make ends meet. Out of that dual perspective emerged the ironic, working-class wit who went on to national acclaim when, for nine television seasons, she portrayed the wife of a construction worker on *Roseanne*.

Upon announcing her intention to seek the Green Party's nomination for president, Barr encountered that which distinguishes
candidates viewed as fringe from candidates viewed as third party.
To those who believed she was running for laughs or who laughed
at her for running, she was a fringe candidate; to those who took
her candidacy seriously, she was a third party candidate. And it
was precisely that debatable distinction that resulted in the Green
Party's rejection of Barr as its nominee. "There is a small cohort [at
the Green Party convention] that will confess, either in an apolo-
getic whisper or in a cranky diatribe, that it's a blessing Roseanne
canceled her planned appearance," the *Washington Post* reported.
"Roseanne Barr, who placed second behind Massachusetts physician Jill Stein in the Green Party's nomination process, is exactly
what party members do not need here. Not when they are trying
to be taken seriously."[10]

After being rebuffed by the Green Party, Barr, with her characteristic wit, mocked both the left-wing Green Party and the right-
wing movement known as the Tea Party by declaring she'd run as
a candidate of the self-created Green Tea Party.[11] Ultimately, however, she received the nomination of the Peace and Freedom Party,
the briefly beleaguered parent of the Freedom and Peace Party that
ran away from home in 1968 to nominate Dick Gregory.

Swerving along the line that distinguishes third party from
fringe, the Peace and Freedom Party had previously nominated
little known candidates, such as a machinist named Herbert G.
Lewin in 1988, and well-known candidates when it could, such as
Eldridge Cleaver in 1968, the famed pediatrician turned antiwar
activist Benjamin Spock in 1972, and consumer advocate Ralph
Nader in 2008. Eight years earlier Nader had been the nominee
of the Green Party in an election where his candidacy may have
tipped the balance to George W. Bush over the Democratic Party's nominee, Al Gore. The Peace and Freedom Party again opted
for a Green Party retread in 2012, this time seeking visibility even
at the risk of ridicule by nominating Barr.

And visibility it got. Not only did newspapers scramble for the
kind of clever headlines cited above, so too was there a scramble
by television interviewers, knowing what a draw Barr would be

by virtue of never knowing what wisecrack would come from her Hollywood Walk of Fame brain. Aiming for voters most likely to have been fans of *Roseanne*, Barr tossed her interview bouquet to Sean Hannity on Fox News. But hold on to your hats, those who oppose Fox News; Hannity demonstrated that he can indeed conduct an interview that is fair and balanced—and cuts to the core. As in these excerpts:

Hannity: I watched you years ago when you did standup. . . . Should I take—is this to be taken seriously or do you really want to be elected president of the United States?

Barr: Yes. I'm very, very serious. . . .

Hannity: All right. I wasn't sure who to expect tonight, because I know you're very funny, you're a comedian, an actress. And I've been following your campaign on the periphery. . . . You say you want to be taken seriously. You've thought about these issues, laying out your ideas. How can people do that, though? I'll put up on the screen just three of your tweets. . . . One says most billionaires are violent pedophiles. . . . How do you get taken seriously when you call billionaires pedophiles? . . .

Barr: I like to get people talking. I am a provocateur, and I do like getting on Twitter and riling people up. You know what, after a while some sane dialogue and sane conclusions come out of that kind of thing. . . . And a lot of people have also said that I'm letting the billionaires off easy. . . .

Hannity: Let me be honest with you. You're too smart to be saying some of these things, if you're serious, that you want to be taken seriously and want to run for the presidency.[12]

No clearer demonstration can be found of a fringe candidate amplifying voices often otherwise barely heard than the fact that even Hannity, a highly successful political commentator with his conservative ear to the ground, failed to give credence in 2012 to claims that resonated with those of a 2016 candidate who would win the presidency. In that next election Donald Trump made claims as outrageous as Barr's claim about billionaires having a predilection for pedophilia—as, for example, Trump's assertion that

President Obama was the founder of the terrorist group known as the Islamic State (ISIS).[13] And Trump justified such claims as Barr did, on the basis of what unnamed people had ostensibly told him. When fueling the demonstrably false conspiracy theory that Obama was not born in the United States, Trump asserted, "You know, some people say that was not his birth certificate," echoing Barr's "a lot of people have also said that I'm letting the billionaires off easy."[14] Many Americans likewise did not view as disqualifying outrageous campaign pledges such as forcing Mexico to pay for the construction of a giant wall along its entire two-thousand-mile border with the United States, nor did they view as disqualifying the degree of rage in Trump's pledge to fight terrorism by attacking the families of terrorists.[15] Barr herself noted these similarities when she declared in 2018, "Trump totally stole my act."[16]

In 2012, however, most Americans clearly viewed Barr's candidacy as fringe when, in "My Platform for President USA," she echoed the rage of Jonathon Sharkey in pledging, "The people must have justice, and so I want to reinstate and enshrine the Blessed and Holy Guillotine, a fast and painless execution of Justice and of execution."[17] That Barr often made ridiculous campaign pledges while insisting she was a serious candidate reflects the mix of connections and disconnections between her and her TV persona on *Roseanne*.

Imagine if her statement on reintroducing the guillotine were a line she delivered to her TV family. Or if she spouted to her TV family this proposal from her platform, aimed at creating a more compassionate society: "Each grandmother is responsible for at least one hundred people around her, as is normal now anyway, and she will answer to the Grandmother at the head of her district. Each District Head answers to the Tribunal Council of Matriarchs. The titular heads of the Worldwide Association of Matriarchal Tribunals will answer to the Head of the World Family, which is of course, Me." One can easily imagine the delightful scene, pungently funny because its absurdity makes a point. Still, given that Barr said she was running for president *to make a point*, why did so many Americans reject such outrageous pledges by Barr but not similarly outrageous pledges made by Trump?

The answer resides in the underlying question: Was Roseanne *Roseanne?*

Not entirely. And never was the distinction more clear than on July 25, 1990, when Barr sang the national anthem at a baseball game between the Cincinnati Reds and the San Diego Padres. Vast numbers of *Roseanne* fans and other Americans were shocked by her televised performance. It was not so much her starting off too high for her vocal range, resulting in her screeching the peak of the song, as it was her appearing to have intended to botch what many consider a sacred song by grabbing her crotch at the end rather than in some way indicating she had inadvertently erred. The Roseanne on *Roseanne,* for all her wisecracking cynicism, would never have done that.

Keep in mind, as mentioned before, that no one was more aware of the differences between Roseanne and *Roseanne* than Barr herself. In a 1989 *New York Times* article, she summed up the public's vision(s) of her, from her emergence as a stand-up comic through to her television show:

> At first, I think, I stood for . . . ordinary folks living ordinary lives in quiet desperation in trailer parks everywhere. Shortly thereafter, I was standing for mother, giving a sort of post-feminist mud pie in the eye to the Super Mom Syndrome. Right after that I was standing for the Little Guy . . . [who] wrestled back some fair share . . . from the American collective media unconscious and liberated it for the dessert-hungry, unwashed masses, making TV a safer place—by gum!—for working Americans. I was also standing for fat people, the forgotten minority. And didn't we have the right to live in denial, like everyone else?[18]

In short, Barr's complaint was that the public saw what it wanted to see—a characteristic not limited to Americans but nevertheless so much a part of our political landscape it is akin to the Rock of Gibraltar. Let's watch as some of our fellow citizens knock their heads against it, in the form of Roseanne/*Roseanne,* and see if anything gets knocked in—or out.

"Once she releases her financial records, everyone will know she is a one-percenter," a reader of Georgia's *Augusta Chronicle* commented after Barr presented her platform for president, going on to ask, "I'm wondering if she'll willingly offer her neck to the guillotine."[19]

A viewer of CNN commented online, "I cannot imagine ANY-ONE voting for a puke like this woman who went so far as to make a farce out of our national anthem." Another CNN viewer more directly revealed the Roseanne/*Roseanne* disconnection as disqualifying with the comment, "I wouldn't vote for Roseanne Barr if she was running for the position of being Roseanne Barr!" Another viewer, however, granted her equality with many of the mainstream presidential contenders—though still seeing the Rose-anne/*Roseanne* one wants to see—in declaring, "Given the current crop of GOP/tea party candidates, she'd fit right in."[20]

Most notable, however, was a comment among those CNN viewers that, four years later, resonated with enough voters to elect Trump: "She won't even need the teleprompter and you will not see her bowing to any foreign leaders. Terrorists are on notice, you don't want to mess with this lady."[21]

There are, of course, considerable differences between Barr and Trump. But in terms of electability, the most significant difference resides in disconnection. Part of the reason Trump connected with so many Americans where Barr connected with so few is that he never claimed to be an average American. The widespread rejection of Barr's candidacy amplified the fact that Americans want to know who their president really is. Unlike Barr, who dubiously said she "was always going to be honest," Trump never made such a claim.

Jimmy McMillan

Rent Is Too Damn High Party

JIMMY MCMILLAN ILLUSTRATES MORE THAN ANY OTHER fringe candidate how, to the degree fringe campaigns attract attention, they are amplifying voices otherwise largely, if not entirely, unheard. When he ran for president in 2012, McMillan was not a newcomer. In 1994 he began what would become repeated candidacies by entering that year's race for New York's governor. Though attention to him was largely confined to that state, McMillan demonstrated his flair for publicity right from the start. And, from the start, that attention revealed elements residing beneath the surface of the political landscape.

"He's a good bet to add some spice to this year's Democratic gubernatorial primary," the *Syracuse (NY) Herald-American* suggested, providing a sample of McMillan's campaign and *cajones* by relating an incident when FBI agents approached him on the steps of the state capital and, for reasons unreported, questioned whether he intended to hurt the governor. "What do you mean hurt?" the report quoted him replying. "He's the main man. He's knocked the businesses out with taxes and regulations. He's punched the poor into the unemployment line. I'm going to hurt him. I'm going after him. In the end, there's going to be two people left standing in that ring. Me and him. And there's going to be one champion, and that will be me."[1]

Apparently that calmed the G-men (no arrest was reported), though the article did say he now faced more imposing obstacles, starting with the fact that "nobody outside his Brooklyn neighborhood . . . knows McMillan." It also noted that "the clenched fist drawn on his head band may scare away as many voters as it attracts." One obstacle the article didn't mention (or did it?—or did it not think it was an obstacle?) was McMillan's race. For most readers the "clenched fist drawn on his head band" said it clearly enough: angry black man.

Throughout the two decades of McMillan's fringe campaigns, his being African American went almost entirely unmentioned. This despite the fact that his soon-to-be-adopted catch-phrase, "The rent is too damn high," was closely associated with urban gentrification, whereby housing gets renovated in order to sell or rent it at higher prices many African Americans could not afford. Through McMillan's fringe campaigns, we can see with considerable clarity whether the nation was moving beyond racial preconceptions—or, more succinctly, whether the clenched fist was still needed.

"Harlem's Jimmy McMillan stole the show at the N.Y. governor's debate Tuesday as the candidate of the Rent is Too Damn High Party," syndicated columnist Agus Hamilton wrote in 2010. "The audience loved him. Everybody wants him to move to L.A. and run for mayor as the candidate of the Lindsay Lohan is Too Damn High party."[2] Others may not find this joke as amusing as I did, but that's not the point. Harlem is. Or more to the point *isn't* where McMillan lived, which was Brooklyn. But Harlem conveyed "African American" without having to say it. And raises the question: Why did he have to convey his race? Which, since he didn't need it to make the joke, begins to reveal the answer as to whether or not the nation was beyond racial preconceptions.

Not Agus Hamilton. Or at least, in his view, some number of his readers.

Returning to 1994, McMillan soon faded from attention in the gubernatorial race, and likewise in 2009 when a piece in the *New York Times* began, "Jimmy McMillan is running for mayor of New York City. The fact that few in the city are aware of his existence, much less his candidacy, did not deter him as he swaggered down Utica Avenue in East Flatbush."[3] New Yorkers in 2009 would correctly suspect that this largely unknown man (according to the article) who "swaggered down Utica Avenue in East Flatbush" was African American.

But shh. Categorizing candidates by race is not the policy of the

New York Times. Or rather, *openly* categorizing them by race. This dirty little secret resonated with McMillan's fringe candidacy and was amplified by the nature of the attention it received in the press.

McMillan's big break came the following year, when he again ran for governor. Much in the way that post-1968 changes in presidential primary rules opened the gates more widely for alternative candidates, a similar effort in New York gave candidates such as McMillan an opportunity to debate on the same stage as that year's major party candidates. It was this debate to which Hamilton was referring when he wrote of McMillan's stealing the show. Clips from that debate soon appeared on the internet, bringing so much national attention to McMillan that his celebrity soon garnered him the prize of being parodied on *Saturday Night Live*.[4] Clips of which, in turn, went viral on the internet. One company began manufacturing a talking doll of McMillan which—you guessed it—said only, "The rent is too damn high!"[5]

The talking doll, however, may prove an antiquated example of popularity and potential impact. Media arts professor Richard L. Edwards cited a music video by the Gregory Brothers released at this time, which used video mashups along with computer technology that altered recordings of McMillan declaring "The rent is too damn high" into melodic attunements to present him as their lead singer. Edwards recognized that the music video was "clearly humorous in intent" and "may seem to be an unlikely conveyer of activism." But he speculated (possibly accurately, God help us), "What began as alternative media logics are now regularly encountered by an electorate that has embraced mashup culture. The profundity of the shift may be seen in the acceptance of 'Auto-Tune the News,'" a hugely successful internet-based series of music videos released by the band.[6]

Needless to say, with all this attention the nation's pundits weighed in as well. Writing about the gubernatorial debate, the columnist Mark Bennett said, "The New York forum was more circus than debate; McMillan's candidacy reflects the current atmosphere." Bennett described that atmosphere as "I vent, therefore I am."[7]

Bennett hit the nail on the head. Long-suppressed rage was

beginning to vent. Its presence was sounded in the 2008 fringe candidacy of Jonathon "The Impaler" Sharkey and further amplified in the far greater attention Jimmy McMillan received in 2010.

Setting up the next nail and hitting it on the head with uncanny prescience, the syndicated *New York Times* columnist Gail Collins wrote, "On the rage-o-meter, this week's gubernatorial debate in New York . . . looked less like a debate than a tryout for some particularly embarrassing reality show." Collins then zoomed in: "The person who got the most post-debate attention was Jimmy McMillan of the Rent is Too Damn High Party. . . . He was very, very, very angry." Displaying further insight, she noted, "We are talking here about undifferentiated anger." Indeed using "The rent is too damn high" as a metaphorical blank to be filled, McMillan's campaign captured the attention of a wide span of Americans with a variety of angers and other discontents. But particularly for those pouring anger into that blank, Collins pointed out that it "creates nothing but a feeling of moral superiority on the part of the irate."[8] A highly combustible brew.

Collins's insights did not stop there. Based in no small part on McMillan's campaign, she began this article by stating, "Rage is not working out," followed by examples of voters electing rage-inducing candidates in primaries who went on to lose the election. She was not wrong, though the political landscape was beginning to quake. Rage soon reached its tipping point in the 2016 election. Still, Collins was not wrong. The nation would discover that even when it wins elections, rage does not work out.

McMillan's 2012 presidential bid did not work out either. Right out of the gate he baffled the news media by combining a serious message with clowning. After McMillan declared his candidacy, a reporter asked him if he had anyone in mind as a running mate. "Mitt Romney," he answered, "or Newt Gingrich." Setting aside the *in your dreams* reasons, the clowning commenced when he explained, "Newt Gingrich has been there before. He is a good liar. People look at him and laugh." As for Romney: "Good looking guy. It'll keep the ladies from looking at me."[9]

With his candidacy subsequently fading from public attention,

McMillan got back in the news with another announcement: he would be dispensing with the Rent Is Too Damn High Party and seeking the presidency as a Republican.

Not surprisingly, Fox News, sometimes referred to as the official organ of the Republican Party, quickly put McMillan in front of the cameras on Sean Hannity's widely watched commentary and interview show. Hannity, however—as when he interviewed Roseanne Barr—again proved himself fully capable of conducting an incisive interview:

Hannity: So [as a Republican], what is the new slogan?

McMillan: The Deficit is Too Damn High.

Hannity: That's your slogan.

McMillan: The same thing I brought with me to the governor's race I'm bringing the same thing to the presidential race, but I just modified it a little bit.

After sparring over the fact that New York has rent control, Hannity turned to the candidate's new slogan:

Hannity: All right, the deficit is too damn high. How are you going to lower the deficit?

McMillan: You lower the deficit by telling the people we are going to pardon all debt—American citizens of all debt.

Hannity: What?

McMillan: Because of what we did with the $800 billion bailouts [of corporations following the 2008 financial crisis].

Hannity: What about people like me that don't have debt?

McMillan: Then it doesn't concern you. But those who have debt—one hundred per cent of people living in poverty because the American government put the people in this hole we're in.

Hannity: Wait a minute. So from the day—if you win the election—the day you are inaugurated, I'm going to accumulate a ton of debt.

McMillan: If you have a debt, your debt would be pardoned. The government put the people in this debt we are in. Someone has to step up and do the right thing for the people. We owe this to the people. Rent is too damn high and the deficit is too damn high and Hannity is too damn smart.[10]

Hannity's shredding of McMillan's campaign platform was not confined to conservatives. A *New York Times* review of a documentary film about McMillan, released during the campaign, noted, "By the end of this smart, subtle film by Aaron Fisher-Cohen, you realize that it's actually a deft look at flash-in-the-pan fame and the emptiness of it. . . . Mr. Fisher-Cohen captures Mr. McMillan's transformation from a guy with a funny look and line into someone who believes his own hype."[11]

McMillan was not the only presidential aspirant in 2012 who could be accused of believing his own hype. "Trump Trumps GOP Hopefuls" a headline read in the *Los Angeles Times* on February 11, 2011, dropping the other shoe in its subhead, "The Developer Shocks Conservatives by Suggesting He May Run for President in 2012." Not, it should be noted, front-page news in that election, the article appeared twenty-two pages into the paper. Though McMillan and Trump were worlds apart on the issue of rent, they were both filled with rage and shared the same belief in their own hype. Vying to return to the spotlight, McMillan soon announced that, should he be nominated by the Republicans, his pick for vice president would be Donald Trump.[12]

In that election Trump never officially declared himself a candidate, and McMillan's campaign finally faded. The fact that the public interest waned for both aspirants indicates that what Collins called "undifferentiated anger" had not yet spread to its fullest extent.

Naked Cowboy

Independent in Underpants

"He was just looking for a little exposure," an Associated Press reporter punned in a 1999 article on the appearance in Lafayette, Louisiana, of a twenty-eight-year-old man singing on the sidewalk wearing only a guitar, a Stetson, and his tighty-whities.[1] Easy pun though it was to pluck, *looking for a little exposure* did indeed foretell what made the Naked Cowboy's 2012 candidacy for president significant.

After announcing his candidacy, the press clamored for the low-hanging fruit of such puns. "'Naked Cowboy' Briefs Public on His Presidential Bid" headlined the account in Elyria, Ohio's *Chronicle Telegram*. "Times Square Cowboy Has Naked Ambition: Presidency" was the pun of choice for Johnstown, Pennsylvania's *Tribune Democrat*. New York's *Daily News* told readers, "Reporters pelted the Naked Cowboy with questions such as will he endorse Fruit of the Loom or Hanes?" Among the more esoteric bons mots, New York's *Village Voice* simply noted the Naked Cowboy's performance attire, then transitioned to his political views with "beneath that exterior."[2] Touché.

You can imagine the views Naked Cowboy expressed in announcing his candidacy in Times Square, where for over a decade he'd been a tourist attraction. But you're probably imagining wrong. He declared his support for sealing our borders more securely to keep out illegal immigrants, mandatory drug tests for welfare recipients, banning unions for government workers, cutting taxes, and abolishing Obamacare. Moreover he clothed these remarks in, well, clothes. Wearing a well-tailored suit, his formerly long blond hair now presidentially trimmed, Robert Burck, the once (and future) Naked Cowboy, told the nation of his dream of being that year's Tea Party candidate. "American politicians," he intoned, "are selling out America and its most cherished institution, that being capitalism."[3]

Was he joking? Was it just a publicity stunt? What possible significance could this guy's candidacy have? As it turns out, quite a lot.

Burck grew up in Greenhills, Ohio, a suburb of Cincinnati created by American politicians during the Great Depression as one of the government-sponsored "greenbelt communities" that provided jobs for idled construction workers and housing for cash-strapped Americans. In Burck's words it was "safe and secure and the woods provided my friends and I with countless things to get into."[4] Upon entering adulthood, however, he couldn't get away from it fast enough—because he believed he was born for greater things.

"I want to be the most celebrated entertainer of all time," he told a reporter in 1999 when he first appeared *au-most naturel* in Times Square. His arrival there was the culmination of a nation-wide nearly buff guitar-plucking tour that included some forty arrests.[5] Having left Cincinnati for Hollywood, Burck had been understandably frustrated after several years seeking singing gigs, auditioning for TV roles, recording CDs to distribute, and working restaurant jobs alongside fellow aspirants for fame. It was then that a friend's casual suggestion that he sing unclad at LA's seaside sexual hotspot, Muscle Beach, struck him like a needed kick in the butt from God.

"I am doing God's work," he wrote, "and it's tough. . . . [But] by God, I will be 'the most celebrated entertainer of all time.'" And so he got back on his feet and out of his clothes. "If I can't find someone with the capacity to get me famous overnight, I'll get famous overnight by my own damn self," he declared in his self-published memoir, *Determination*.[6] From his Times Square base he became so popular with visitors to the Big Apple he attracted the attention of journalists, which in turn caught the eye of Madison Avenue ad men. Not only underwear maker Fruit of the Loom but other corporate heavyweights such as Pepsi, Chevrolet, Pizza Hut, and

Citibank lined up outside this new celebrity's (un)dressing room
to sign him up for ad campaigns.

But the Naked Cowboy sought a grander campaign. "I have
put another national vibe of my personality across the cosmos,"
he confided in a diary entry later published in his book. "I just
want more, and so I ask, what is the next thing that must be done
to continue toward my destiny?"[7]

Answer: run for president.

His initial answer, however, was to run for mayor. Which he
did in 2009, launching his campaign with the slogan "Nobody
Has Done More with Less." But Burck soon discovered that putting his vibe across the cosmos was a lot easier than putting it
across the New York City Conflicts of Interests Board, a niche in
the cosmos that Burck, like pretty much the rest of us, had never
heard of. Under New York election laws, the Board demanded that
Burck reveal even more of himself—things like his income and its
sources. Which, in those years, ranged from $100,000 to $250,000
a year. Likewise his vibe didn't jibe with the New York Board of
Elections, which notified him that, in order to get his name on the
ballot, he had to collect 7,500 verifiable voter signatures.[8]

Burck dropped out of the race. But genuinely determined when
he'd asked himself what was next in his destiny, the following year
he took another shot at politics, this time with his sights on the
White House. Along with his announcement in Times Square,
he spread the word on his website, announcing to the multitudes
who came to view him there, "Naked Cowboy for President 2012."

Yet by February 2011 the website no longer mentioned his presi-
dential bid. And the 439 names registered with the Federal Election
Commission as candidates for president in 2012 included neither
Robert Burck nor Naked Cowboy. Returning us to the question:
Was it just a publicity stunt? Yes. Which then returns us to the
question: Was his candidacy of any significance? Nevertheless yes.

You can call Burck lots of things—egotistical comes to mind—
but not stupid. Though to assert that America's most cherished
institution is capitalism leads one to wonder if he'd ever read the
Declaration of Independence and the Constitution, where it goes

unmentioned. Rather than quibble, however, let's turn to an unquestionably cherished American: Ralph Waldo Emerson. "I am persistent like Emerson's 'Hero,'" Burck wrote in his diary.[9] Clearly he did not lack ego, but also clearly he was no dummy, as demonstrated by his familiarity with Emerson's 1841 essay "Heroism."

Nor was he so starry-eyed as to be unsuited, as it were, to deal with the day-to-day details of the working world dealt with by those who wear suits to work. When faced with competition on Times Square by a newcomer named Naked Cowgirl, he had his attorney send her a cease-and-desist letter asserting she was violating his trademark and demanding that she sign a "Naked Cowboy Franchise Agreement." When the Naked Cowgirl, a former striptease dancer named Sandy Kane, disagreed, Burck took her to court. It may sound nuts, but there is yet to be a nut lawyers haven't taken a crack at. The case became so entangled in legalities the two sides ended up agreeing to a settlement.[10]

Nor was Burck man enough to put the spurs only to cowgirls. In 2008 he sued the corporation that manufactures M&Ms when an ad for the candy featured a guitar-playing M&M wearing a cowboy hat. It was, he claimed, a Naked Cowboy M&M. Here too the case became so entangled in court rulings the two sides decided to settle it in private. The Naked Cowboy's legal posse also went after the advertising giant Clear Channel and CBS.[11]

While intelligent and litigious are not synonyms, evidence of Naked Cowboy's intelligence surfaced in the *Village Voice* article on his presidential announcement. Reporter Martin Tanzer observed that, after Burck had just declared he would make English "the universal language," he descended the podium and moments later was giving an interview in Spanish to a Latin American news outlet. "This guy is complex!" Tanzer, quite correctly, assessed.[12]

It is here that we find the significance of Naked Cowboy's fringe candidacy. Drilling down into Tanzer's observation, even more can be assessed—starting with the not particularly startling but nonetheless often overlooked fact that each of our presidents, from George Washington on, was or is complex. More important, however, their complexity is in precisely the ways the Naked Cowboy expressed.

Burck, for instance, is genuinely sensitive to the feelings of others. But in complex ways, such as calling for English to be the universal language, then speaking fluent Spanish with those for whom it is their first language. On a more personal level, Burck wrote of the woman he loved during the years of his struggle for fame, "I wasn't giving her the attention she deserved. . . . [She] was the only source of connection I've ever really had to a fulfilled existence. The excuse I would use was that I had a higher obligation to humanity, which I humbly admit I do, but she, I somehow consistently forgot, was my favorite human."[13]

The *excuse he admittedly used*—that being a higher obligation to humanity—which he *humbly admitted he had*. If you could put that spin on a baseball and get batters to buy it, you could rule the World (Series). Or try this on for its presidential fit: "How many people can I inspire to achieve their goals by continually focusing on achieving mine? . . . Every time the Naked Cowboy succeeds, everyone whom I reach succeeds. . . . Everyone who knows my plans and expectations will be elevated by my efforts."[14]

Here, however, is a difference between a candidate such as the Naked Cowboy and a candidate who has a chance of winning the White House: the candidates who win don't say these things. But have they thought them? Lincoln did, as we saw when exploring the candidacy of Live Forever Jones. To have the determination necessary to become the president of the United States, how could one not? Which is a naked—and admittedly uncomfortable—truth. Beneath their political accoutrements, most, if not all, American presidents are naked cowboys.

And someday soon, dagnabbit (as the Naked Cowboy himself complained), cowgirls.

Deez Nuts

Games with Balls Candidate

DURING THE 2016 ELECTION SEASON THE FRINGE CANDIDATE Deez Nuts attracted a spate of attention, even though the candidate's internet-based platform had nothing to do with that name. "I believe anyone who is found as an illegal immigrant in this country must be deported back to their country of origin, with the lone exception of being a minor," it stated. "The reason we are in a budget crisis is because the two main parties refuse to compromise on this issue." The platform additionally supported gay marriage, waffled on abortion, and supported tax incentives to corporations for hiring Americans.[1]

Obviously the attention was due to the candidate's provocative pseudonym rather than this not particularly provocative platform. Except it would not be so obvious to the Federal Election Commission, whose 2016 presidential candidate filings included Ceedeez Nuts, Bofa Deez Nuts, Deez W. Nutz, Hold Ma Nutz, along with their more celebrated relative, Deez Nuts. More celebrated because Deez Nuts is the phrase previously used by rapper Dr. Dre on his album *The Chronic*; it went on to become a catchphrase.

Gaining further visibility after launching his (presumably not her) *Deez Nuts for President 2016* website, the candidate landed in an opinion poll conducted in North Carolina that included the question "Do you have a favorable or unfavorable opinion of Deez Nuts?"[2] To give the Tar Heels their due, 81 percent said they were not sure. Another 13 percent had an unfavorable opinion, most likely taking offense at the name. However, 6 percent answered favorable—just enough to set the press sniffing. Tracking down Deez Nuts, the nation's journalistic hounds soon discovered he was an Iowan named Brady Olson.

And fifteen years old.[3]

Lights, camera, action. For the next two months, the puckishly freckled boy wonder was the darling of news reports nationwide, including *USA Today*, *Time* magazine, CBS News, and NBC News.[4]

And then was news no longer. Beyond the ruse, not only was his platform nothing new, nor, finally, was the fact that teenagers are often among the nation's best in pulling pranks. This one, however, was a doozy.

What is significant, however, is the way this fringe candidate achieved nationwide recognition—that being the poll in North Carolina. Why was the question asked? Possibly, though unlikely, it was included in an effort to gauge voter resentment—unlikely because resentment so clearly could have been at the candidate's name rather than at electoral politics. More likely it was included in an effort to get the polling organization's results noticed in the press. Which, indeed, happened. In this respect it stands out as an example of an ostensibly objective data-gathering organization competing with other polling organizations by adding a bit of spice to its data to entice attention from traditional news media, cable networks, and internet news sites. All of which were also competing with each other, as we've seen, by increasing the proportion of entertainment value in reporting news.

"I loathe this trend," the *Washington Post* columnist Chris Cillizza wrote in response to such data from another polling organization in 2016. It revealed that millennials preferred Darth Vader to Donald Trump as president. "Writing about President Vader, unless you run a Star Wars blog, isn't a path to the future," Cillizza told readers. "It's a step, or several steps, backward."[5]

Cillizza was right. Such findings are funny, but their impact is not. Emanating from a behavioral science that has earned the public's trust, zany data propagate what could be termed *mythinformation*.[6] Each of these bits of *mythinformation* contributes, even if just that bit, to altering perceptions of political reality—and perceptions, it bears mentioning, of science.

By 2016 both political reality and science were on shaky ground when the nation elected as its president the star of a reality TV show who did not believe the overwhelming scientific evidence that humans were causing climate change.

Andrew Basiago

Time Travel Candidate

"Self-proclaimed time traveler Andrew D. Basiago claims he has seen the future and it includes his election to the White House," an online news outlet reported in 2016.[1] Also positing his belief in an alien civilization on Mars, Basiago's fringe candidacy received limited notice. Still, its resemblance to the 1960 campaign of the Universal Flying Saucer Party candidate Gabriel Green is such that it invites comparison.

To a greater extent than Green, Basiago had received attention prior to announcing his run for the White House. Nearly two dozen articles about him or mentioning him appeared between 2009 and 2015 in his hometown *Seattle Examiner*. But his reputation was not confined to Seattle. Separate reports of his views on time travel also appeared during these years in Illinois (*Chicago Examiner*), Michigan (*Detroit Examiner*), New Mexico (*Albuquerque Examiner*), North Carolina (*Winston-Salem Examiner*) South Carolina (*Charleston Examiner*), Florida (*Panama City Examiner*), and even Hawaii (*Honolulu Examiner*).[2]

Likely you've spotted a pattern. These local editions of the *Examiner* were part of a larger entity, Examiner.com. Expanding upon the post-1968 election trend of increasing access to candidates, this internet site did likewise for those seeking to be journalists by publishing articles from self-proclaimed reporters whose facts, the executive editor of Examiner.com stated, "don't get edited."[3] Consequently *Examiner* reports on Basiago included headlines such as "Head on Mars: Photo Shows Odd Artifact Resembling Barack Obama?"

In that particular report Basiago "confirmed" that he and Obama, when they were teenagers, participated in "the CIA's Mars visitation program," code-named Project Pegasus. Among the other young people in the program, Basiago asserted, was Bill Richardson, later to become the governor of New Mexico, U.S. secretary of energy, and ambassador to the United Nations. Need there be more proof than the titles alone that these youngsters were being groomed, or grooved, for Earth leadership—especially now that Basiago was about to be elected president (as he claimed to know from time travel)?[4]

There were, need I say, skeptics. Foremost among them were journalists who wrote for outlets other than Examiner.com. A column in the *Santa Fe New Mexican* titled "Beam Me Up, Xoe!" ridiculed Basiago's claims. In that same state's *Alamogordo Daily News*, a column titled "Governor's Past Is Beyond Belief" pointed out that the name "Pegasus Project" had already been revealed—in Marvel Comics.[5]

The most widespread attention Basiago received prior to his candidacy resulted from an article in the *Huffington Post* in which he was quoted saying he had teleported to the past and future eight times as part of the CIA's secret project, including a trip to Ford's Theater the night Lincoln was assassinated.[6] An encapsulated version of the *Huffington Post* report subsequently appeared in newspapers nationwide under the heading "Things People Believe."[7]

Unlike Green, public attention to Basiago was not limited to his cosmic views. Neither a street-corner crazy nor living in his parents' basement, he was a practicing attorney who had studied at Cambridge University and held an additional degree in urban planning. Indeed Basiago had published numerous articles on urban environmental sustainability in scholarly journals, putting forth views that were subsequently cited by others in that field.[8]

These articles had drawn to a close by 2008, the year he authored "The Discovery of Life on Mars," an article published under the auspices of the Mars Anomaly Research Society (or, yes, MARS)—of which he was the president.[9] Nevertheless these views too attracted some number of followers. Respectful references to Basiago's claims appeared in enough books (several being self-published) that their number is more significant than their quality. Similarly, in *Mysterious Magazine* Makia Freeman, a senior researcher at

ToolsforFreedom.com, wrote, "The idea of a flat earth has attracted and converted some high-profile names, such as Andrew Basiago, the man who claims he teleported to Mars as part of Project Pegasus in the 1960s and 1970s." In this 2015 article Freeman scored a scoop when he reported, "Basiago, by the way, revealed . . . that he intends to join the 2016 presidential race."[10]

And then the attention all but ended. Possibly Basiago's enthusiasts clammed up from concern that failure to win the election—a victory he said he had already witnessed—would dismantle all his claims. In addition, just as his campaign commenced, his main source of attention, Examimer.com, was closing down, having been bought by another media conglomerate. In the traditional media his candidacy went virtually unmentioned. Other than a piece in the online edition of *Esquire*, which linked his candidacy to his time travel statements in the *Huffington Post*, coverage was limited to his being among those listed in a few newspapers in Florida, the one state where he'd managed to qualify as a certified write-in candidate.[11] Internet blogs paid a bit more attention, though even on the internet the campaign never went viral.

All told, Basiago's presidential candidacy was similar but not identical to Green's. Its two main differences were that Basiago also earned a reputation among scholars and the rise of the internet, which provided him with greater access to the public. Yet in that newer medium we spot their greatest similarity. Among the online news reports about or mentioning Basiago were the headlines "UFO Sighting: NASA Cover-up?" (*Chicago Examiner*, November 11, 2014), "Second Whistleblower Emerges to Confirm Reality of Time Travel" (*Seattle Examiner*, December 31, 2009), and "White House Press Association, Press Secretary Robert Gibbs Block ET, UFO Press Questions to Obama" (*Seattle Examiner*, January 23, 2010). Both Green and Basiago campaigned on platforms devoted to revealing purported government cover-ups of recent astonishing events.

While Green was not the first fringe candidate to amplify a belief in cosmic revelations, he was the first to suggest the federal government was hiding such revelations. Likewise his era was the first in which the federal government created a perma-

nent secretive information-gathering agency, the CIA. In addition
Green's era was the first in which the federal government's efforts
to combat communism entailed warnings of secret communist
cells operating throughout the United States. By 2016 government
secrecy had further expanded with the creations of the Defense
Intelligence Agency, National Security Agency, and Department
of Homeland Security.

Secrecy, however, creates its own blank to be filled, one an individual's fears and needs will participate in filling. Moreover in the
years between the candidacies of Green and Basiago, revelations of
secret government-sponsored medical testing of untreated syphilis on uninformed African Americans, secret testing of LSD by
the army on uninformed soldiers, and testing of radiation exposure from atomic blasts on underinformed soldiers lend credence to rumors of other cover-ups and conspiracies in the federal
government.[12]

But not unbounded credence. The limited degree of attention
that Basiago's fringe candidacy received provides a measure of the
degree to which Americans in 2016 were willing to consider extraordinary claims of government cover-ups. On the other hand, the
similarities between Basiago's 2016 candidacy and the 1952 Green
candidacy (and, in turn, the similarities between the fears underlying Green's candidacy and those underlying that of Live Forever
Jones) reveal that end-of-the-world anxiety, countered in each
instance by some form of miraculous rescue, has continued for
centuries in the United States—indeed throughout recorded time.

Zoltan Istvan

Transhumanist Party

In some respects Zoltan Istvan is to Live Forever Jones as Andrew Basiago was to Gabriel Green. But where Americans dismissed Jones's belief that we can live forever, Istvan's views, which include living forever, are not as easily brushed aside.

The first thing not easily brushed aside is his name. "If you were going to invent a human being to run for president of the United States as the first-ever candidate from the Transhumanist Party, his name would probably be Zoltan," Alexis Madrigal quipped in an otherwise serious *Huffington Post* article on this 2016 presidential candidate.[1] His name, however, is not the moniker of a mad pseudoscientist; it's Hungarian, given him by his parents, who immigrated to the United States prior to his birth in 1973.

While a student at Columbia University, Istvan was introduced to views on transhumanism, a topic born in the nineteenth-century Industrial Revolution with works such as Mary Shelley's *Frankenstein* and later reenergized by breakthroughs in microchips and nanotechnology. After graduating, Istvan became a war correspondent for *National Geographic* and other news outlets. "I had seen a lot of terrible things," he later recalled. "It got me thinking very deeply about life and death. . . . Something in my head shifted—this idea that I don't want to die—and I started to think about how I could dedicate myself to not dying."[2] He started to think, in other words, about transhumanism.

Being a field on the cusp of what is today science and science fiction, transhumanism has attracted a wide variety of adherents who describe it in various ways. During his presidential campaign, Istvan described it as a view that recognizes that "technology could potentially double our lifetimes, in the next twenty to forty years, through radical science like gene editing, bionic organs, and stem cell therapy. Eventually, life extension technology like this will probably even wipe out death and aging altogether."[3]

Not all transhumanists would describe it that way. "The guy is a freaking loon," fellow adherent Solomon Kleinsmith declared of Istvan. "He's really done a huge amount of damage to the Transhumanist cause by taking his wingnut bullshit to that label."[4] Be that as it may, Istvan's campaign advocated that, rather than hiding from or dismissing such possibilities, the nation needs to prepare for them. In one of his numerous columns in the *Huffington Post* he warned,

> We're all headed to a transhumanist world. Of course some won't want to join, but it's sort of like the Internet. If you don't use the Internet, then you are missing out on a major piece of the new world. Transhumanism will be like that. Without upgrading your bodies, you'll be totally left behind, both intellectually and physically. Can you imagine if you're the only one in fifty years who doesn't have a bionic eye that can stream media info into your brain, see 100 miles clearly, and also see ninety per cent of the light spectrum (gases, microbes, etc.)?[5]

Whether or not it's inevitable, it's not just for kooks. Writing in the *Washington Post* about the inclusion of transhumanism in a document issued by the National Intelligence Council, reporter Christine Emba pointed out, "Some claim, not unfairly, that these modifications aren't so different from much more accepted technologies such as pacemakers."[6] Pacemakers are almost Old School, dating back to the 1950s. In the years since, technology has gone on to develop artificial hearts, cochlear implants, intraocular lenses, interactive prosthetics, and a growing list of electronic body parts currently being tested.

In 2013 Istvan ventured into transhumanism's spotlight when he self-published a novel titled *The Transhumanist Wager*. Self-published works are rarely reviewed or, for that matter, purchased. Not so in this instance. It sold like hotcakes and, to date, has been the subject of analysis in nearly a dozen books—and that's not counting discussions of Istvan in self-published books.[7] The following year he sought to capitalize on the buzz his book created by forming the Transhumanist Party, in preparation for his presidential run. He then fit out an old bus to look like a giant coffin on wheels, its sides emblazoned with "IMMORTALITY BUS WITH TRANSHUMANIST ZOLTAN ISTVAN," and set out on a cross-country effort to win votes.

Or not.

Or not in 2016. "Since I almost certainly won't be elected," he told reporters, "I have the opportunity to come up with some extraordinary policies. Some are predictions, but some aren't. They're policies that the larger parties will eventually be discussing."[8]

The columnist Martin Wisckol reacted, "I've seen my share of wild-eyed would-be politicians. This guy didn't have that look. He was calm, measured. He wasn't ranting."[9] Similarly in his *Huffington Post* article Madrigal wrote, "Zoltan has helped create a forum for people to start thinking about what the world could be like in ten, twenty, or thirty years, and what politics might be necessary to meet those challenges. . . . I wouldn't rule out the possibility that, in the next decade, the issues Zoltan cares most about will end up on the national stage."

Not everyone in the press agreed. Or was able to resist the entertainment potential—though, in fairness, as legitimate journalists they did include at least one sentence mentioning technological advancements potentially posing major political and ethical challenges. For instance, the *Buffalo News* in New York reported, "When it comes to campaign promises that are bold and innovative, even revolutionary, Zoltan Istvan Gyurko stands alone." (Third names in Hungarian are traditionally equivalent to our middle names.) "What other candidate for president is advocating government-supported immortality, or a new bill of rights for humanlike robots and cyborgs of the future?" The article then transitioned with the comparison, "And if you think Gyurko is not your kind of politician, how about Michael Ingbar and his slogan, Make America Dance Again?"[10]

Wisecracks also frequently headlined articles on Istvan's campaign. "Zoltan's Cyborg Utopia: The Transhumanist Party Presidential Candidate Wants Us to Live Forever" called to readers

from atop a news report in a Massachusetts newspaper. A syndicated column bore the title "A Man Named Zoltan Is Running for
President, Too, and He Wants Our Bodies." That column was by
the humorist Dave Barry, and its significance is that, even though
Barry's primary purpose was humor, he managed to convey as
much about Istvan's candidacy as ostensibly serious news reports
seeking to be amusing. "If I understand him correctly," he wrote—
immediately establishing a nonjudgmental view more associated
with reporters than comics—"the Transhumanists want to use
science to replace our weak and frail limbs and organs and skeletons with high-tech mechanical body parts, so we can live forever."
Not a bad summary. And if you've ever wondered what makes a
humorist such as Barry so successful, note in this example how
nonjudgmental factuality was not an obstacle to his comic talent,
as he followed up, "I asked Istvan where he stands on the issue of
low-flow toilets, which I strongly oppose, as an American and as
a human being."[11]

Then note this: fanatics rarely have a sense of humor. Istvan did.
"I have a very interesting position on that," he replied. "We're trying to upgrade humans to machines. We think pooping and pee-
ing is a waste of time."

On Election Day the number of write-in votes Istvan may have
received was so negligible as to go unmentioned. But he did not
take this to mean his presidential campaign had failed. "The real
goal is to try to work and build the Transhumanist Party so that
it has a much better shot at 2020 and 2024," he told *Esquire* magazine. "That doesn't mean it's going to win in 2020 and 2024, of
course, but I think we can bring the Transhumanist Party on par
with the Libertarian Party or the Green Party, with the sizes of
other third parties that can actually make a difference."[12] If, as he
indicated he would, he repeatedly seeks the presidency, he may
not only be a perennial presidential candidate; he may become
our first eternal presidential candidate.

That remark may look like a joke but, *as with all fringe candidates for president*, not be a joke after all.

In Exiting—Watch Your Step

FIRST A WORD ABOUT, AS OF THIS WRITING, THE CLOWN in the White House. Since this is a touchy subject, don't take it from me; take it from the conservative periodical *Old Guard* ("Devoted to the Principles of 1776 and 1787"), whose editor wrote, "Shall we speak of . . . an ignoramus as a scholar? Of an obscene joker and clown as a well-bred man of refinement and taste? . . . To say that we shall not speak of Lincoln coarsely is to forbid us to mention his name."

I should point out the article was written in 1864.[1]

The number of references to Abraham Lincoln as a clown was exceeded only by the number of references, when he sought the presidency in 1860, to his being a candidate with fringe views who, through a combination of electoral circumstances, managed to squeeze through to the White House. Nor was this view confined to the South. When Lincoln sought reelection, an Ohio newspaper repeated its view of him as fringe with even more fervor. "We have tried him four years," it declared. "He has destroyed the Union, violated the Constitution, trampled upon the laws, made the name of America a hissing and a byword through the earth, made our rivers to flow with blood, covered the land with green graves and devoured the substance of the people."[2]

But come on, when we speak of the clown in the White House, we know who we mean. Here again, however, don't take it from me but from the conservative author Thomas R. Meinders, who wrote, "Thanking Obama for killing bin Laden is like going into McDonald's and thanking Ronald McDonald for the hamburger. It's the guy cooking the burger that should get the credit, not the clown."[3]

Theodore Roosevelt too was called a clown in the White House.[4] In this respect Donald Trump, so often viewed and depicted as a clown candidate who managed, also through a combination of electoral circumstances, to win the White House, is not the first president to be viewed as such. What is significant about Trump's victory in terms of fringe candidates is that he was not a fringe candidate. He was the nominee of a major political party.

But how Trump came to be the nominee of a major political party can be found in fissures deep within the nation's political landscape that were amplified by fringe candidates.

Dating back as far as 1848, the candidacy of John Donkey reveals that voters were already recognizing and resenting meaningless campaign double-talk. The attention paid to the wealthy entrepreneur George Francis Train in 1872 reveals the curiosity of many for a successful businessman rather than a professional politician running the country—but also reveals that the political landscape was as yet scaled tightly against entertaining braggadocio. Fringe candidates in 1968 contributed to widening fissures, and those who gained attention through post-1968 changes in primary election rules were further enabled to reveal more fissures. Not long after, fringe candidates benefited from entertainment increasingly sharing the stage with journalism as competition intensified among the traditional news media, cable TV, and the internet. In 2016 enough of these fissures intersected to erupt into a mainstream path to the presidency for Donald Trump.

To be clear, fringe candidates did not cause these changes, though many played a role in exposing and enlarging them. Those whose candidacies received widespread attention attracted that spotlight because their campaigns resonated with and amplified lesser-heard voices for change—voices that represented political fissures.

With the election of Trump, many Americans may feel our revels now are ended. These fringe candidates, as I foretold when taking your political tickets, are clowns and Quixotes, but rather than fading into air, they have manifested themselves in later major party candidates—one of whom, widely viewed as a clown or modern-day Don Quixote, came to occupy the Oval Office.[5]

But are our revels ended?

Bear in mind, many Americans in earlier eras also felt the fun was over, that our democracy was done. And they were wrong. Nevertheless it's a question worth asking, even if again and again.

In the course of this trip we have seen that the variety of odd banners with which fringe candidates have headed into the presidential fray have been as significant to this nation's story as Don Quixote's has been for all humanity. Indeed the crazy quilt of quests one could assemble with the banners of fringe candidates was part of what made this nation's bed at its inception, when Thomas Jefferson described our collective quixotic quest in that paradoxical phrase "to form a more perfect union." With those slightly wacky words, and the Constitution of which they are a part, the United States became the first nation in history in which laughter and political lunacy officially became patriotic acts.

Whether or not our revels are ended will be determined by the kind of presidents we elect in the future. Fringe candidates for president will provide the hints.

NOTES

Before We Begin

1. The seed for the Democratic Party donkey was planted by those opposed to Andrew Jackson who thought it a real knee-slapper to call him Andrew Jackass. Pun-averse opponents of Jackson also used a donkey, depicting Jackson riding one—a reference to a then-remembered statement by Benjamin Franklin regarding poor men who ride donkeys to the polls. Not until 1870, however, was a donkey used to represent the Democratic Party. It (and the elephant as a representation of the Republican Party) were the inspiration of Thomas Nast, star cartoonist for *Harper's Weekly*. Conceivably Nast was influenced by John Donkey, though that donkey and the publication that created him had long since been put to pasture. See Monaghan, "Origin of Political Symbols," 205–12.

2. Untitled, *Joliet (IL) Signal*, July 11, 1848.

3. Unedited footage of Queer Nation commercial for presidential candidate Joan Jett Blakk, 1992, Bill Stamets Collection, c.2005-08, Chicago Film Archives.

4. "Crazy Candidates," *Fort Wayne (IN) Daily Sentinel*, May 28, 1872.

5. Federal Election Commission, "2012 Candidate Summary," "2016 Candidate Summary," https://www.fec.gov/data/candidates/.

The First Fringe Candidates

1. "Election of 1828," *American Presidency Project*, http://www.presidency.ucsb .edu/showelection.php?year=1828,

2. Hubbell and Adair, "Robert Munford's 'The Candidates.'"

John Donkey

1. John Donkey, "Important Presidential Correspondence," *The John-Donkey*, March 18, 1848, 183.

2. John Donkey, "To the Public," *The John-Donkey*, April 22, 1848, 262.

3. Cf. "Address by John Donkey," *Portage Sentinel* (Ravenna OH), May 3, 1848; "John Donkey in the Field!," *North Carolina Standard* (Raleigh), May 3, 1848; "Address by John Donkey," *Democratic Banner* (Louisiana MO), May 8, 1848; "John Donkey in the Field!," *Spirit of Jefferson* (Charles Town VA, now WV), May 23, 1848.

4. "Sure Enough!," *Democratic Banner* (Louisiana MO), June 26, 1848.

5. "Thomas Dunn English Dead," *New York Times*, April 2, 1902; Hutchisson, *Poe*, 190; "Poe Letters and Manuscripts Found in a Pillow-Case," 823–24.

6. "Death of G. G. Foster," *New York Times*, April 18, 1856.

Joseph Smith

1. Smith, *History of the Church*, 210.

2. Donkey, "To the Public," 262.

3. "The Election," *Baton Rouge Gazette*, April 6, 1844.

4. Smith, *History of the Church*, 188.

5. "Another Candidate for President," *Whig Standard* (Washington DC), March 13, 1844.

6. "A New Advocate for a National Bank," *Washington (DC) Globe*, reprinted in *North Carolina Standard* (Raleigh), March 27, 1844.

7. Smith, *History of the Church*, 206.

8. "Very Important and Curious from the Mormon Empire," *New York Herald*, January 26, 1844.

9. "The Mormons," *Whig Standard* (Washington DC), February 28, 1844.

10. "Life in Nauvoo," *New York Daily Tribune*, May 28, 1844.

11. "The Mormon War," *Cleveland Herald*, June 27, 1844.

12. Smith, *History of the Church*, 211.

Leonard "Live Forever" Jones

1. "The Victim of an Idea," *New Orleans Crescent*, September 6, 1868.

2. "The Victim of an Idea."

3. "Endless Life," *Register of Debates*, 97–98.

4. "Letter from Charlestown," *New Albany (IN) Daily*, April 22, 1868.

5. "The Victim of an Idea."

6. "Debate on Kossuth Resolution," *Southern Press* (Washington DC), January 27, 1852.

7. "The Victim of an Idea"; "Death of Live-Forever Jones," *Daily Ledger* (New Albany IN), August 31, 1868; "Death of Live-Forever Jones," *St. Cloud (MN) Journal*, September 10, 1868.

8. "The Victim of an Idea."

9. "A Strange Character," *Wyoming Democrat* (Tunkhannock PA), October 21, 1868.

10. While it is a widely believed myth that the explorer Ponce de Leon searched for the Fountain of Youth, for actual examples see Haber, "Anti-Aging Medicine."

11. Mooney, "The Ghost Dance Religion," 788, 797, 908, 967, 983.

12. Pritchard, "Religious Change," 297–330; Pritchard, "The Burned-Over District Reconsidered," 243–65; Rowe, "A New Perspective."

13. "Popery in the United States," *Boston Investigator*, April 26, 1843. For the dispute regarding Lafayette, see Gilbert du Motier, Marquis de Lafayette, Wikiquote, https://en.wikiquote.org/wiki/Gilbert_du_Motier,_Marquis_de_Lafayette.

14. "Live Forever Jones," *Hickman (KY) Courier*, September 19, 1868.

15. "Millerism as Amended," *Niles National Register* (Washington DC), April 6, 1844, 96.

16. "The Victim of an Idea."

17. Lamon, *Life of Abraham Lincoln*, 242.

18. "The Victim of an Idea."

George Francis Train

1. Untitled, *Bossier Banner* (Bellevue LA), January 6, 1872. Front-page images of Trump as a clown in the *New York Daily News* also include "Sideshow Don," April 11, 2011; "Dawn of the Brain Dead: Clown Comes to Life with N.H. Win," February 10, 2016; "Clown's Dopey Hair Trigger," May 21, 2016.

2. "Second Appearance," *New Orleans Republican*, June 22, 1872; "George Francis Train at Tammany Hall," *New York Times*, December 27, 1869; "Transcript: Donald Trump at G.O.P. Convention," *New York Times*, July 22, 2016, https://www.nytimes.com/2016/07/22/us/politics/trump-transcript-rnc-address.html?_r=0.

3. Train, *My Life*, 72.

4. Train, *My Life*, 77.

5. Downey, "George Francis Train," 251–61.

6. "Fourth of July in Australia," *Boston Post*, October 8, 1853. For Train as correspondent, see Wright, *The Forgotten Rebels*, 30.

7. Train, *My Life*, 132; Holland, "George Francis Train," 25; Vivian Yee, "Donald Trump's Math Takes His Towers to Greater Heights," *New York Times*, November 1, 2016, https://www.nytimes.com/2016/11/02/nyregion/donald-trump-tower-heights.html.

8. "Letter from Chicago," *New Orleans Republican*, May 26, 1872; Train and Nichols, *People's Candidate*, 3.

9. Train, *Spread Eagleism*, viii–ix.

10. Train, *Spread Eagleism*, ix–x.

11. Train, *Young America in Wall Street*, 344–45.

12. "Not Bad," *Sugar Planter* (West Baton Rouge LA), February 13, 1858.

13. "The Two Conventions," *National Republican* (Washington DC), October 10, 1862; "The Conflict Commenced in Boston—George Francis Train Mobbed by Sumner's Supporters—No Free Speech," *Richmond Dispatch*, October 11, 1862; "Massachusetts Politics," *New York Times*, October 26, 1862.

14. Train and Nichols, *People's Candidate*, 4; Downey, "George Francis Train," 253.

15. Train and Nichols, *People's Candidate*, 21.

16. Bryan McGovern to author, March 1, 2017. Train was arrested aboard ship when he arrived at Cork, causing a diplomatic dust-up as an American citizen was being arrested by British authorities on the basis of statements he had made in the United States that were not illegal in the United States. Train was subsequently released.

17. "George Francis Train for Congress," *New York Herald*, October 10, 1868; "The Vote in the Fifth Congressional District," *New York Times*, November 6, 1868.

18. "George Francis Train on the Chinese," *Cairo (IL) Evening Bulletin*, July 9, 1869.

19. "Train," *Public Ledger* (Memphis TN), April 7, 1871.

20. For examples of racist jokes, see "Local Affairs," *Albany (OR) Register*, July 24, 1869; "Wit, Humor and Wisdom," *Monticello (IA) Express*, January 4, 1872.

21. "The World on the Notabilities at Chicago," *Cleveland Morning Leader*, September 2, 1864.

22. "Train Oil," *Washington Standard* (Olympia), July 17, 1869.

23. Untitled, *Idaho World* (Idaho City), April 25, 1872.

24. "All Sorts of Paragraphs," *Monticello (IA) Express*, January 4, 1872.

25. "Personal," *New Albany (IN) Ledger*, January 6, 1872.

26. "Train's Ovation," *Public Ledger* (Memphis), April 7, 1871.

27. "Train—The Next President on the Rostrum," *Nashville Union and American*, November 18, 1871.

28. "Local Affairs—Tuesday Night," *Albany (OR) Register*, July 24, 1969.

29. Leip, *Atlas of Presidential Elections*.

30. "Special Dispatches—The Vote in Different Parts of the State," *Knoxville (TN) Chronicle*, November 6, 1872.

31. "New York—George Francis Train Judged Insane," *Chicago Tribune*, May 21, 1873; "New York News," *Helena (MT) Weekly Herald*, April 3, 1873; "Bermischte Depeschen aus New-York" [Various Dispatches from New York], *Der Deutsche Correspondent* (Baltimore), April 15, 1873.

32. "Is Train Insane?," *New York Times*, April 16, 1873.

33. "The Train Lunacy Investigation," *New York Times*, April 23, 1873; "The Train Lunacy Case," *New York Times*, April 29, 1873.

34. "Train Pronounced Sane," *New York Times*, May 7, 1873; "The Courts—George Francis Train," *New York Herald*, May 21, 1873; "Train," *Knoxville (TN) Chronicle*, May 21, 1873.

35. "The Political Campaign of 1872," 419; Zinn, *A People's History*, 204.

36. "The Political Campaign of 1872," 401, 402, 419.

37. "George Francis Train's Lecture," *New York Times*, April 30, 1877.

38. "Train on the Platform," *New York Times*, September 26, 1887.

39. "Citizen Train Wouldn't Stand Up," *New York Times*, April 28, 1894.

40. "Citizen Train as a Rope Skipper," *New York Times*, July 18, 1893.

41. "Train in Chicago," *New York Times*, October 8, 1887.

Victoria Woodhull

1. "A Train on the Track," *Memphis Appeal*, March 22, 1871; "Don't Accept," *New Northwest* (Portland OR), July 5, 1872.

2. Untitled, *New Orleans Republican*, February 19, 1871.

3. Untitled, *Idaho World* (Idaho City), April 13, 1871.

4. Untitled, *New Orleans Republican*, June 23, 1872; "Paragrams," *Pacific Commercial Advertiser* (Honolulu), August 17, 1872.

5. Untitled, *Democrat* (New Albany OR), June 14, 1872.

6. Untitled, *Hickman (KY) Courier*, April 6, 1872.

7. "A Petticoat President," *Weekly Panola (MS) Star*, February 11, 1871; "A Petticoat Politician," *New York Herald*, May 27, 1870; "Is This an Honest Administration?," *New National Era* (Washington DC), April 11, 1872.

8. "The Free Love Queen," *Sumter Watchman* (Sumterville SC), June 14, 1871.

9. Untitled, *Eaton (OH) Weekly Democrat*, February 8, 1872.

10. Untitled, *Ottawa (IL) Free Trader*, September 16, 1871.

11. Cf. "Blood, Woodhull, Clafin," *New York Herald*, May 16, 1871; "Mrs. Woodhull Explains," *Janesville (WI) Gazette*, August 31, 1871.

12. In the midst of the 1872 presidential campaign, Woodhull's ex-husband was dying from complications resulting from substance abuse and appealed to her for shelter. Demonstrating profound mercy and kindness, she and her second husband again provided him a place in their home, where he soon passed away. See "The Death of Dr. Woodhull," *Chicago Tribune*, April 15, 1872.

13. Untitled, *Painesville (OH) Journal*, November 25, 1871.

14. "The Grand Fisk Ovation," *Charleston (SC) Daily News*, November 27, 1871; "Woman's 'Rights,'" *Belmont (OH) Chronicle*, November 30, 1871.

15. Woodhull, *Principles of Social Freedom*, 12, italics in original.

16. Woodhull, *Principles of Social Freedom*, 14, 19–20, 11.

17. Woodhull, *Principles of Social Freedom*, 21–22.

18. "Concentrated Nastiness," *Lexington (KY) Caucasian*, February 3, 1872.

19. Woodhull, *Principles of Social Freedom*, 24.

20. "'Victoria' on the Stump," *New York Herald*, February 21, 1872.

21. "The Queen of Quacks," *Chicago Tribune*, September 17, 1871; "The Grand Fisk Ovation . . . Demosthenes at Steinway Hall," *Charleston (SC) Daily News*, November 27, 1871.

22. Untitled, *Evening Star* (Washington DC), September 12, 1871.

23. Woodhull, *Principles of Social Freedom*, 3.

24. Edwards, *Personal Recollections*, 85.

25. "The New York Convention," *New Northwest* (Portland OR), May 31, 1872.

26. "Northern Society," *Nashville Union and American*, June 8, 1871.

27. "The Beecher-Woodhull Scandal," *Intelligencer* (Wheeling WV), January 13, 1873.

28. "Vivacious Vic," *Saint Paul (MN) Daily Globe*, May 12, 1892; "The Women's Victoria," *Pittsburgh Dispatch*, October 22, 1892.

James B. Walker

1. Untitled, *Cincinnati Star*, April 25 1876. For the American Party, see "An American Party," *Wisconsin State Journal* (Madison), June 24, 1876.

2. "Political," *Brownstown (IN) Banner*, December 12, 1872.

3. "The American Party," *Northern Tribune* (Cheboygan MI), December 2, 1876.

4. "From the New York American," *Illinois Gazette* (Shawnee-town), March 22, 1828.

5. "Anti-Masonic Convention," *National Intelligencer* (Washington DC), October 1, 1831; "Anti-Masonic Nominations," *New York Spectator*, October 1, 1831; "National Anti-Masonic Convention," *Gettysburg (PA) Star*, October 4, 1831.

NOTES TO PAGES 46–56

6. "Secret Societies," reprinted from *Cincinnati Enquirer* in *Portsmouth (OH) Times*, June 18, 1870.

7. "Crazy Candidates," *Fort Wayne (IN) Daily Sentinel*, May 28, 1872.

8. "The Masonic Bugaboo," *Chicago Tribune*, November 20, 1874, reprinted in *Indianapolis Journal*, November 24, 1874; *Boonsville (IN) Enquirer*, November 28, 1874.

9. Untitled, *Bloomington (IL) Daily Leader*, February 20, 1875.

10. While never in the national spotlight, James B. Walker was highly respected among those who knew him. His retirement ceremony, which recounted his career, was written up and sent to Illinois newspapers. Cf. "Wheaton—James B. Walker," *Chicago Tribune*, August 1, 1875.

11. Kutlowski, "Anti-Masonry Reexamined"; Bullock, "A Pure and Sublime System."

12. Roberts, "The Crusade against Secret Societies," 399.

13. "The Political Campaign of 1872," 401, 419.

Mark Twain

1. Cf. "A Presidential Candidate," *St Mary's Beacon* (Leonardtown MD), May 8, 1879; *Ouachita Telegraph* (Monroe LA), July 4, 1879; *Carbon Advocate* (Lehightown PA), July 5, 1879; *Evening Star* (Washington DC), July 14, 1879.

2. "Campaign Post," *Boston Post*, September 6, 1876.

3. "Reformer or Tax-Dodger?," *New York Times*, September 2, 1876; "No Excuse for Tilden," *New York Times*, September 4, 1876.

4. "The Courier Journal Says," *Memphis Public Ledger*, October 20, 1876; "Hayes's Defective Memory," *Alpena (MI) Weekly Argus*, October 25, 1976; "The LeRoy Charge against Gov. Hayes," *Watertown (WI) Republican*, October 25, 1976.

5. "Gen. Hayes," *Eaton (OH) Democrat*, October 7, 1875.

6. "A Word to Workingmen," *Lima (OH) Democrat*, October 5, 1876; "For Workingmen," *Bartholomew Democrat* (Columbus IN), October 6, 1876.

7. Garfield was caught up in a shady investment structure to help finance construction of the Union Pacific Railroad. For his testimony before a congressional investigating committee, see "Credit Mobilier," *Memphis Daily Appeal*, January 15, 1873; Peskin, *Garfield*, 354–59.

8. "Samuel L. Clemens," *National Republican* (Washington DC), October 3, 1876; Morris, *Fraud of the Century*, 142–44.

9. "Mark Twain Home, an Anti-Imperialist," *New York Herald*, October 16, 1900.

10. "Mark Twain," reprinted from *New York World* in *St. Paul (MN) Globe*, October 21, 1900.

11. "Mark Twain Home Again," *New York Times*, October 16, 1900.

George Edwin Taylor

1. Cf. "A Law to Stop Lynching," *New York Times*, August 18, 1899; "Negro on Lynching," *Trenton (NJ) Evening Times*, April 27, 1899; "Negro Appointment Plan," *New York Times*, January 25, 1903; "Negroes Working for Crum," *New York Times*, February 4, 1903.

2. Cf. "National Colored Labor Convention," *New Era* (Washington DC), January 13, 1870; "Washington," *Knoxville (TN) Chronicle*, February 18, 1871; "The Negro in Politics," *Manning (SC) Times*, August 1, 1888.

3. "Indorse Roosevelt," *Wilmar (MN) Tribune*, July 13 1904; "Negroes Name a Ticket," *Free Lance* (Fredericksburg VA), July 12, 1904.

4. "Candidate for President Arrested," *St. Paul (MN) Globe*, July 14, 1904.

5. Untitled, *Fulton County News* (McConnellsburg PA), July 27, 1904, italics added.

6. "Many Parties in the Field," *Arizona Silver Belt* (Globe City), July 28, 1904.

7. Wellman, "Bringing Order to a Disorderly Place," 1117–28.

8. "Bill Scott," *St. Louis (MO) Palladium*, July 16, 1904; Mouser, *Black Gambler's World*, 92.

9. Miller, *Guide into the South*, 99, 148, 216, 277, 307, 465; "Quarters of Negroes Destroyed by Fire," *Defiance (OH) Express*, March 9, 1904; "Vengeance on Negroes," *Weekly Tribune* (Moulton IA), April 26, 1904; "'Tip' Harrison on Roosevelt," *Atlanta Constitution*, November 20, 1904; "White People of South," *Atlanta Constitution*, December 4, 1904.

10. "Taylor Has Novel Career," *Omaha Daily Bee*, July 25, 1904.

11. "Negro Candidate for President of the US," *Tacoma (WA) Times*, August 7, 1904; "Negro Candidate for President of U.S.," *Logansport (IN) Reporter*, August 10, 1904; "Negro Candidate for President of U.S.," *Spokane Press*, August 23, 1904.

12. "Letter of Acceptance," *Evening Democrat* (Ottumwa IA), September 14, 1904; "Accepts the Honor," *Ottumwa (IA) Courier*, September 15, 1904.

13. "What Taylor Thinks," *Evening Times-Republican* (Marshalltown IA), September 3, 1904; "Taylor Writing Acceptance," *Omaha Bee*, September 4, 1904; "A National Negro Party," *Hawaii Star* (Honolulu), September 21, 1904.

14. George E. Taylor, "The National Liberty Party's Appeal," *Independent*, October 13, 1904, 844–66.

15. Taylor, "The National Liberty Party's Appeal," 845.

16. "Campaign Will Be Aggressive," *Ottumwa (IA) Weekly Democrat*, September 1, 1904.

17. "Says Taylor Is a Tool," *Ottumwa (IA) Weekly Courier*, September 17, 1904.

18. "Associated Press Dispatches," *St. Paul (MN) Appeal*, May 7, 1904.

19. Untitled, *Cedar Falls (IA) Gazette*, April 5, 1904; Mouser, *For Labor, Race, and Liberty*, 122–23.

20. "Republican Party vs. All Other Parties," *Iowa State Bystander* (Des Moines), September 23, 1904.

21. "Colored Man Fails to File His Nomination Papers," *Marshalltown (IA) Times-Republican*, October 10, 1904; "Sparks Not on Ticket," *Ottumwa (IA) Weekly Courier*, October 11, 1904.

22. Mouser, *For Labor, Race, and Liberty*, 117, 125, 127.

23. Untitled, *Stark County Democrat* (Canton OH), September 20, 1904.

24. Mouser, *For Labor, Race, and Liberty*, 159.

25. "Topics of the Times," *Times-Republican* (Marshalltown IA), November 29, 1904.

26. Mouser, *For Labor, Race, and Liberty*, 129.

27. "Iowa News," *Oxford Mirror* (Oxford Junction IA), April 25, 1907; "Politicians and Politics," *Bismarck (ND) Daily Tribune*, April 30, 1907; "Once Ran for President," *Washington Post*, April 12, 1907.

Will Rogers

1. Will Rogers, "I Accept the Nomination," *Life*, May 31, 1928, 3.

2. "Will Rogers for President," *Life*, May 31, 1928, 4.

3. Will Rogers, "Our Candidate Insults the Voters," *Life*, September 21, 1928, 3.

4. Will Rogers, "Our Candidate Won't Sling Mud," *Life*, October 12, 1928, 5.

5. Will Rogers, "Our Candidate Has No Religion," *Life*, October 19, 1928, 3.

6. L. J. Quinby, "A Laughing President," letter to the editor, *Baltimore Sun*, January 1, 1928.

7. L. J. Quinby was the author of three respectable, though less than best-selling, books, including *Natural Basis of Morals and Ethics*. His bread and butter came from what he wrote under the pen name Wallace Clifton. These included his more titillating *Three Paths: Biography of a Man Who Tried Them All* and scenarios he ground out for silent films. In that world of agents and promoters, his career overlapped that of Will Rogers, who had appeared in twenty-five films prior to 1928.

8. "Will Rogers Endorsed," *New York Times*, January 22, 1928; "Will Rogers Named as Candidate for Presidency of U.S.," *Burlington (IA) Hawk-Eye*, January 22, 1928.

9. "Will Rogers Not a Candidate This Year; His Phrase Is 'I Do Not Contemplate,'" *New York Times*, February 3, 1928.

10. Rogers, "I Accept the Nomination," 3.

11. Will Rogers, "Is Will Rogers Too Big for the Presidency?," *Life*, June 28, 1928, 4.

12. Henry Ford, "Henry Ford Tells Why He Indorses Will Rogers," *Life*, June 21, 1928, 4.

13. "Senators to Discuss the Value of Radio," *New York Times*, October 23, 1928.

14. *Waterloo (IA) Times-Tribune* cited in "An Insult," *Life*, September 6, 1928, 37; *Corvallis Gazette* cited in Rogers, "Is Will Rogers Too Big for the Presidency?," 4.

15. Leip, *Atlas of Presidential Elections*.

Gracie Allen

1. "Gracie's Checking Account," *The George Burns and Gracie Allen Show*, CBS television, season 1, episode 5, December 7, 1950.

2. Burns, *Gracie*, 188, 190.

3. "Listen! With Slocum," *Washington Post*, February 26, 1940.

4. Burns, *Gracie*, 186.

5. Burns, *Gracie*, 186.

6. "Listen! With Slocum," *Washington Post*, March 9, 1940.

7. Burns, *Gracie*, 188.

8. "Jimmie Fidler in Hollywood," *Washington Post*, March 17, 1940.

9. "Walter Winchell on Broadway," *Burlington (NC) Times-New*, April 5, 1940.

10. "Surprise Party Candidate Captures S.L.," *Salt Lake Tribune*, May 11, 1940.

11. Burns, *Gracie*, 191; "Gracie Tells of Platform," *Mason City (IA) Globe-Gazette*, May 15, 1940; "Venus de M. Has No Arms; Gracie Lacking Elsewhere," *Nebraska State Journal* (Lincoln), May 17, 1940.

12. Allen, *How to Become President*, 38, 54, 56, 58.

13. Burns, *Gracie*, 190; United Press International, "Mrs. Big-Gracie Nominated by Surprise Party," *Washington Post*, May 19, 1940.

14. Allen, *How to Become President*, 26.

15. Allen, *How to Become President*, 26, 49.

16. Allen, *How to Become President*, 19.

17. "Sampascoopies," *Lowell (MA) Sun Times*, June 18, 1940.

18. "Joke Over, Gracie Pulls Out of Race," *Charleston (WV) Gazette*, June 30, 1940; "Gracie Allen Ends Phoney Campaign," *Nevada State Journal* (Reno), June 30, 1940.

19. Mae West, the sexy stage and film star, was famous for zingers that zapped others, but she paid a price other sex symbols in her era did not. Her movies were routinely placed on the Legion of Decency's list of indecent films, and despite excellent box office, she was never given her own radio or television show.

20. Russell, "Self-Deprecatory Humor"; Wagner, "Have Women a Sense of Humor?"; Mellencamp, "Situation Comedy."

21. Burns, *Gracie*, 190.

22. Allen, *How to Become President*, 51.

John Maxwell

1. "Gracie Reports," *Pampa (TX) News*, September 16, 1948.

2. "What Next?," *Milwaukee (WI) Sentinel and Gazette*, September 26, 1850.

3. "Vegetarians Issue 12-Point Platform," *New York Times*, July 22, 1948; Russell Porter, "Splinter Parties in Presidency Race," *New York Times*, October 31, 1948.

4. United Press International, "Calls on Vegetarians over World to Drop George B. Shaw," *Amarillo (TX) Daily News*, August 31, 1948; "Earl Wilson: Great Vegetarian Controversy," *Zanesville (OH) Recorder*, August 20, 1948.

5. Harold Williams, "The Passing Show: Spinach for All," *Long Beach (CA) Press-Telegram*, May 25, 1948.

6. Philip S. Marden, "Saturday Chat," *Lowell (MA) Sun*, November 19, 1949.

7. Cf. "Ration, Where's Thy Sting?," *Tucson (AZ) Citizen*, January 29, 1943.

8. "Vegetarian Says Meat Strike May Help," *Circleville (OH) Herald*, January 17, 1946; Edward Ellis, "Meat Strike May Bring Longer Life," *Dubuque (IA) Telegraph-Herald*, January 17, 1946; "Two Sides to Everything, Even the Meat Strike," *Ames (IA) Tribune*, January 17, 1946; "Hails Meat Strike as Aid to Health," *Moorhead (MN) Daily News*, January 17, 1946; "Vegetarian Pleased by Meat Strike," *Kenosha (WI) Evening News*, January 17, 1946.

9. "Meat Prices Set New Highs," *New York Times*, September 9, 1947; "Meat, Butter Resume Price Rise," *New York Times*, November 4, 1947; "Retail Meat Costs Up 2 to 6 Cents," *New York Times*, July 14, 1948.

10. "81-Year-Old Candidate for the Presidency to Run on Strictly Vegetarian Diet," *New York Times*, July 30, 1947. The age cited may be a typesetting error; by all other reports, Maxwell would have been eighty-five years old.

11. "Meat Strike May Bring Longer Life."

12. Associated Press report, "Vegetarian Eyes Presidency," *Hagerstown (MD) Morning Herald*, June 18, 1948.

13. On relationship with Townsend, "Good-bye Doctor," *Lowell (MA) Sun*, February 24, 1938; radio show in Chicago, "Townsend Club to Hear Dr. John Maxwell," *Oak Leaves* (Oak Park IL), March 31, 1938; columnist in Milwaukee and restaurant, "John Maxwell to Speak," *Blue Island (IL) Sun-Standard*, December 22, 1938; CBS appearance, "Radio," *Huronite* (Huron SD), May 13, 1948; "No Meat, No Drink," *Time*, August 11, 1947, 22.

14. Timotheus T., "About Town and Country," *Harrisburg (IL) Daily Register*, May 25, 1948.

15. "The Vegetarian Party," *Altoona (PA) Mirror*, June 29, 1948.

16. "Lettuce-Nibblers Will Put Up Doctor for President," *Wisconsin Rapids Daily Tribune*, July 29, 1947; "Meat Tee-totaler Candidate for Party," *Berkeley (IA) Gazette*, July 30, 1947; "Politico-Gastric Note," *St. Louis (MO) Dispatch*, reprinted in *Helena (MT) Independent-Record*, September 12, 1948.

17. On his being a naturopath physician, "Meat Strike May Bring Longer Life"; birth in England, "Ineligible Candidates," *Canandaigua (NY) Daily Messenger*, July 12, 1948; "'Splinter' Parties in Presidency Race," *New York Times*, October 31, 1948.

18. Associated Press, "Candidate of Vegetarians Writes In His Own Name," *New York Times*, November 3, 1948.

19. "So They Say," *Kenosha (WI) News*, September 1, 1948.

20. Jim Stingl, "Lettuce Adorn Vegetarian Presidential Candidate's Final Plot," *Milwaukee Journal-Sentinel*, September 10, 2010; on placing of gravestone, Jim Stingl, "Historian Votes for Proper Send-Off," *Milwaukee Journal-Sentinel*, November 16, 2013, http://archive.jsonline.com/news/milwaukee/historian-votes-for-proper-send-off-b99143430z1-232212791.html/.

Homer Tomlinson

1. "Tomlinson Is Confident of Election by Miracle," *Bluefield (WV) Daily Telegraph*, February 18, 1960.

2. "Clergymen Establish Picket Line," *Hammond (IN) Times*, November 5, 1937; "Bobbed Hair Is Compromise with Satan," *Greenville (MS) Delta Star*, November 9, 1937.

3. "1940 Fair Exceeds Ten Million Mark," *New York Times*, August 26, 1940; "Couple Wedded in Parachute," *Massillon (OH) Evening Independent*, August 26, 1940.

4. "5th Av. Fox Chase Causes Jail Term," *New York Times*, January 8, 1922; "'Welcome' for Queen Made a Movie Stunt," *New York Times*, October 1, 1926.

5. "Tomlinson Is Confident of Election by Miracle"; "Church of God Overseer to Run for President," *Southern Illinoisan* (Carbondale), September 8, 1950; Ward

Cannel, "What Homer Wants Is to Be King of U.S.," *El Paso (TX) Herald-Post*, February 23, 1960.

6. United Press International, "'I Am the King,' Tomlinson Says," *Anniston (AL) Star*, September 4, 1954; Associated Press, "Bishop Proclaims Himself New King of Whole World," *Kingsport (TN) Times-News*, September 5, 1954.

7. "Miter in the Ring," *Washington Post*, September 6, 1951.

8. "In Seeking Presidency, Bishop Will Fast 21 Days," *New York Times*, August 11, 1951; "Bishop Runs for President," *San Antonio (TX) Light*, August 10, 1951; "Bishop to Stump U.S. as Presidential Candidate," *Hattiesburg (MS) American*, August 18, 1951.

9. In addition to Tomlinson, those candidates were Riley Alvin Bender, Farrell Dobbs, Don Dumont, Albert S. Falk, Vincent Hallinan, Stuart Hamblen, Eric Hass, Chauncey Himmelman, Herbert C. Holdridge, Darlington Hoopes, Ellen Linea Jensen, Henry Krajewski, Robert McCormick, Reginald B. Naugle, Frederick Proehl, and Gerald L. K. Smith. Cf. "Woods Full of Unknown GOP Hopefuls," *Washington Post*, July 8, 1952; "The Political Picture," *Atlanta (GA) Daily World*, September 3, 1952.

10. United Press International, "Crowns Himself 'King' of Iowa," *Washington (IA) Evening Globe*, March 17, 1960; Associated Press, "President Hopeful Crowns Himself as King of Iowa," *Arizona Republic* (Phoenix), March 18, 1960.

11. "King of All Nations," *Findlay (OH) Republican Courier*, November 14, 1955; "Tomlinson Is Barred from Emperor's Tomb," *Norwalk (OH) Reflector*, December 28, 1955; "U.S. Sect Leader Sitting in Red Square Proclaims Himself King of Russia," *New York Times*, July 13, 1958.

12. "What Homer Wants Is to Be King of U.S."

13. "Tomlinson Is Confident of Election by Miracle."

14. "King of the World Begins Campaign for Presidency," *Edwardsville (IL) Intelligencer*, June 3, 1963.

15. Among the many newspapers carrying this report were "Church of God Bishop Leads Peace Rally at Childersburg," *Anniston (AL) Star*, September 14, 1952; "Bishop Tomlinson Beats a Sword Into a Plowshare," *Washington Post*, September 15, 1952; "Beats Sword into Plowshare," *Jefferson City (MO) Post-Tribune*, September 15, 1952.

16. "Arkansas Now Has a 'King,'" *Blytheville (AR) Courier News*, May 19, 1960.

17. Floyd Carl Jr., "The Washington County Carousel," *Northwest Arkansas Times* (Fayetteville), December 15, 1960.

18. William Whitworth, "Profile: The Tide of Times," *New Yorker*, September 24, 1966, 69.

19. Whitworth, "Profile," 108.

20. Associated Press, "'King of the World' Quits, to Work for 'Golden Age,'" *The Robesonian* (Lumberton NC), September 24, 1963.

21. Associated Press, "Church of God Party Changed," *Fairbanks (AK) Daily News Mirror*, August 22, 1960; "Roving with Boyle—Not the Same Church of God," *Wilson (NC) Daily Times*, March 24, 1960; "Pastor Refutes Claims of 'King,'" *Florence (SC) Morning News*, April 13, 1960.

22. Associated Press, "Small Attendance at Convention," *Joplin (MO) Globe*, March 22, 1964.

23. "Theocratic Party Plans Clergy Cabinet," *Florence (SC) Morning News*, April 25, 1964; "Theocratic Party Favors 10 Per Cent Income Tax," *Raleigh Register* (Beckley WV), April 30, 1964; "Theocratic Candidates Campaign," *Lawrence (KS) Daily Journal-World*, May 21, 1964.

24. *Minneapolis Star* editorial, reprinted in *Austin (TX) Daily Herald*, September 21, 1968.

25. Associated Press, "Tomlinson Runs Again for President," *Abilene (TX) Reporter-News*, March 25, 1968.

26. Associated Press, "Bishop Tomlinson Offers Garden of Eden Platform," *Joplin (MO) Globe*, August 30, 1968.

27. "Runs on Commandments," *New York Times*, August 17, 1951.

28. "Church Leader Say He Plans a Third Party," *Joplin (MO) News Herald*, March 14, 1960.

29. Ward Cannel, "Homer Runs for President but Really Seeks Kingdom," *Brainerd (MN) Daily Dispatch*, March 17, 1960.

30. As early as 1787 the Protestant theologian Johann Eichhorn built upon emerging theories that Genesis and Exodus were compilations of texts from competing political and theological factions in ancient Israel. This branch of scholarship continued and expanded with works such as Benjamin Bacon's *The Genesis of Genesis* (1892), onward to Richard Elliott Friedman's *Who Wrote the Bible?* (1997) and numerous others.

31. Bill Daniel, "King of the World Seeks Presidency of U.S. on Church of God Ticket," *Billings (MT) Gazette*, June 22, 1960.

Gabriel Green

1. Jack Smith, "Flying Saucer Man Runs for President," *Los Angeles Times*, August 10, 1960.

2. United Press International, "Candidate Gets Idea from Planets," *Albuquerque (NM) Journal*, March 4, 1972.

3. United Press International, "Los Angeles 'Selected' for Arrival on Earth of Men from Mars," *Rio (TX) News-Herald*, November 5, 1956.

4. "Army Tells Plans for New Rocket Weapon, Space Ships," *Twin Falls (ID) Telegram*, January 30, 1946; "Supersonic Flying Saucers Sighted by Idaho Pilot," *Chicago Tribune*, June 26, 1947.

5. "Flying Saucers Seen by Others," *Montana Standard* (Butte), June 29, 1947.

6. "Ten Workers Lose Jobs in Loyalty Probe," *Lubbock (TX) Morning Avalanche*, June 28, 1947; "Flying Saucers May Be Russian," *Daily Mail* (Hagerstown MD), December 22, 1947.

7. "Drew Pearson Says," *Idaho State Journal* (Pocatello), November 27, 1949.

8. "Pact Defense," *Soda Springs (ID) Sun*, January 5, 1950; "Race in Outer Space," *Times-News* (Twins Falls ID), October 14, 1957; "Russians Launch Rocket at Moon," *Montana Standard* (Butte), September 13, 1959.

9. David Lawrence, "Mystery of the Flying Saucers," *Evening Star* (Washington DC), November 2, 1955.

10. "Space People Destroyed Red Rocket," *Pasadena Independent*, September 17, 1959.

11. "So They Say," *Register News* (Mt. Vernon IL), August 4, 1959.

12. "Space People Have Candidate," *Oxnard (CA) Press-Courier*, August 10, 1960.

13. Marx and Engels, *Manifesto of the Communist Party*, 20–25.

14. Hal Draper, "Afternoon with the Space People," *Harper's*, September 1960, 37–40.

15. "America Needs a Space Age President," campaign ad for Gabriel Green, *Los Angeles Mirror News*, July 22, 1960, http://files.abovetopsecret.com/files/img /nz57686c79.jpg.

16. Peters, "UFOs," 261–78, 297.

17. "Newest UFOs Blink Lights," *Billings (MT) Gazette*, September 16, 1973; Warren Brown, "Carter Laughs Off His 'UFO Sighting,'" *Washington Post*, May 12, 1976.

18. Exodus 19:16–19, King James Version, cited in Lewis, *The Gods Have Landed*, xi.

19. Jung, *Flying Saucers*, 2–7.

20. "Write-In 'Space Age' Candidate Withdraws," *Kenosha (WI) News*, October 24, 1960.

21. "Flying Saucer Clubs Head Contends for Presidency," *Hayward (CA) Daily Review*, March 4, 1972.

22. Marx, "Money, the Universal Whore," 205.

23. On the founding of the Universal Party, "Political Party Out of Luck," *Reno (NV) Gazette*, September 7, 1964; Green candidacy, Carla Fisher, "Iowa Ballot 7 Columns," *Burlington (IA) Hawk-Eye*, October 22, 1972; platform of the Universal Party, *Our Campaigns*, http://www.ourcampaigns.com/PartyDetail.html?PartyID=1605.

24. Don Cole, "Presidential Candidate Has Space Contacts," *Arizona Daily Sun* (Flagstaff), April 10, 1972.

25. "James Dent: The Gazetteer," *Charleston (WV) Gazette*, March 20, 1972.

26. United Press International, "Candidate Gets Ideas from Planets," *Albuquerque (NM) Journal*, March 4, 1972.

27. Mark Henry, "Verbose Encounters at Giant Rock," *Riverside (CA) Press-Enterprise*, August 3, 1996.

Louis Abolafia

1. "Artist, 24, Fasting to Gain Recognition," *New York Times*, December 21, 1965; "In Seeking Presidency Bishop Will Fast 21 Days," *New York Times*, August 11, 1951.

2. "Nemesis Pickets Dali Show," *New York Herald Tribune*, December 19, 1965; Zalman, "Dali, Magritte, and Surrealism's Legacy," 24–38.

3. "Gubernatorial Aspirant Throws Beret in Ring," *New York Times*, August 19, 1966.

4. Herbert Gold, "Where the Action Is," *New York Times*, February 19, 1967; Bernard Weinraub, "10,000 Chant 'L-O-V-E,'" *New York Times*, March 27, 1967; Steven A. O. Golden, "Inhibitions and Movies Unreel as a Love-In Turns Itself On," *New York Times*, May 3, 1967.

5. "Campaigns for Presidency on 'Love' Ticket," *Dubuque (IA) Telegraph-Herald*, May 3, 1967.

6. "Hippie Seeking Presidency Stages Campaign Happening," *Hayward (CA) Daily Review*, May 3, 1967; "Platform of Love for U.S. President," *Burlington (IA) Hawk-Eye*, May 5, 1967; "Help a Humble Beatnik Earn an Honest Living," *Corona (CA) Daily Independent*, May 3, 1967; photo caption from *Bradford (PA) Era*, May 4, 1967.

7. "Hippie Seeking Presidency Stages Campaign Happening," *Hayward (CA) Daily Review*, May 3, 1967.

8. "Abolafia for President," *New Yorker*, May 13, 1967.

9. Don McNeill, "Abolafia for President: A Case of Self-Propulsion," *Village Voice*, May 11, 1967.

10. Tom Tiede, "He Sees World Going to Pot," syndicated article cited from *Burlington (NC) Times-News*, February 1, 1968.

11. Sylvie Reice, "The Swinging Set," *Steubenville (OH) Herald-Star*, April 15, 1968; Kay Bartlett, "Runaways in Hippieland," *Baltimore Sun*, September 22, 1968.

12. Mike Jahn, "New York Current," *Bucks County (PA) Courier Times*, January 30, 1968.

13. Associated Press, "If Elected, He'll Be Mr. President-Baby," *Long Beach (CA) Independent Press Telegram*, May 26, 1967.

14. United Press International, "Love-In Rally," *Berkshire (MA) Eagle*, May 29, 1967.

15. Sculptures of Founding Fathers in togas include Horatio Greenough's statue of George Washington at the Smithsonian's National Museum of American History; Giuseppe Ceracchi's bust of Washington in the Metropolitan Museum of Art; Francesco Lazzarini's statue of Benjamin Franklin, the original at the Library Company of Philadelphia and its more widely known replica above the entrance to the American Philosophical Society in Philadelphia; another of Franklin, sculpted in the workshop of H. Micali, at the American Antiquarian Society, Worcester, Massachusetts; and two different busts of Alexander Hamilton in a toga by Ceracchi, one at Thomas Jefferson's Monticello, the original of the other now lost but reproduced at the Treasury Department.

16. Marcuse, *Eros and Civilization*, xxi; attribution to Abolafia, Alan Feuer, "These Stars May Show Skin, but the Focus Is on the Suits," *New York Times*, June 18, 2006.

17. National Archives, "Statistical Information about Casualties of the Vietnam War," https://www.archives.gov/research/military/vietnam-war/casualty-statistics.html.

18. Capp, "Hippie Economics," 64–67.

19. Associated Press, "Galbraith Says He'll Back Humphrey as 'Better Man,'" *New York Times*, October 21, 1968.

20. "Galbraith Reviewed with Brush and Pen," *Washington Post*, August 30, 1967; Donald Fritts, "Capp 'Discovers' Hippie Candidate," *Bakersfield Californian*, September 15, 1967; "You Should Buy and Read: The Hippie Economics," *Emporia (KS) Gazette*, September 16, 1967; "Hippie Economics," *Sandusky (OH) Register*, November 11, 1967; *Congressional Record*, 90th Congress, 2nd Session, A5691.

21. Bell-McClure wire service, "N.Y. Hippies Wonder What Happened to Summer of Love," *Fond du Lac (WI) Commonwealth Reporter*, July 26, 1968.

22. Kenneth F. Case, "Case's Column," *Ludington (MI) Daily News*, August 8, 1968.

23. "View from Here," *Northwest Arkansas Times* (Fayetteville), October 22, 1968.

24. Muriel Dobbin, "On the Campaign Fringe," *Baltimore Sun*, November 4, 1980; United Press International, "Candidate Just Grins . . . and Bares It!," *Roswell (NM) Daily Record*, December 20, 1979.

25. Graham and Greenfield, *Bill Graham Presents*, 255.

26. Emanuel Perlmutter, "Hippie Threats Win a Theater," *New York Times*, October 24, 1968.

27. Associated Press, "Scene of Debate 'Shouts' Civic Pride," *Lubbock (TX) Avalanche-Journal*, October 7, 1976.

28. "What's New in Art," *New York Times*, July 10, 1966.

Pat Paulsen

1. Digby Diehl, "Of Thee I Sing, Pat Paulsen," *New York Times*, October 20, 1968.

2. "Auto Safety," *Smothers Brothers Comedy Hour*, CBS, February 26, 1967.

3. Erskine Johnson, "First Appearance: Got 17,000 Letters," *Abilene (TX) Reporter-News*, May 10, 1967.

4. "Should the Use of Firearms Be Restricted?," *Smothers Brothers Comedy Hour*, CBS, March 19, 1967.

5. Newspaper Enterprise Association, "'Generals' Night' Premiere Hollywood's 1st '67 Glitter," *Lima (OH) News*, February 25, 1967.

6. Charles Lucy, "Doctors Try to Beat Candidates of Socialized Medicine," *El Paso Herald-Post*, October 28, 1950.

7. "Should Doctor's Fees Be Regulated?," *Smothers Brothers Comedy Hour*, CBS, September 24, 1967.

8. Grant Marshall, "Taken for Granted," *Burlington (IA) Hawk-Eye*, October 6, 1967.

9. Stan Maays, "Smothers Brothers as Supreme Court?," *North Adams (MA) Transcript*, December 23, 1967.

10. *Smothers Brothers Comedy Hour*, CBS, February 11, 1968.

11. Associated Press, "Satire Become TV Specialty," *Robesonian* (Lumberton NC), January 16, 1968.

12. Williams and Kragen, *Pat Paulsen for President*, 46–47.

13. "Are Our Draft Laws Unfair?," *Smothers Brothers Comedy Hour*, CBS, October 29, 1967.

14. Hal Humphrey, "Viewing TV: Paulsen for President Special Planned," *Beckley (WV) Register and Post*, June 1, 1968; "Election Special: Pat Paulsen for President Sweat Shirts," Woolco department store ad, *Amarillo (TX) Daily News*, September 28, 1968; on campaign dinners, Associated Press, "Paulsen Steps Up Presidential Campaign," *Coshocton (OH) Tribune*, July 25, 1968.

15. Marian Dern, "Pat Paulsen: Comic, Candidate," *TV Week*, June 23, 1968, 15.

16. Ernie Kreiling, "A Closer Look at Television," *Van Nuys (CA) News*, June 6, 1968; Osborne-Thompson, "Tracing the 'Fake' Candidate," 67.

17. "Candidate Intentionally Funny," *Kenosha (WI) News*, September 6, 1968; Richard Robinson, "Pat Splurges," *Freemont (CA) Argus*, September 12, 1968.

18. Tony Cillo, "Pat Paulsen Views Meaty," *Long Beach (CA) Press-Telegram*, October 14, 1968.

19. Associated Press, "Comic Paulsen Opens 'Drive' at Convention," *Evening Star* (Washington DC), August 5, 1968.

20. "Candidate Intentionally Funny."

21. "Paulson Won't Stand Pat," *Evening Star* (Washington DC), August 28, 1968.

22. "Candidate Intentionally Funny."

23. George Gent, "Smothers Show Censored Anew," *New York Times*, January 27, 1968.

24. George Gent, "Seeger Will Sing 'Big Muddy' on TV," *New York Times*, February 15, 1968.

25. Lawrence Laurent, "More Than Controversy Aids Smothers," *Washington Post*, February 27, 1968.

26. Nat Hentoff, "The Smothers Brothers: Who Controls TV?," *Look*, June 24, 1969, 27–29.

27. "A 'Serious' Candidate," *Racine (WI) Journal-Times*, January 31, 1972; on the legal challenge, Associated Press, "Actor, Comic Lose Pace Campaigning," *Bluefield (WV) Daily Telegraph*, March 6, 1972; Associated Press, "Pat Paulsen Withdraws from Presidential Race," *San Antonio (TX) Express*, April 19, 1972.

28. Carr, "On the Edge of Tastelessness," 20.

Eldridge Cleaver

1. Cleaver, "Revolution in the White Mother Country," 13–15.

2. Cleaver, "The Land Question and Black Liberation," 284.

3. Wallace Turner, "Black Panthers, White Power," *New York Times*, July 20, 1968.

4. Rout, *Eldridge Cleaver*, ix.

5. Leip, *Atlas of Presidential Elections*.

6. Willard Clopton, "Shift to Militancy Seen in Peace Protests," *Washington Post*, September 3, 1967.

7. Associated Press, "Peace Party Nominates E. Cleaver," *Mitchell (SD) Daily Republic*, August 19, 1968.

8. The approximation reflects the number of U.S. newspaper articles of the two events in the database Newspaper Archive (accessed May 10, 2017). Four newspapers in the database carried reports of Cleaver's announcement that he intended to seek the presidency; forty-eight reported on his wanting Rubin as a running mate.

9. David Dietz, "Black Panther Author Tells View on Weapons, 'Pigs,'" *San Rafael (CA) Independent Journal*, July 3, 1968.

10. "Cleaver Leads Gregory in Race," *Pasadena Independent*, August 5, 1968.

11. James J. Kilpatrick, "Donnybrook Hour Approaches," *Thomasville (GA) Times-Enterprise*, August 22, 1968.

12. Gene Oishi, "Agnew Can Be Scapegoat but Not Hero," *Baltimore Sun*, November 3, 1968.

13. Combined New Service, "Cleaver Gives First UC Lecture; No Obscenity in 'Scholarly' Talk," *Long Beach (CA) Press-Telegram*, October 7, 1968. Cf. *scholarly* in quotation marks in relation to Cleaver's lectures, "Cleaver Resumes Attacks on Reagan, Rafferty, Etc.," *Hayward (CA) Daily Review*, October 10, 1968.

14. Cf. Barthelemy, *Black Face, Maligned Race*; Smith, "Hot Bodies and 'Barbaric Tropics'"; Adler, "The Rhetoric of Black and White in *Othello*"; Buxton, "The Significance (or Insignificance) of Blackness."

15. "Cleaver Dares Gov. Reagan to Duel," *Arizona Republic* (Phoenix), October 5, 1968.

16. Cleaver, *Target Zero*, 38; Rout, *Eldridge Cleaver*, vii.

17. "Panthers Accuse Police of Murder," *Long Beach (CA) Independent*, April 8, 1968; Associated Press, "Clash between Police and Black Panthers," *Glens Falls (NY) Times*, April 8, 1968.

18. "Dumbfounding Ruling by a Court," *San Mateo (CA) Times*, June 15, 1968.

19. United Press International, "Legislature Faces Security Crisis," *Bakersfield Californian*, May 4, 1967.

20. "Black Panther Author Tells View on Weapons, 'Pigs.'"

21. Associated Press, "Militancy Is Here to Stay," *Long Beach (CA) Press-Telegram*, October 4, 1968.

22. Rout, *Eldridge Cleaver*, 95.

Dick Gregory

1. "Keeping the Record Straight," *Albuquerque (NM) Journal*, August 21, 1968.

2. "Low Comedy," *Washington Post*, January 4, 1968.

3. Diggs Datrooth, "National Hotline," *Chicago Defender*, February 3, 1960; Connie Woodruff, "On the Scene," *New York Amsterdam News*, November 2, 1968; Eliot Asinof, "Dick Gregory Is Not So Funny Now," *New York Times*, May 17, 1968.

4. "Police Seize 48 in Protest at Chicago," *Baltimore Sun*, August 13, 1963; "Gregory on Hunger Strike," *Albuquerque (NM) Tribune*, November 17, 1965.

5. Gregory, *Write Me In!*, 14.

6. Ernest Boynton, "Bang-Bang Is a Threat to the Nation," *Chicago Defender*, December 16, 1967.

7. "Onion for the Day," *Chicago Defender*, June 5, 1968.

8. Phyllis Battelle, "Dick Gregory Not Feeling Too Funny," *Lowell (MA) Sun*, March 4, 1965.

9. Dick Gregory, "Let's First Make It Right," excerpts from speech at Yale University, *Charleston (WV) Gazette Mail*, March 3, 1968.

10. "Dick Gregory Pioneers as a Negro Comedian," *Southern Illinoisan* (Carbondale), September 25, 1960.

11. Chapel, "Humor in the White House," 45.

12. Gatch, "Dick Gregory's 'One Vote' Note."

13. United Press International, "Dick Gregory Pamphlets Are Seized," *Brazil (IN) Daily Times*, October 23, 1968.

14. "Greg $$ Elude G-Men," *Chicago Defender*, October 24, 1968.

15. Wilkie Connor, "The Paperbacks: Comedian's Bid for the Presidency Is No Joke," *Gastonia (NC) Gazette*, July 7, 1968.

16. Leip, *Atlas of Presidential Elections*.

17. Those candidate were Shirley Chisolm (1972), Margaret Wright (1976), Clifton DeBerry (1980), Andrew Pulley (1980), Jesse Jackson (1984, 1988), Larry Holmes (1984, 1988), Dennis L. Serrette (1984), Edward Winn (1984, 1988), Lenora Fulani (1988, 1992), James Warren (1988, 1992), Ronald Daniels (1982), Joan Jett Blakk (1992), Helen Halyard (1992), Isabell Masters (1992, 1996), Alan Keyes (1996, 2000, 2008), James Harris (1996, 2000, 2004), Monica Moorehead (1996, 2000), Randall A. Venson (2000), John Parker (2004), Al Sharpton (2004), and Carol Moseley Braun (2004).

Pigasus

1. Tom Buckley, "The Battle of Chicago: From the Yippies' Side," *New York Times*, September 15, 1968.

2. Hoffman, *Revolution for the Hell of It*, 32.

3. John Kifner, "Hippies Shower $1 Bills on Stock Exchange Floor," *New York Times*, August 25, 1967.

4. Associated Press, "Hippies Toss Cash in Exchange," *Tucson (AZ) Daily Citizen*, August 25, 1967.

5. Hoffman, *Revolution for the Hell of It*, 32–33.

6. Krassner, *Confessions*, 162.

7. Raskin, *For the Hell of It*, 128–29.

8. Raskin, *For the Hell of It*, xxi.

9. John Chamberlain, "Old Rooseveltian Glue Losing Much of Magic," *Kittanning (PA) Times*, August 29, 1968; see also Kemble, "The Democrats after 1968."

10. Buckley, "The Battle of Chicago."

11. "City vs. Hippies," *Santa Fe New Mexican*, August 23, 1968; Richard Ciccone, "Yippies' Candidate Can't Run," *Mitchell (SD) Daily Republic*, August 24, 1968.

12. David Smothers, "Yippies Are Sideshow in Chicago," *Lubbock (TX) Avalanche-Journal*, August 23, 1968.

13. Nicholas von Hoffman, "Yippies Trot Out Candidate," *Washington Post*, August 24, 1968.

14. Rubin, *DO IT!*, 83.

15. "Yippies' Candidate Can't Run." The likelihood of Hugh "Wavy Gravy" Romney being the one quoted in this article is based on his telling an interviewer eight years later that he previously ran a pig for president who was the first "black and white candidate." See Pat Ryan, "Wavy Gravy Makes Debut," *Austin Texan*, October 22, 1976.

16. "Yippies Present a Pig as Presidential Choice," *New York Times*, September 29, 1968.

17. United Press International, "Americans Have Many Choices on General Election Ballots," *Nevada State Journal* (Reno), November 4, 1968.

18. Chazalon, "'Thea'tricks'"; "Mocking the Judge," *Billings (MT) Gazette*, February 7, 1970; J. Anthony Lukas, "Two of Chicago 7 Don Black Robes," *New York Times*, February 7, 1970.

19. David E. Rosenbaum, "Yippie Leader Arrested," *New York Times*, October 4, 1968; "Yippie Adjudged Guilty," *New York Times*, November 22, 1968; Bart Barnes, "Court Overturns Conviction for Flag Desecration," *Washington Post,* March 30, 1971.

20. Associated Press, "Anti-War Yippies Disrupt House Un-American Probers," *Salina (KS) Journal*, October 2, 1968.

21. Raskin, *For the Hell of It*, 240–41, 245, 253; John T. McQuiston, "Abbie Hoffman, 60's Icon, Dies," *New York Times,* April 14, 1989.

22. David S. Broder, "GOP Set to Join Democrats' Efforts to Revamp Conventions," *Washington Post*, March 6, 1969; David S. Broder, "Top Democrats Meet to Plan Party Reforms," *Washington Post*, April 26, 1969.

23. Chazalon, "'Thea'tricks.'"

Aftershocks

1. Wavy Gravy, *Something Good for a Change*, 227–28.

2. Dennis McDougal, "Bringing Back the '60s on the Wavy Gravy Train," *Los Angeles Times*, November 17, 1987.

3. Jay Miller, "A Perfect Candidate for the Nobody-Cares Folks," *Santa Fe New Mexican*, October 12, 1988.

4. Raskin, *For the Hell of It*, 108; Richard Sealey, "The Poly-Tickle Rally of the Century," *Santa Fe New Mexican*, September 30, 1988.

5. Wavy Gravy, *Something Good for a Change*, 229–30; Jack Stamm, "Hippies on a 'Dopeless High' in Tesuque Canyon Rites," *Santa Fe New Mexican*, June 24, 1968.

6. Barnard L. Collier, "300,000 at Folk-Rock Fair," *New York Times*, August 17, 1969.

7. Barnard L. Collier, "200,000 Thronging to Rock Festival," *New York Times*, August 16, 1969.

8. Associated Press, "Pop Fans to Descend on Texas," *Montana Standard* (Butte), August 30, 1969; Eric Spitznagel, "Q&A: Wavy Gravy, 75, on His Ben & Jerry's Break-up and Most Cherished Arrest Memory," *Vanity Fair*, May 19, 2011, http://www.vanityfair.com/hollywood/2011/05/qa-wavy-gravy-75-on-his-ben-jerrys-break-up-and-most-cherished-arrest-memory.

9. "Local News," *Clay County (IN) Enterprise*, July 18, 1972.

10. Gendin, "Why Vote?," 123–32.

11. United Press International, "In Hollywood," *Piqua (OH) Daily Call*, May 12, 1932.

12. Frank Sanello, "Puppets on 'Spitting Image' Lampoon Politicos," *Franklin (PA) News-Herald*, August 28, 1986.

13. Michael Sterling, "Wavy Gravy Alias Hugh Romney," *Austin Texan*, February 20, 1975; United Press International, "Nobody for President," *San Antonio (TX) Light*, July 13, 1976; United Press International, "Flourishing Political Flee Market Has Emerged Outside Statler Hilton," *Dunkirk-Fredonia (NY) Evening Observer*, July 14, 1976.

14. Georgie Anne Geyer, "The Way Radicals End," *Biloxi (MS) Sun-Herald*, August 21, 1976.

15. Associated Press, "Nobody Kicks Off Campaign," *Neenah (WI) Daily Northwestern*, October 13, 1976.

16. Associated Press, "Wavy Gravy Brings Nobody's Drive to State," *Farmington (NM) Daily Times*, October 20, 1976.

17. United Press International, "'Nobody' for President Campaign Hits Texas," *Amarillo (TX) Globe-Times*, October 27, 1976.

18. "Young Republicans Want Conservative," *Reno (NV) Evening Gazette*, March 17, 1975; on enactment in Nevada, "Copout Option," *Mt. Carmel (IL) Republican Register*, February 23, 1976; Kentucky proposal, "Ballot Choice Too Wide Open," *Charleston (WV) Gazette*, November 4, 1975; California proposal, John Pachtner, "Bill Would Allow Vote for Nobody," *Freemont (CA) Argus*, March 2, 1977.

19. Art George, "A Social Worker in Freak's Clothing," *Oakland (CA) Tribune*, July 28, 1974.

20. Jay Miller, "The Perfect Candidate for the Nobody-Cares Folks," *Santa Fe New Mexican*, October 12, 1988.

Joan Jett Blakk

1. *Drag in for Votes*, directed by Gabriel Gomez and Elspeth Kydd, independent film, 1991.

2. *Drag in for Votes*.

3. Cook, "Race Activists," 150–51; Jeffreys, "Joan Jett Blakk for President," 186–95.

4. Baim, *Out and Proud*, 183.

5. "Some Guys Have All the Fun," *Milwaukee Journal*, June 8, 1992.

6. Irene Lacher, "Leave It to Shivela to Put Camp Back in Campaign Series," *Los Angeles Times*, August 16, 1992; "Convention '92," *Houston Chronicle*, July 14, 1992.

7. Nationwide news coverage of Ben-Shalom included "Lesbian Struggles to Serve in Army," *New York Times*, August 10, 1989; Nora Zamichow, "Isolation Painful for Partners of Gays in Service," *Los Angeles Times*, February 3, 1991; Ruth Marcus, "Justices Decline to Review Anti-Homosexual Policies," *Washington Post*, February 27, 1990.

8. *All Things Considered*, National Public Radio, April 25, 1993.

9. Bawer, *A Place at the Table*, 39; on the controversy over Blakk, Bogad, "Sturm und Drag."

Vermin Supreme

1. *All Things Considered*, National Public Radio, February 14, 1992.

2. Molly A. K. Conner, "He Reigns Supreme," *Concord (NH) Monitor*, January 15, 2012.

3. C. J. Ciarmella, "There's Finally a Documentary about Perpetual Candidate Vermin Supreme," *Vice*, March 25, 2015, https://www.vice.com/en_ca/article/qbegq5 /someone-finally-made-a-documentary-about-vermin-supreme-324.

4. *Who Is Vermin Supreme? An Outsider Odyssey*, directed by Steve Onderick, independent film, 2014.

5. Katie Gunther Kodat, "Peace March Growing as It Nears Goal," *Baltimore Sun*, November 7, 1986; Andrea Pawlyna, "The Foot Soldiers of Peace March Near Journey's End," *Baltimore Sun*, November 13, 1986.

6. Conner, "He Reigns Supreme."

7. Sandy Banisky, "The Name Is Mr. Vermin," *Baltimore Sun*, November 4, 1987.

8. "Gallimaufry," *Baltimore Sun*, November 9, 1987.

9. "Gallimaufry."

10. "The Name Is Mr. Vermin."

11. Kennedy, *Dangerous Joy*, 119–20.

12. Associated Press, "Demonstrators Fill L.A. Streets," *Cedar Rapids (IA) Gazette*, August 14, 2000.

13. Pagan Kennedy, "Merry Prankster Performance Artist Vermin Supreme," *Boston Globe*, January 11, 2004.

14. "Zombie Preparedness: Dark Horse Issue?," *National Journal*, December 20, 2011, NewsBank-Access World News, http://infoweb.newsbank.com.

15. For mandatory tooth brushing, Myra Eder, "For Some, Convention Is Center of Universe," *Orland Park (IL) Star*, September 1, 1996; zombies powering turbines, Robyn Urback, "Vermin Supreme, Man with a Boot on His Head," *National Post*, November 25, 2015, http://nationalpost.com/opinion/robyn-urback-vermin-supreme-man-with-a -boot-on-his-head could-be-the-most-sensible-presidential-candidate/wcm/d5957f51 -2eb9-40ba 80c5-a8/6f4cd6383; free pony for everyone, Seth Brown, "The Pun Also Rises," *Bennington (VT) Banner*, June 23, 2015, http://www.benningtonbanner.com /stories/the-pun-also-rises-vermin-supreme-in-2016,300113.

16. Kennedy, *Dangerous Joy*, 115.

17. For anarchist, Gene Collier, "Finally, a Candidate Who Vows to Do Something about the Weather," *Pittsburgh Post-Gazette*, August 15, 2000; for friendly tyrant, Erin Duggin, "Anyone Can Run in N.H.," *Syracuse (NY) Post-Standard*, February 1, 2000; for ultimate goal, "He Reigns Supreme."

18. *Who Is Vermin Supreme?*

19. "Your Voice/Your Vote," ABC News, http://abcnews.go.com/Politics/video /presidential-candidate-vermin-supreme-tells-abc-news-campaign-36121810.

20. "Finally, a Candidate Who Vows to Do Something about the Weather."

21. Kennedy, *Dangerous Joy*, 117, 121.

22. Annie Garau, "Vermin Supreme Support Grows in Bloomington," *Xavier Crosswire* (Cincinnati OH), April 1, 2016.

23. Marla McKenna, "Vermin Supreme—A Choice We Can Live With," *Charlottesville (VA) Daily-Progress*, June 22, 2016.

24. Mike Argento, "Vote for Vermin Love Supreme! Get a Pony!," *York (PA) Daily Record*, December 13, 2015.

Jonathon "The Impaler" Sharkey

1. Bibeau, *Sundays with Vlad*, 162; Pizza, *Paganistan*, 70–72.
2. *Impaler*, directed by Tray White, Trivial Productions, 2007.
3. Dane Smith, "'Impaler' Sinks His Teeth into Governor's Race," *Minneapolis Star Tribune*, January 12, 2006.
4. "'Impaler' Sinks His Teeth into Governor's Race."
5. Ed Kemmick, "Magikal Impaler Announces Candidacy," *Billings (MT) Gazette*, January 13, 2006, http://billingsgazette.com/news/opinion/blogs/city-lights/magikal -impaler-announces-candidacy/article_8ad6f296-72cb-5df1-8a89-7dbd09acb28a.html.
6. *Fox & Friends*, Fox News, January 16, 2006.
7. *The Situation with Tucker Carlson*, MSNBC, January 16, 2006.
8. Jackie Nielsen, "The Vampire on the Campaign Trail," *Iowa State Daily* (Ames IA), January 18, 2006, http://www.iowastatedaily.com/opinion/article_3319aa2a-f6ad -588e-8ba2-35856616e052.html.
9. Will Tubbs, "We're No. 2!," *Leesville (LA) Daily Leader*, February 13, 2006, NewsBank-Access World News, http://infoweb.newsbank.com.
10. "The Bottom Line," *San Antonio (TX) Express-News*, January 23, 2006.
11. Jason Offutt, "Ballots Are Still Better Than Bullets," *Independence (MO) Examiner*, January 28, 2006, NewsBank-Access World News, http://infoweb.newsbank.com.
12. "People in the News," *Duluth (MN) News Tribune*, February 1, 2006, NewsBank-Access World News, http://infoweb.newsbank.com.
13. Jonathan Casiano, "He's Got a Big Stake in Presidential Future," *Newark (NJ) Star-Ledger*, March 30, 2007.
14. Peter Shilling, "Impaler: The Documentary," *Minneapolis Star Tribune*, May 24, 2007; Lavanya Ramanathan, "The Devil Made Him Do It," *Washington Post*, September 27, 2007.
15. Laycock, *Vampires Today*, 160; *News Channel 5 This Morning*, WTVF (Nashville TN), October 2, 2006; "'Impaler' Pledges to Impale Bush," *Metro* (London, UK), March 13, 2007, http://metro.co.uk/2007/03/13/impaler-pledges-to-impale-bush-162726/.
16. *Impaler*.

Stephen Colbert

1. Neil White, "Colbert Running," *State* (Columbia SC), October 18, 2007; for favorite son, Jacques Steinberg, "Colbert Consulted Parties before Announcing Run," *New York Times*, October 18, 2007; for peaches, Cokie Roberts and Steven V. Roberts, "Stephen Colbert Is a Real Fake," *Port Arthur (TX) News*, November 5, 2007.
2. Candidate books written during this time include Hillary Clinton, *It Takes a Village*; Barack Obama, *The Audacity of Hope*; John Edwards, *Home: The Blueprints of Our Lives*; John McCain, *Hard Call: Great Decisions and the Extraordinary People Who Made Them*; Mike Huckabee, *From Hope to Higher Ground: 12 Steps to Restoring America's Greatness*; Fred Thompson, *Government at the*

Brink: The Root Causes of Government Waste and Mismanagement; Mitt Romney, *Turnaround*; Ron Paul, *Revolution: A Manifesto*; Rudy Giuliani, *Leadership*.

3. *Good Morning America*, ABC, October 9, 2007.

4. *Larry King Live*, CNN, October 11, 2007.

5. *The Daily Show with Jon Stewart*, Comedy Central, October 16, 2007.

6. Associated Press, "Stephen Colbert Tosses Satirical Hat into Presidential Race," *Alton (IL) Telegraph*, October 18, 2007.

7. Howard Kurtz, "Primary-Time TV with Colbert the Candidate," *Washington Post*, October 17, 2007, emphases added.

8. Michael Cavna, "Comedians of Clout," *Washington Post*, June 12, 2008.

9. Laura Capitano, "Candidate Colbert, Do You Dare?," *Florida Times-Union* (Jacksonville), October 23, 2007; Marisha Pietrowski, "The Stephen Colbert Buzz," *BG News* (Bowling Green State University OH), October 25, 2007, https://issuu.com/bgviews/docs/2007-10-25.

10. Jones, "The Stephen Colbert Problem," 295–323.

11. "Farewell, Stephen," *Henderson (NC) Daily Dispatch*, November 3, 2007.

12. Eric Boehlert, "Stephen Colbert's Joke Is on the Press," *Kokomo (IN) Tribune*, November 6, 2007.

13. Baumgartner and Morris, "One 'Nation,' under Stephen?"

14. LaMarre et al., "The Irony of Satire."

15. Faina, "Public Journalism Is a Joke."

16. *Citizens United v. Federal Election Commission*, 558 U.S. 310 (2010).

17. Juliet Eilperin, "Waning War on Cash in Politics," *Washington Post*, April 30, 2013.

18. Benacka, *Rhetoric, Humor, and the Public Sphere*, 110–11.

19. Alexandra Petri, "Run, Stephen, Run!," *Washington Post*, January 14, 2012.

Frank Moore

1. Dan Geringer, "When It Comes to Sex, Artist Has to Laugh," *Philadelphia Daily News*, May 21, 1987; Corey Nicholl, "Frank Moore," *Berkeleyside* (Berkeley CA), October 17, 2013, http://www.berkeleyside.com/2013/10/17/frank-moore-shaman-artist-teacher-writer-musician/.

2. Allan Parachini, "Federal Official Seeks Dates of Four Artists' Shows Back to '84," *Los Angeles Times*, June 25, 1990.

3. The Douginator, "Interview with a Presidential Candidate: Frank Moore," *Arabian Monkey*, July 5, 2006, http://www.frankmooreforpresident08.com/blog/2007/07/interview-with-presidential-candidate.html; Corey Nicholl, "Frank Moore Gathers Presidential Electors Nationwide for Groundbreaking Write-in Campaign," *Indy Media Center*, February 23, 2008, https://www.indybay.org/newsitems/2008/02/23/18481148.php; Cara Dagett, "Meet Frank Moore," *Colorado Independent*, March 28, 2008, http://www.coloradoindependent.com/3467/meet-frank-moore-he-just-makes-sense.

4. "Presidential Ballot Finalized in Montana," *Sidney (MT) Herald*, September 9, 2008; Martin Wisckol, "Ron Paul Qualifies as Write-in Candidate," *Orange County*

Register (Santa Ana CA), October 29, 2008, https://www.ocregister.com/2008/10/29/ron-paul-qualifies-as-write-in-candidate/; "A Final Look at Several Races on the Ballot," *Red Bluff* (CA) *Daily News*, November 3, 2008, NewsBank-Access World News, http://infoweb.newsbank.com.

5. "When It Comes to Sex, Artist Has to Laugh."

Keith Russell Judd

1. Jennifer S. Lee, "Living the 8-Bit Dream in a 32-Bit World," *New York Times*, July 22, 1999; Associated Press, "Chief Scientist Picked for Antimissile Effort," *New York Times*, October 31, 1987.

2. Sarah Moore, "Inmate Eyes Spot on the Ballot," *Beaumont* (TX) *Enterprise*, November 20 2007.

3. Joline Gutierrez Krueger, "Ex-Candidate Gets 17 Years in Prison," *Albuquerque Times*, September 28, 1999.

4. Jonathan McDonald, "Man Gets 17 Years for Mailing Threats in Letters to Odessan," *Odessa* (TX) *American*, September 29, 1999; "Ex-Candidate Gets 17 Years in Prison."

5. "Voters Go to the Poll," *Carol County* (IN) *Comet*, November 1, 2000.

6. "Cargo, Chavez to Face Runoff in Albuquerque Mayoral Vote," *Santa Fe New Mexican*, October 6, 1993; Mark Oswald, "Capital Chronicle," *Santa Fe New Mexican*, May 23, 1994; "Musician Joins Race for Mayor's Job," *Albuquerque Journal*, July 3, 1997.

7. Kevin Landrigan, "No Cigar," *Nashua* (NH) *Telegraph*, October 21, 2007; Sarah Moore, "Inmate Eyes Spot on Ballot," *Beaumont* (TX) *Enterprise*, November 20, 2007.

8. "Texas Prison Candidate Cons Way onto Idaho Primary Ballot," *Walla Walla* (WA) *Union-Bulletin*, April 16, 2008; "If Elected, Presidential Candidate Can't Serve," *Tulsa* (OK) *World*, April 17, 2008; "Inmate Makes 'Mockery' of Idaho Ballot," *Santa Fe New Mexican*, April 17, 2008.

9. The precise number of signatures was 1 percent of the eligible voters in Idaho. The state's new law stipulated that a presidential candidate could either collect the signatures or pay a $1,000 fee. Judd's financial disclosures indicated he was able to pay the fee from funds that appear to be from an inheritance. Cf. "Inmate Eyes Spot on the Ballot."

10. *Vote Smart*, https://votesmart.org/candidate/biography/15574/keith-judd#.WkZoxDdG3IU. Biographical information about Judd that appeared in many of the news reports was credited to this website in at least one of them.

11. "Inmate Makes 'Mockery' of Idaho Ballot."

12. Betsy Z. Russell, "Idaho Settles Suit over Ballot," *Spokane* (WA) *Spokesman-Review*, July 20, 2011.

13. Geoff Earle, "Jailbird Shocker in W.Va. Vote," *New York Post*, May 10, 2012.

14. Don Surber, "The Left Name-Calling Continues," *Charleston* (WV) *Daily Mail*, May 16, 2012.

15. Letter to the Editor, *Salisbury* (NC) *Post*, May 13, 2012, NewsBank-Access World News, http://infoweb.newsbank.com.

16. Hoppy Kercheval, "About That Embarrassing Vote for a Felon," *Charleston (WV) Daily Mail*, May 17, 2012.

17. "We're All Inmate 11593-051 Now," *Investor's Business Daily*, May 10, 2012.

18. *Hannity*, Fox News, December 13, 2011.

Roseanne Barr

1. John Lahr, "Dealing with Roseanne," *New Yorker*, July 17, 1995, 43–60.

2. Gilbert, *Performing Marginality*, 142–45, 161; Lee, "Subversive Sitcoms"; Dresner, "Roseanne Bar"; Auslander, "Brought to You by Fem-Rage"; Russell, "Self-Deprecatory Humor." The sparsity of Barr's books in university libraries can be seen in the fact that, in the Washington DC metropolitan area, only one of her books (*My Lives*) is currently in the collection of only the University of Maryland–College Park library.

3. *Hannity*, Fox News, September 24, 2012.

4. Associated Press, "Names and Faces," *Schenectady (NY) Gazette*, February 4, 2012.

5. Rick Steelhammer, "Raising the Barr of Election Insanity," *Charleston (WV) Gazette*, February 5, 2012; "President Roseanne Barr?," *Fort Lauderdale (FL) Sun Sentinel*, September 19, 2012.

6. Christie D'Zurilla, "Roseanne Barr Is Running for President as a Green Party Candidate," *Waterbury (CT) Republican-American*, February 4, 2012.

7. Barr, *Roseannearchy*, 4.

8. Allen, *How to Become President*, 41.

9. Hunter Walker, "Roseanne in the Rose Garden?," *New York Observer*, June 6, 2012, http://observer.com/2012/06/roseanne-in-the-rose-garden/.

10. Monica Hesse, "Patiently Waiting for the Green Light," *Washington Post*, July 16, 2012.

11 Beau Yarbrough, "Internal Affairs: Roseanne Barr Forms 'Green Tea Party,'" *San Jose (CA) Mercury News*, June 9, 2012, http://www.mercurynews.com/2012/06/09/internal-affairs-roseanne-barr-forms-green-tea-party-and-vows-to-soldier-on/.

12. *Hannity*, Fox News, September 24, 2012.

13. Donald Trump interview, *The Hugh Hewitt Show*, August 10, 2016, http//:www.hughhewitt.com/donald-trump-makes-return-visit/.

14. "Once Again, It's Silly Political Season Time," *Colorado Springs Gazette*, August 15, 2013.

15. Cf. "Trump, Christie, Sanders," *Face the Nation*, CBS, December 6, 2015, http://www.cbsnews.com/news/face-the-nation-transcripts-december-6-2015-trump-christie-sanders/.

16. *Jimmy Kimmel Live!*, ABC, March 22, 2018.

17. Roseanne Barr, "My Platform for President," *Roseanneworld*, March 3, 2012, http://www.roseanneworld.com/2012/03/03/my/.

18. Roseanne Barr, "What Am I Anyway? A Zoo?," *New York Times*, July 31, 1989.

19. "Rants & Raves," *Augusta (GA) Chronicle*, February 15, 2012.

20. "CNN Political Ticker: Roseanne Sets Sights on White House," CNN, August 5, 2011, http//:politicalticker.blogs.cnn.com/2011/08/05/roseanne-sets-sights-on-white -house/.

21. For Trump on not needing teleprompters, Robert Costa and Philip Rucker, "All 33 Times Donald Trump Jabbed the Bushes in One 35-Minute Interview," *Washington Post*, August 27, 2015, https://www.washingtonpost.com/news/post-politics /wp/2015/08/27/all-33-times-donald-trump-jabbed-the-bushes-in-one-35-minute -interview/?utm_term=.8210056dee63; for Trump on not bowing to foreign leaders, Glenn Kessler, "Trump's NATO-Funding Claims Too Simple, Hyperbolic," *Washington Post*, April 3, 2016.

Jimmy McMillan

1. Patrick Lakamp, "Gubernatorial Hopeful Walks on the Fringe," *Syracuse (NY) Herald-American*, May 8, 1994.

2. Agus Hamilton, "Jokes to Go!," *Joplin (MO) Globe*, October 26, 2010.

3. Bao Ong and Sam Roberts, "One Word Battle," *New York Times*, October 7, 2009.

4. *Saturday Night Live*, NBC, October 23, 2010.

5. Associated Press, "Rent Candidate Doll," *Roswell (NM) Daily Record*, November 2, 2010.

6. Edwards, "Flip the Script," 34–35; David Montgomery, "Auto-Tune the News Taps into SD for Political Humor," *Capital Journal* (Pierre SD), September 16, 2009, http://www.capjournal.com/news/auto-tune-the-news-taps-into-sd-for-political -humor/article_fbd88d57-e25a-53a9-9454-e600dccc98e2.html.

7. Mark Bennett, "Will 'Enthusiastic Discontent' Give Rise to a New Political Party in America?," *Terre Haute (IN) Tribune-Star*, October 24, 2010.

8. Gail Collins, "The Fury Failure," *North Adams (MA) Transcript*, October 22, 2010.

9. "The Race before the Race," *National Journal*, January 31, 2011, NewsBank-Access World News, http://infoweb.newsbank.com.

10. *Hannity*, Fox News, March 8, 2011.

11. Neil Genzlinger, "Damn," *New York Times*, August 12, 2011.

12. Catherine Duazo, "Former N.Y. Mayoral Candidate McMillan Speaks," *Daily Princetonian*, April 29, 2011, NewsBank-Access World News, http://infoweb.newsbank .com.

Naked Cowboy

1. Associated Press, "Playgirl Model 'Naked Cowboy' Gets Chilly Reception in Louisiana," *Orange (TX) Leader*, January 12, 1999.

2. Deepti Hajela, "'Naked Cowboy' Briefs Public on His Presidential Bid," *Elyria (OH) Chronicle Telegram*, October 7, 2010; "Times Square Cowboy Has Naked Ambition: Presidency," *Johnstown (PA) Tribune Democrat*, October 5, 2010; Aliyah Shahid, "Naked Cowboy, Times Square Staple, to Run for President," *New York Daily News*, October 7, 2010, http://www.nydailynews.com/news/politics/naked -cowboy-times-square-staple-run-president-2012-tea-party-candidate-article-1 .191364; Myles Tanzer, "No Longer Naked Cowboy Announces 2012 Bid for Pres-

ident," *Village Voice*, October 6, 2010, https://www.villagevoice.com/2010/10/06
/no-longer-naked-cowboy-announces-2012-bid-for-president/.

3. "Naked Cowboy's Next Gig: Run for President," NBC News, October 6, 2010,
http://www.nbcnews.com/id/39543094/ns/us_news-weird_news/#.WXNFf-mQzIU.

4. Burck, *Determination*, 12.

5. Associated Press, "Even New Yorkers Turned Their Heads," *Syracuse (NY) Post-
Standard*, October 9, 1999.

6. Burck, *Determination*, 34, 98.

7. Burck, *Determination*, 18–19.

8. Alison Leigh Cowan, "Naked Cowboy Drops Out," *New York Times*, September 5, 2009.

9. Burck, *Determination*, 117.

10. Associated Press, "Naked Cowboy vs. Naked Cowgirl," *Aiken (SC) Standard*,
June 28, 2010.

11. Dan Slater, "The Naked Cowboy Sues the Naked M&M," *Wall Street Journal*,
February 13, 2008, http//:blogs.wsj.com/law/2008/02/13/the-naked-cowboy-sues
-the-naked-mm; Dan Slater, "Naked Cowboy's Lawsuit Drives M&M Outta Dodge,"
Wall Street Journal, February 15, 2008, https://blogs.wsj.com/law/2008/02/15/naked
-cowboys-lawsuit-drives-mm-outta-dodge/; Robert Trigaux, "In Naked Cowboy
vs. Clear Channel Communications, Who Has Trademark Rights?," *Tampa Bay
(FL) Times*, June 1, 2009; Eriq Gardner, "CBS Beats New York's Naked Cowboy in
'Bold and the Beautiful' Lawsuit," *Hollywood Reporter*, February 24, 2012, http://
www.hollywoodreporter.com/thr-esq/cbs-naked-cowboy-lawsuit-bold-and-the
-beautiful-294639.

12. Tanzer, "No Longer Naked Cowboy."

13. Burck, *Determination*, 29.

14. Burck, *Determination*, 44.

Deez Nuts

1. "Deez Nuts for President 2016," https://deeznutsforpresident2016.yolasite.com/.

2. The poll was conducted by Public Policy Polling, a left-leaning organization,
albeit with a substantial record of accurate data collection.

3. Ben Collins and Emily Shire, "Presidential Sensation Deez Nuts Is a 15-Year-Old
Iowa Farm Boy," *Daily Beast,* August 19, 2015, http://www.thedailybeast.com
/presidential-sensation-deez-nuts-is-a-15-year-old-iowa-farm-boy.

4. Kyle Munson, "At Home on the Farm with Deez Nuts," *USA Today*, August
26, 2015, https://www.usatoday.com/story/news/politics/elections/2015/08/26/deez
-nuts-iowa-interview/32391651/; Tessa Berenson, "Deez Nuts Speaks: Meet Brady
Olson, the 15-Year Old Presidential Candidate," *Time*, August 24, 2015, http://time
.com/4007941/deez-nuts-president-2016/; CBS News, August 20, 2015; NBC News,
September 1, 2015.

5. Chris Cillizza, "Why I Hate Polls about How Darth Vader Would Beat Donald
Trump in 2016," *Washington Post*, December 16, 2015, https://www.washingtonpost.com

/news/the-fix/wp/2015/12/16/i-hate-polls-about-how-darth-vader-would-beat-donald
-trump-in-2016/?utm_term=.dcf3438d71b8. The polling organization was Ipsos.

6. Stein, *Vice Capades*, 196–200.

Andrew Basiago

1. Dmitry Belyaev, "Time Travel Expert Andrew D. Basiago Is Running for President," *Metro*, May 25, 2016, NewsBank-Access World News, http://infoweb.newsbank
.com.

2. Examples of articles in the various local editions of Examiner.com are Alfred Lambremont Webre, "Secret DARPA Time Travel Program May Hold Key to Understanding the Deep Politics of 9/11," *Seattle Examiner*, March 16, 2010; Jeffrey Pritchett, "Alta Dillard & Chad Dillard: The Ufology Revolving Doors 1st M.A.B.U.S. Case!," *Panama City (FL) Examiner*, April 21, 2011; Clare Kolewski, "Taking the Persecution of Christians to the Next Level," *Detroit Examiner*, October 24, 2013; "UFO Sighting: NASA Cover-up?," *Chicago Examiner*, November 11, 2014; Norman Byrd, "Head on Mars: Photo Shows Odd Artifact Resembling Barack Obama?," *Charleston (SC) Examiner*, November 30, 2014; "Humans on Mars: Obama Makes Pledge in State of the Union," *Honolulu Examiner*, January 21, 2015; Dustin Pardue, "Time Travel, the Beatles, and an Amazingly Suspicious Cassette Tape," *Winston-Salem (NC) Examiner*, February 2, 2015. All are archived in NewsBank-Access World News, http://
infoweb.newsbank.com.

3. Executive editor Jim Pimentel quoted in Matt Smith, "Blogos-Free," *SF Weekly*, December 5, 2007, http://www.sfweekly.com/news/blogos-free/.

4. Neel V. Patel, "Confessed Time Traveler Andrew Basiago Is Running for President, Knows He'll Win," *Inverse*, April 21, 2016, https://www.inverse.com/article/14577
-confessed-time-traveler-andrew-basiago-is-running-for-president-knows-he-ll-win.

5. Steve Turrell, "Beam Me Up, Xoe!," *Santa Fe New Mexican*, July 23, 2010; Jay Miller, "Governor's Past Is Beyond Belief," *Alamogordo (NM) Daily News*, August 20, 2010. On first appearance of Pegasus Project in Marvel Comics, "The Stars Are Wrong," *Realm of Kings* 1, no. 1 (January 2010).

6. David Moye, "Seattle Attorney Andrew Basiago Claims U.S. Sent Him on Time Travels," *Huffington Post*, April 28, 2012, http://www.huffingtonpost.com/2012/04/28
/andrew-basiago-seattle-attorney-time-travels_n_1438216.html.

7. Cf. "Things People Believe," *Hartford (CT) Advocate*, July 5, 2012.

8. Biographical details from Peter Larsen, "Road to Recovery, Ruin—Rebuilding Results Mixed on Street Ravaged by Tremblor," *Los Angeles Daily News*, January 15, 1995.

9. Basiago, "Discovery of Life on Mars."

10. Freeman, "Is This the 2nd Biggest Conspiracy of All?"

11. Peter Wade, "Meet the Time-Traveling Presidential Candidate," *Esquire*, April 30, 2016, http://www.esquire.com/news-politics/news/a44479/time-traveling-presidential
-candidate-andrew-basiago/.

12. Brandt, "Racism and Research"; Moreno, "Bioethics and the National Security State"; *Human Experimentation*, 3–10.

Zoltan Istvan

1. Alexis C. Madrigal, "Meet the Only U.S. Presidential Candidate Promising Immortality," *Huffington Post*, February 8, 2016, http://www.huffingtonpost.com/entry/zoltan-istvan-transhumanist-president_us_56b7c39ee4b08069c7a7b1d0.

2. Vicki Larson, "Transhumanist Novel by Zoltan Istvan Sparks Intense Dialog among Futurists," *Marin Independent Journal* (San Rafael CA), December 19, 2013, http://www.marinij.com/general-news/20131219/transhumanist-novel-by-zoltan-istvan-sparks-intense-dialog-among-futurists; Daniel Rothberg, "Meet the Transhumanist President Candidate Who Won't Be Onstage Tonight," *Las Vegas (NV) Sun*, October 13, 2015, https://lasvegassun.com/news/2015/oct/13/meet-the-transhumanist-presidential-candidate-who/.

3. Zoltan Istvan, "To Ensure a Future of Transhumanism," *Huffington Post*, February 24, 2016, http://www.huffingtonpost.com/zoltan-istvan/should-atheists-confront-_b_9303396.html.

4. Solomon Kleinsmith, "How Many Votes Did Zoltan Istvan Get in the 2016 Presidential Election?," *Quora*, November 28, 1016, https://www.quora.com/How-many-votes-did-Zoltan-Istvan-get-in-the-2016-Presidential-Election.

5. Zoltan Istvan, "Interview: Zoltan Istvan on Transhumanism and His U.S. Presidential Campaign," *Huffington Post*, July 6, 2016, http://www.huffingtonpost.com/zoltan-istvan/an-interview-on-transhuma_b_10798942.html.

6. Christine Emba, "Will Technology Allow Us to Transcend the Human Condition?," *Washington Post*, May 16, 2016, https://www.washingtonpost.com/news/in-theory/wp/2016/05/16/will-technology-allow-us-to-transcend-the-human-condition/?utm_term=.c9f7a7837983.

7. Analyses of *The Transhumanist Wager* in traditional publications include O'Connell, *To Be a Machine*; Bartlett, *Radicals Chasing Utopia*; Hauskeller, *Mythologies of Transhumanism*; Fuller, "Wherein Lies the Value of Equality"; Harris, *Solitudo*; Stolyarov; "Business as an Agent of Human Progress."

8. Hunter Styles, "Zoltan's Cyborg Utopia: The Transhumanist Party Presidential Candidate Wants Us to Live Forever," *Easthampton (MA) Valley Advocate*, June 10, 2015, http://valleyadvocate.com/2015/06/10/zoltans-cyborg-utopia/.

9. Martin Wisckol, "Zoltan, a Presidential Candidate for the Future," *Orange County Register* (Santa Ana CA), July 22, 2016, http://www.ocregister.com/2016/07/22/zoltan-a-presidential-candidate-for-the-future/.

10. Phil Fairbanks, "Candidacy Is 'Phenomenal Teaching Moment,'" *Buffalo (NY) News*, November 7, 2016.

11. Dave Barry, "A Man Named Zoltan Is Running for President, Too, and He Wants Our Bodies," *Miami Herald*, July 20, 2016, http://www.miamiherald.com/living/liv-columns-blogs/dave-barry/article90792612.html.

12. John Hendrickson, "Can This Man and His Massive Robot Network Save America?," *Esquire*, May 19, 2015, http://www.esquire.com/news-politics/interviews/a35078/transhumanist-presidential-candidate-zoltan/.

In Exiting

1. "Editor's Table," *Old Guard* 2, no. 8 (August 1864): 191–92.

2. "In Tribulation," *Holmes County Farmer* (Millersburg OH), September 22, 1864.

3. Meinders, *Americans against Obama*, 42.

4. "Levi Scifres," *Salem (IN) Democrat*, August 15, 1900.

5. Please forgive me, William Shakespeare and Shakespeareans, especially Professor William Slights.

BIBLIOGRAPHY

Adler, Doris. "The Rhetoric of Black and White in Othello." *Shakespeare Quarterly* 25, no. 2 (1974): 248–57.

Allen, Gracie. *How to Become President*. New York: Duell, Sloan and Pearce, 1940.

Auslander, Philip. "'Brought to You by Fem-Rage': Stand-up Comedy and the Politics of Gender." In *Acting Out: Feminist Performances*, edited by Lynda Hart and Peggy Phelan. Ann Arbor: University of Michigan Press, 1993.

Bacon, Benjamin. *The Genesis of Genesis*. Hartford CT: Student Publishing, 1892.

Baim, Tracy, ed. *Out and Proud in Chicago: An Overview of the City's Gay Community*. Chicago: Surrey Books, 2008.

Barkun, Michael. *A Culture of Conspiracy: Apocalyptic Visions in Contemporary America*. Berkeley: University of California Press, 2013.

Barr, Roseanne. *My Lives*. New York: Ballantine Books, 1994.

———. *Roseannarchy: Dispatches from the Nut Farm*. New York: Gallery Books, 2011.

———. *Roseanne: My Life as a Woman*. New York: Harper & Row, 1989.

Barthelemy, Anthony G. *Black Face, Maligned Race*. Baton Rouge: Louisiana State University Press, 1987.

Bartlett, Jamie. *Radicals Chasing Utopia: Inside the Rogue Movements Trying to Change the World*. New York: Perseus/Hachette, 2017.

Basiago, Andrew. "The Discovery of Life on Mars." Mars Anomaly Research Society, 2008. https://exopolitics.blogs.com/files/mars---andrew-d.-basiago---the -discovery-of-life-on-mars---12-12-08.pdf.

———. "Economic, Social, and Environmental Sustainability in Development Theory and Urban Planning Practice." *Environmentalist* 19, no. 2 (1998): 145–61.

———. "The Limits of Technological Optimism." *Environmentalist* 14, no. 1 (1994): 17–22.

———. "Methods of Defining 'Sustainability.'" *Sustainable Development* 3, no. 3 (1995): 109–19.

Baumgartner, Jody C., and Jonathan S. Morris. "One 'Nation,' under Stephen? The Effects of *The Colbert Report* on American Youth." *Journal of Broadcasting & Electronic Media* 52, no. 4 (2008): 622–43.

Bawer, Bruce. *A Place at the Table: The Gay Individual in American Society*. New York: Touchstone Books, 1993.

Benacka, Elizabeth. *Rhetoric, Humor, and the Public Sphere: From Socrates to Stephen Colbert*. New York: Lexington Books, 2017.

Bibeau, Paul. *Sundays with Vlad: From Pennsylvania to Transylvania, One Man's Quest to Live in the World of the Undead*. New York: Three Rivers Press, 2007.

Bogad, L. M. "Sturm und Drag: The Fabulous Camp-pains of Miss Joan Jett Blakk." In *Electoral Guerrilla Theatre: Radical Ridicule and Social Movements*, edited by L. M. Bogad. New York: Routledge, 2005.

Brandt, Allan M. "Racism and Research: The Case of the Tuskegee Syphilis Study." *Hastings Center Report* 8, no. 6 (1978): 21–29.

Bullock, Steven C. "A Pure and Sublime System: The Appeal of Post-Revolutionary Freemasonry." *Journal of the Early Republic* 9, no. 3 (1989): 259–73.

Burck, Robert. *Determination: The Legend of the Naked Cowboy*. Los Angeles: Naked Cowboy Enterprises, 2010.

Burns, George. *Gracie: A Love Story*. New York: G. P. Putnam's Sons, 1998.

Buxton, Richard. "The Significance (or Insignificance) of Blackness in Mythological Names." In *Myths, Martyrs, and Modernity*, edited by Jitse Dijkstra, Justin Kroesen, and Yme Kuiper. Boston: Brill, 2010.

Capp, Al. "The Hippie Economics." *Nation's Business* 55, no. 9 (1967): 64–67.

Carr, Steven Alan. "On the Edge of Tastelessness: cbs, the Smothers Brothers and the Struggle for Control." *Cinema Journal* 31, no. 4 (1992): 3–24.

Chapel, Gage William. "Humor in the White House: An Interview with Presidential Speechwriter Robert Orben." *Communications Quarterly* 26, no. 1 (1978): 44–49.

Chazalon, Elodie. "'Thea'tricks': Forms of Resistance in the 1968 United States and After." *Orda Revue: L'Ordinaire des Amériques* 217 (2014). http://orda.revues .org/1602.

Cleaver, Eldridge. "The Land Question and Black Liberation." 1968. In *African American Political Thought*, vol. 2, edited by Marcus D. Pohlmann. New York: Routledge, 2003.

——. "Revolution in the White Mother Country and National Liberation in the Black Colony." *North American Review* 253, no. 4 (1968): 13–15.

——. *Target Zero*. New York: Palgrave Macmillan, 2006.

Congressional Record—Appendix. 90th Congress, 2nd Session. Washington dc: Government Printing Office, 1968.

Cook, Charles Orson. "Race Activists and Fringe Parties with a Message." In *African Americans and the Presidency*, edited by Bruce A. Glasrud and Cary D. Wintz. New York: Routledge, 2010.

Dorset, Lyle W. *Billy Sunday and the Redemption of Urban America*. Grand Rapids mi: W. B. Eerdmans, 1991.

Downey, Dennis B. "George Francis Train: The Great American Humbug." *Journal of Popular Culture* 14, no. 2 (1980): 251–61.

Dresner, Zita Z. "Roseanne Bar: Goddess or She-Devil." *Journal of American Culture* 16, no. 2 (1993): 37–44.

Edwards, H. Sutherland. *Personal Recollections*. London: Cassell, 1900.

Edwards, John, ed. *Home: The Blueprints of Our Lives.* New York: Collins, 2006.

Edwards, Richard L. "Flip the Script: Political Mashups as Transgressive Texts." In *Transgression 2.0: Media, Culture, and the Politics of a Digital Age,* edited by Ted Gournelos and David J. Gunkel. New York: Continuum International, 2012.

Eichhorn, Johann. *Introduction to the Old Testament.* Condensed English version. Translated by George Tilly Gallop. Privately printed, 1888. Originally published in German in 1787 as *Einleitung ins Alte Testament.*

Faina, Joseph. "Public Journalism Is a Joke." *Journalism* 14, no. 4 (2012): 541–55.

Freeman, Makia. "Is This the 2nd Biggest Conspiracy of All?" *Mysterious Magazine* 2 (Summer 2015): 12–15.

Friedman, Richard Elliott. *Who Wrote the Bible?* San Francisco: Harper, 1997.

Frisken, Amanda. *Victoria Woodhull's Sexual Revolution: Political Theater and the Popular Press in Nineteenth-Century America.* Philadelphia: University of Pennsylvania Press, 2004.

Fuller, Steve. "Wherein Lies the Value of Equality When Equality Is No Longer 'Natural'?" In *Understanding Inequality: Social Costs and Benefits,* edited by Amanda Machin and Nico Stehr. Wiesbaden, Germany: Springer Fachmedien, 2016.

Gatch, Loren. "Dick Gregory's 'One Vote' Note." *Paper Money* 297 (May June 2015). https://sites.uco.edu/la/political-science/files/gatch/Dick-Gregory.pdf.

Gendin, Sidney. "Why Vote?" *International Journal of Politics and Ethics* 1, no. 2 (2001): 123–34.

Gilbert, Joanne R. *Performing Marginality: Humor, Gender, and Cultural Critique.* Detroit: Wayne State University Press, 2004.

Graham, Bill, and Robert Greenfield. *Bill Graham Presents: My Life Inside Rock and Out.* Cambridge MA: Da Capo Press, 2004.

Gregory, Dick. *Write Me In!* New York: Putnam, 1968.

Haber, Carole. "Anti-Aging Medicine: The History: Life Extension and History: The Continual Search for the Fountain of Youth." *Journal of Gerontology: Biological Sciences* 59, no. 6 (2004): B515–B522.

Harris, Michael. *Solitude: In Pursuit of a Singular Life in a Crowded World.* New York: Thomas Dunne/St. Martin's Press, 2017.

Hauskeller, Michael. *Mythologies of Transhumanism.* New York: Palgrave Macmillan, 2016.

Hoffman, Abbie. *Revolution for the Hell of It.* 1968. 2nd ed. New York: Thunder's Mouth Press/Avalon, 2005.

Holland, Patricia G. "George Francis Train and the Woman Suffrage Movement, 1867–70." *Books at Iowa* 46, no. 1 (1987): 8–29.

Hubbell, Jay B., and Douglas Adair. "Robert Munford's 'The Candidates.'" *William and Mary Quarterly* 5, no. 2 (1948): 217–57.

Human Experimentation: An Overview of Cold War Era Programs. Testimony before National Security Subcommittee, Committee on Government Operations, House of Representatives, 103rd Congress, 2nd Session. Washington DC: General Accounting Office, 1994.

Hutchisson, James M. *Poe*. Jackson: University of Mississippi Press, 2005.

Jeffreys, Joe E. "Joan Jett Blakk for President: Cross-Dressing at the Democratic National Convention." *Drama Review* 37, no. 3 (1993): 186–95.

Jones, Clifford A. "The Stephen Colbert Problem: The Media Exemption for Corporate Political Advocacy and the 'Hail to the Cheese Stephen Colbert Nacho Cheese Doritos® 2008 Presidential Campaign Coverage.'" *University of Florida Journal of Law and Public Policy* 19 (2008): 295.

Jung, Carl. *Flying Saucers: A Modern Myth of Things Seen in the Sky*. Translated by F. C. Hull. 1959. Princeton NJ: Princeton University Press, 1979.

Kemble, Penn. "The Democrats after 1968." *Commentary* 47, no. 1 (1969): 35–41.

Kennedy, Pagan. *The Dangerous Joy of Dr. Sex and Other True Stories*. Santa Fe NM: Santa Fe Writers Project, 2008.

Krassner, Paul. *Confessions of a Raving, Unconfined Nut: Misadventures in the Counterculture*. 1993. 2nd edition. Berkeley CA: Soft Skull Press, 2012.

Kutlowski, Kathleen Smith. "Anti-Masonry Reexamined: Social Bases of the Grassroots Party." *Journal of American History* 71, no. 4 (1984): 269–93.

LaMarre, Heather L., Kristen D. Landreville, and Michael A. Beam. "The Irony of Satire: Political Ideology and the Motivation to See What You Want to See." *International Journal of Press/Politics* 14, no. 2 (2009): 212–31.

Lamon, Ward H. *The Life of Abraham Lincoln*. Boston: James R. Osgood, 1972.

Laycock, Joseph P. *Vampires Today: The Truth about Modern Vampirism*. Westport CT: Praeger, 2009.

Lee, Janet. "Subversive Sitcoms: *Roseanne* as Inspiration for Feminist Resistance." *Women's Studies* 21 (1992): 87–101.

Leip, David. *Atlas of Presidential Elections*. http://uselectionatlas.org/.

Lenowitz, Harris. *The Jewish Messiahs: From Galilee to Crown Heights*. New York: Oxford University Press, 1998.

Lewis, James R., ed. *The Gods Have Landed: New Religions from Other Worlds*. Albany: State University of New York Press, 1995.

Marcuse, Herbert. *Eros and Civilization: A Philosophical Inquiry into Freud*. Boston: Beacon Press, 1966.

Mark, David. *Going Dirty: The Art of Negative Campaigning*. New York: Rowman & Littlefield, 2006.

Marx, Karl. "Money, the Universal Whore." 1844. In *Political Thought*, edited by Michael Rosen and Jonathan Wolff. New York: Oxford University Press, 1999.

Marx, Karl, and Frederick Engels. *Manifesto of the Communist Party*. English translation of 1848 edition. Chicago: Charles H. Kerr, 1906.

Meinders, Thomas R. *Americans against Obama: What Americans Think*. Bloomington IN: iUniverse, 2011.

Mellencamp, Patricia. "Situation Comedy, Feminism and Freud: Discourses of Gracie and Lucy." *Text and Performance Quarterly* 17, no. 4 (1997).

Melton, J. Gordon. "The Contactee Survey." In *The Gods Have Landed: New Religions from Other Worlds*, edited by James R. Lewis. Albany: State University of New York Press, 1995.

Miller, James L. D. *A Guide into the South*. Vol. 1. Atlanta: Index Publishing, 1910.

Monaghan, Jay. "Origin of Political Symbols." *Journal of the Illinois State Historical Society* 37, no. 3 (1944): 205–12.

Mooney, James. "The Ghost Dance Religion." In *Fourteenth Annual Report of the Bureau of Ethnology to the Smithsonian Institution—1892-3*, part 2. Washington DC: Government Printing Office, 1896.

Moreno, Jonathan D. "Bioethics and the National Security State." *Journal of Law, Medicine & Ethics* 32, no. 2 (2004): 198–208.

Morris, Roy, Jr. *Fraud of the Century: Rutherford B. Hays, Samuel Tilden, and the Stolen Election of 1876*. New York: Simon & Schuster, 2003.

Mouser, Bruce. *A Black Gambler's World of Liquor, Vice, and Presidential Politics: William Thomas Scott*. Madison: University of Wisconsin Press, 2014.

——. *For Labor, Race, and Liberty: George Edwin Taylor, His Historic Run for the White House, and the Making of Black Politics*. Madison: University of Wisconsin Press, 2011.

O'Connell, Mark. *To Be a Machine: Adventures among Cyborgs, Utopians, Hackers, and the Futurists Solving the Modest Problem of Death*. New York: Doubleday, 2017.

Osborne-Thompson, Heather. "Tracing the 'Fake' Candidate in American Television Comedy." In *Satire TV: Politics and Comedy in the Post-Network Era*, edited by Jonathan Gray, Jeffrey Jones, and Ethan Thompson. New York: New York University Press, 2009.

Peskin, Allan. *Garfield: A Biography*. Kent OH: Kent State University Press, 1978.

Peters, Ted. "UFOs: The Religious Dimension." *Cross Currents* 7, no. 23 (1977): 261–97.

Pizza, Murphy. *Paganistan: Contemporary Pagan Community in Minnesota's Twin Cities*. New York: Routledge, 2016.

"Poe Letters and Manuscripts Found in a Pillow Case." *Current Opinion* 70, no. 6 (1921): 823–24.

"The Political Campaign of 1872." *North American Review* 115, no. 237 (1872): 401–22.

Pritchard, Linda K. "The Burned-Over District Reconsidered: A Portent of Evolving Religious Pluralism in the United States." *Social Science History* 8, no. 3 (1984): 243–65.

——. "Religious Change in Nineteenth Century America." In *The New Religious Consciousness*, edited by Charles Y. Glock and Robert N. Bellah. Berkeley: University of California Press, 1976.

Raskin, Jonah. *For the Hell of It: The Life and Times of Abbie Hoffman*. Berkeley: University of California Press, 1996.

Red Channels: The Report of Communist Influence in Radio and Television. New York: Counterattack, 1950.

Register of Debates in Congress of the Second Session of the Twenty-second Congress. Vol. 9. Washington DC: Gales and Seaton, 1833.

Roberts, Clarence N. "The Crusade against Secret Societies and the National Christian Association." *Journal of the Illinois State Historical Society* 64, no. 4 (1971): 382–400.

Rout, Kathleen. *Eldridge Cleaver*. Boston: Twain/G. K. Hall, 1991.

Rowe, David L. "A New Perspective on the Burned-Over District: The Millerites in Upstate New York." *Church History* 47, no. 4 (1978): 408–20.

Rubin, Jerry. DO IT! *Scenarios of the Revolution*. New York: Ballantine Books, 1970.

Russell, Danielle. "Self-Deprecatory Humor and the Female Comic: Self-Destruction or Comedic Construction?" *Third Space: A Journal of Feminist Theory & Culture* 2, no. 1 (2002). http://journals.sfu.ca/thirdspace/index.php/journal/article/viewArticle/d_russell/68.

Saliba, John A. "Religious Dimensions of UFO Phenomena." In *The Gods Have Landed: New Religions from Other Worlds*, edited by James R. Lewis. Albany: State University of New York Press, 1995.

Schiller, Aaron Allen, ed. *Stephen Colbert and Philosophy: I Am Philosophy (And So Can You!)*. Chicago: Open Court, 2009.

Smith, Jon. "Hot Bodies and 'Barbaric Tropics': The U.S. South and New World Natures." *Southern Literary Journal* 36, no.1 (2003): 104–20.

Smith, Joseph. *History of the Church of Jesus Christ of Latter-day Saints*. Vol. 6. Salt Lake City: Church of Jesus Christ of Latter-day Saints, 1912.

Stein, Mark. *Vice Capades: Sex, Drugs, and Bowling from the Pilgrims to the Present*. Lincoln: University of Nebraska Press, 2017.

Steward, Patrick, and Bryan McGovern. *Fenians: Irish Rebellion in the North Atlantic World, 1858–1876*. Knoxville: University of Tennessee Press, 2013.

Stolyarov, Gennady, II. "Business as an Agent of Human Progress in *Time Will Run Back*, *Methuselah's Children*, and *The Transhumanist Wager*." In *Capitalism and Commerce in Imaginative Literature: Perspectives on Business from Novels and Plays*, edited by Edward W. Younkins. Lanham MD: Lexington Books, 2016.

Train, George Francis. *An American Merchant in Europe, Asia, and Australia*. New York: G. P. Putnam, 1857.

——. *My Life in Many States and in Foreign Lands*. New York: D. Appleton, 1902.

——. *Spread Eagleism*. New York: Derby & Jackson, 1859.

——. *Young America in Wall Street*. New York: Derby & Jackson, 1857.

Train, George Francis, and John Wesley Nichols. *The People's Candidate for President, 1872*. New York: Train League, 1872.

Wagner, Kristen Anderson "'Have Women a Sense of Humor?': Comedy and Femininity in Early Twentieth Century Film." *Velvet Light Trap* 68 (Fall 2011): 35–46.

Wavy Gravy. *Something Good for a Change*. New York: St. Martin's Press, 1992.

Wellman, Matthew Anthony. "Bringing Order to a Disorderly Place." *Louisiana Law Review* 38, no. 4 (1978): 1117–28.

Williams, Mason, with Jinx Kragen. *Pat Paulsen for President*. Beverly Hills CA: Kragen/Fritz, 1968.

Wojcik, Daniel. *The End of the World as We Know It*. New York: New York University Press, 1997.

Woodhull, Victoria. *The Principles of Social Freedom as Delivered in Steinway Hall, Monday, November 20, 1871*. New York: Woodhull, Clafin, 1872.

Wright, Clare. *The Forgotten Rebels of Eureka*. Melbourne, Australia: Text, 2014.

Zalman, Sandra. "Dali, Magritte, and Surrealism's Legacy, New York c. 1965." *Journal of Surrealism and the Americas* 6, no. 1 (2012): 24–38.

Zinn, Howard. *A People's History of the United States*. New York: Harper Perennial, 2003.

INDEX